To my wife Mary, to my children,
Cristina, Martín, and Carmen
and to Mary Pistolesi, a teacher

F. OFFICE M. GEMENT

IN H. Y LODGING OPERATIONS

.ATT A. CASADO

Disclaimer: Although the author has prepared this book to the best of his ability, he does not guarantee the accuracy of its contents. The author shall not be held liable for any loss of profit or other commercial damage said to be incurred by the use of the information herein.

Although names are given to people, all are fictional, and related to no person either past or present.

Properties mentioned in the text may or may not exist in the cities in which the author has placed them. Their names are used only as examples, and attributes and situations described are merely hypothetical and not known by the author to be true. Any relationship to real occurrences is purely coincidental.

Edited by Mary Elizabeth Natali

ISBN-10 1494943646
ISBN-13 9781494943646

Cover Image Photo Credit:
Courtesy of InterContinental Hotels Group

TABLE OF CONTENTS

PART 3: ROOMS RATES AND RESERVATIONS

PART 4 FRONT OFFICE OPERATIONS

PREFACE

The hospitality business, like all businesses in the 21st century, is evolving very rapidly because of development of new technologies, globalization, changes in the work force, evolving expectations of guests, and changing trends in marketing and management. In this book, I try not just to give a framework to teach prospective hoteliers the traditional skills necessary to run the front desk and manage its personnel smoothly, but also to make readers aware of those changes and the options they have. The purpose of ***Front Office Management in Hospitality Lodging Operations*** is to provide instructors of front office courses with the necessary tools to teach this core class central to the curriculum of hospitality programs. The book was written on the premise that the position of front office manager in lodging operations is one that requires proficiency in the areas of management and administration, as well as a thorough knowledge of professional and technical skills. Recruiters for lodging companies view front office managers as first-line administrators capable of directing the department by themselves, without direct intervention from the property's upper management. For this reason, students of 4-year, 2-year, and technical hospitality programs who wish to become lodging professionals, must be instructed in the particular skills that the industry demands.

ORGANIZATION OF THE TEXT

This book presents three types of expertise necessary to become a competent front office manager: *management of service, sale of guestrooms,* and *knowledge of technical operations.*

Part 1: Introduction to Front Office Management is aimed at preparing future front office managers to be department heads by covering management concepts and responsibilities as they apply to the front office department. It also describes the steps needed to structure the department. Chapters 1 and 2 explain the role of front office manager and provide information about the design of the front office in lodging establishments. Chapter 3 provides a perspective of the application of technology to front office operations.

Part 2: Professional Aspects of Front Office Management discusses the technical skills needed for running the front office department, including discussions on effective communication, customer service, and issues related to personnel management.

Part 3: Room Rates and Reservations covers aspects related to the most important function of the front office—that of achieving optimum occupancy. The processes of determining room rates, explaining selling techniques, and describing the reservation function are explained in chapters 7, 8 and 9.

Part 4: Front Office Operations explains in detail the check-in process, management of guest and non-resident accounts, and aspects of check-out procedures.

Part 5: Front Office Financial Controls, Security, and job-seeking strategies for graduates. Chapter 13 focuses on the department's operations budget, profit and loss statement, and variance analysis. Control of productivity and how to establish cash controls are also discussed. Chapter 14 addresses risk management in lodging, including how to minimize theft and crime and how to manage safety. Chapter 15 explains the strategies necessary to get a management-training position in the hospitality industry in general and in the front office department in particular. It covers techniques for compiling a perfect resume, interviewing for a position, and how to select the most appropriate job offer.

Each chapter includes a list of objectives, an overview, and a variety of practical situations or cases that reflect the types of problems and experiences students will face when they join a front office operation. I have compiled these examples from my own experience gained in an extensive career as hotelier and as an instructor of hospitality classes taught in higher education programs. The situations and cases are intended for discussion and resolution in the classroom. For this reason, most of them are concise and aimed at preparing students to deal with operational and low-level management situations common in the beginning stages of front office positions.

TEXT FEATURES

Each chapter of Front Office Management in Hospitality Lodging Operations includes the following features:

Learning Objectives help students identify the skills and knowledge they will require upon completing the chapter.

The **Chapter Overview** summarizes the content and topics covered in the chapter.

Key Terms highlight the specialized terminology presented in each chapter. A list of terms is provided at the end of each chapter fully defined in the **Glossary.**

Discussion Questions are included at the end of each chapter to foster class discussions or to be used as homework assignments.

Practical Situations focus on realistic day-to-day, practical problems front office managers commonly face.

Operational **Case Studies** provide scenarios involving technical dilemmas front office managers need to solve when managing the department.

Graduates from hospitality lodging programs have little trouble finding jobs. If they are enthusiastic workers, there is the potential to climb the ladder faster than can their peers with many other degrees. They are likely to meet people from all walks of life and from around the globe. The adventurous graduate can even use his new skills to see the world. As a young front office manager at a resort in Aguadulce, Spain, that hosted crews from spaghetti westerns, I spent time getting to know Sean Connery, Bridget Bardot and a number of other actors and movie directors. As assistant manager at the Royal Court in London, I became acquainted with the Beatles. As a pursuer (who essentially performs the tasks of a hotel manager on board) of an American cruise ship, I visited exotic destinations in the South Pacific.

No two days are alike in this profession. With this book, I hope to help teach students skills to do their jobs and to meet the often unpredictable challenges that face them in this their chosen dynamic profession.

Matt A. Casado, Ed.D., C.H.A., C.H.E
Professor Emeritus
Northern Arizona University

CHAPTER 1

THE FRONT OFFICE MANAGER IN HOSPITALITY LODGING OPERATIONS

CHAPTER OBJECTIVES

- Learn how management concepts apply to the position of front office manager.
- Discuss the necessity of achieving high productivity at the front office while also considering the needs of the employees in the department.
- Understand the duties of the front office manager as department head.
- Explain the role of the front office manager as department coordinator.
- List the managerial responsibilities of the front office manager.

OVERVIEW

This chapter explains how management concepts can be applied to the role of front office manager. As a manager, you must be able to combine concern for production with concern for people in order to run the department effectively. The traditional functions of management can be followed as a guide to organize and coordinate the department, plan and direct activities, and control results.

As a department head, the front office manager must be proficient in technical, people-related, and conceptual skills. As a manager, the person in charge of the front office must understand the concepts of time management, problem resolution, quality control, and decision making, and operate within the precepts of industry-accepted codes of ethics.

THE FRONT OFFICE MANAGER IN LODGING OPERATIONS

MANAGEMENT CONCEPTS AS THEY APPLY TO THE FRONT OFFICE MANAGER

Because the front office is at the hub of activities where most guest transactions take place, students are eager to be recruited for positions in this department where they will meet a constant stream of guests from all walks of life. On a personal level, I have, for example, checked in and interacted with many celebrities, such as movie stars Brigitte Bardot and Sean Connery, as well as cellist Gaspar Cassado and film directors Sergio Leone and John Guillermine. The Beatles used to stay at a hotel in London where I was assistant to the general manager. I found from my experience that it is as important for the front office to be as alert to celebrities' needs and privacy concerns as it is to attend to the needs of families and business travelers.

The responsibilities of the front office manager include staffing, training, and running the front office, maximizing occupancy and room revenue, providing customer service to guests, administering the resources allotted to the department, making technical decisions about how to optimize the use of technology, and maintaining cooperative relationships with other departments. Students interviewing for positions at the front desk must have the skills to communicate with all kinds of travelers and be able and willing to deal with complex situations that front-line employees must often face. Before being promoted to the position of front office manager, you will need to master the management skills and special traits that follow. It is the responsibility of a manager to create and maintain an environment in which people can work toward the goals of the company. As the manager of a department that is considered to be the heart of a lodging operation, the front office manager must possess strong managerial skills in order to perform this task well. Also the front office manager must be concerned with the productivity of the work force and with the interaction with people (both guests and employees) and must be able to efficiently coordinate effort in the workplace.

PRODUCTIVITY OF THE FRONT OFFICE

The overall goal of management in a profit-making operation is to increase the owner's equity by maximizing profits. So, in turn, one of the major concerns of the front office manager should be to maximize the productivity and efficiency of front office employees. Managers must set standards of production and require employees to reach these levels of performance. If productivity levels are found to be above the standard, management could choose to pay bonuses to workers as an incentive to maintain productivity quotas. If productivity levels are below the standard, production methods have to be improved. For instance, the front office manager can analyze the average time required to efficiently check in guests and use that time as the department's standard for that task. When productivity and quality exceed the standards for this activity, special recognition or extra compensation could be given for maintaining the productivity quotas. If performance of this task falls below pre-established levels, the **front office clerks** should be retrained or the method used to check in guests re-evaluated. This approach of setting optimum standards fosters productivity and can increase the profits of the company which, in turn, could pay its employees higher wages.

CONCERN FOR PEOPLE

Some factors other than the physical aspect of a job can have an effect on productivity, namely, the workers' social interactions and personal relationships. It has been demonstrated that in order to increase productivity in the workplace, human relations factors must be considered. That is, an organization consists first and foremost of the people working in it and management must be greatly concerned with the social and psychological aspects of the relationship between the company and its employees. This concept can be easily understood and applied from a front office management perspective. For instance, if the department manager does not consider the social needs of the workers a priority, workers in turn will not develop a sense of loyalty to their manager. If a reservations clerk who is scheduled to work the morning shift cannot find a babysitter for mornings, management should do everything possible to schedule this worker in the evening. If this were done, the employee would feel gratitude and therefore be more willing to return the favor by improving productivity. In other words, productivity can be greatly improved if management takes care of its workers. The dynamics of human behavior lead to the premise that management must be aware that workers, besides being units of production, are social entities in their own right.

MANAGING PEOPLE EFFECTIVELY IN THE WORKPLACE

As discussed above, management must view workers as human components in the organization's social system. Although it is true that front office managers must develop a keen sense for production in the workplace (after all, the main reason for lodging companies to stay in business is to generate a profit), they must also see front office employees as individuals. In other words, the ability to manage people effectively affects positively the productivity of the workforce. This is important because without adequate productivity, profits decline, forcing management to pay insufficient wages and to provide inferior benefits.

Clearly, then, adding concern for people to the management equation is imperative. However, the real skill lies in finding a proper balance; for example, a front office manager determined to please workers at any cost may not be totally successful because employees easily sense when a manager is "too nice" and they may take advantage of that. A case in point would be a front office manager agreeing to pay too much overtime or allowing employees to call in with any excuse not to show up for work leaving the shift under-staffed.

THE FRONT OFFICE MANAGER AS COORDINATOR

Another function of the front office manager should be to see to it that all parts of the front office are integrated as a whole. Five accepted principles of management that apply to the lodging industry in general and to the front office department in particular are:

- Planning
- Organizing
- Directing
- Coordinating
- Controlling

PLANNING

One of the main functions the manager of the front office department must perform is deciding which tasks are essential at any given time to keep the department running at peak efficiency. As the occupancy of the property varies from month to month, and even from day to day, forecasting labor must be done in advance to minimize costs. The definition of planning is simple: deciding where one should go and how to get there. Planning, however, is not always easy for it requires the predetermination of strategies and policies necessary to fulfill company goals. When forecasting the need for employees, for instance, the front office manager must skillfully schedule according to the property's upcoming occupancy. With heavy check-ins or check-outs all employees are needed, but only part of the staff is required when occupancy is low.

Creativity is an important element of the planning function; it requires the ability of a manager to develop and implement different, more efficient solutions to operational problems. A creative front office manager is flexible in judging employee initiatives, encouraging workers to develop new ways to improve the efficiency of the department. A highly structured, bureaucratic department might be efficient in production but could stifle or limit innovation. Creativity in planning should allow for diversity of ideas without attempting to rigidly structure the behavior of employees.

Planning involves the achievement of short- and long-range objectives. A **short-range objective** might be to bring down the labor cost by one percentage point the following month.

A **long-range objective** might be to increase the productivity of front desk clerks, uniformed personnel, or valet-parking attendants by 5 percent over last year's results by the end of the current fiscal year.

ORGANIZING

The organization of the front office is necessary in order to establish a pattern of relationships with other operational units and among the different components of the department itself. The organization of the front desk, reservations, concierge, and uniformed employees includes the determination of tasks, skills, and personnel necessary to achieve the objectives of the department. It is the responsibility of the front office manager to structure the department so that all work can be finished efficiently and accurately. The first necessary step when structuring the front office department is to determine the pattern of authority by drawing an organizational chart. This follows the principle of **unity of command** which states that workers should be given orders only by their own direct supervisor. To this effect, the **span of control** must be clearly defined; this relates to the number of subordinates that a supervisor can oversee effectively. In the front office department, when employees are well trained and dependable, the span of control can be quite broad.

Defining relationships within the department is also important because strong cooperation must exist among its different units. For instance, communicating the status of available rooms to be sold to the members of an incoming shift or warning of the arrival of an important meeting planner that evening will alert the clerks on how to perform their jobs effectively. In addition, if the status of the rooms is not accurate when changing shifts, overbooking may occur causing the displacement of guests to other establishments. This is always very inconvenient to travelers and usually results in the loss of some guests forever.

Another organizational task is that of creating descriptions of the jobs to be done (list of tasks) and the qualifications of workers who are to perform the jobs. Matching the right person for each job that must be accomplished is a priority in the organization of the front office department. The importance of selecting people who are capable of performing their tasks efficiently is obvious.

DIRECTING

This managerial function involves achieving the goals of the department by explaining to employees what needs to be accomplished, then facilitating their efforts to do the job. Crucial to effective direction is the ability of the manager to train, motivate, supervise, and discipline employees. Competent front office managers are able to obtain higher levels of productivity from their workforce than can managers who are not adequately trained to direct people.

Without proper direction, employees tend to duplicate efforts, focus on the wrong priorities, and apply effort to the wrong purpose. An example of improper direction would be permitting drivers of the shuttle van to take guests to nearby restaurants (usually for tips) when there are incoming guests waiting at the airport to be picked up. Another example of poor management would be to play favorites with employees as this leads to discontent among those who see themselves as not favored. An efficient front office manager should emphasize both the economic-technical system and the human aspects of administration.

COORDINATING

The front office manager must match the individual work of the staff to the common goals of the operation. The person in charge of the front office must coordinate work schedules and the overall communication among the different units of the department. This function is carried out through a series of briefings, meetings, and committee work where daily operational matters, intradepartmental issues, and hotel-wide concerns are addressed.

Lodging operations require a large degree of interdepartmental coordination. It is the job of the front office manager to integrate the department in the operation as a whole, making sure that communication flows to and from the front office and the different operational units of the property. A case in point would be that of attending a meeting in which the arrival of a large convention to the hotel is discussed. It would be up to the front office manager to learn the number of people in the group, arrival time, type of accommodation booked, and other requirements and to communicate this information to front office employees for proper follow up. Not only must the front desk be prepared for the group's arrival, but so must the uniformed staff, valet-parking attendants, the concierge desk and the shuttle vans if the property is located near an airport.

Coordination can be achieved by linking all activities together under a central authority. In the front office department, however, it would be difficult to cope individually with all the coordinating problems that might arise every day. The coordinating function must be supported by a system of procedures designed to carry out much of the routine work automatically, for instance, using information logs, memos, and routing slips. It is also important to achieve voluntary coordination on the part of front office employees. If they see the need for coordination and they are willing to find means to integrate their activities with other participants, departmental coordination will be smooth.

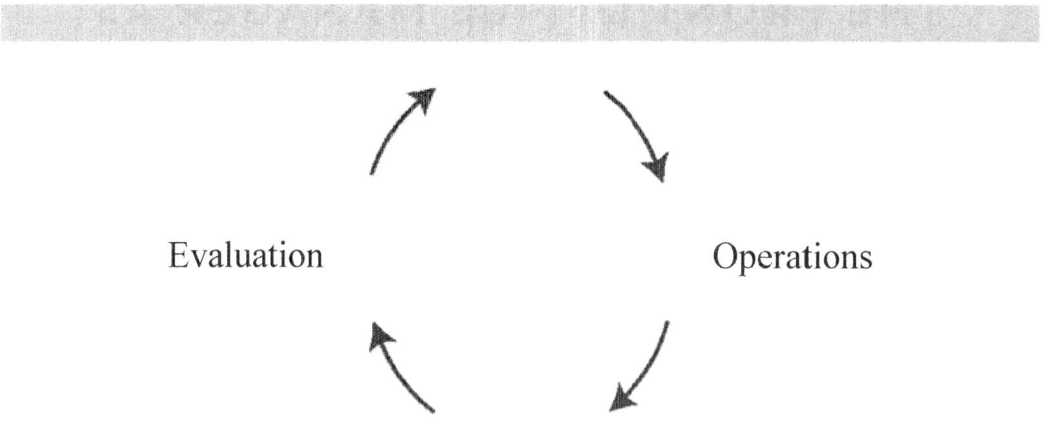

FIGURE 1.1 THE CYCLE OF CONTROL

CONTROLLING

The purpose of control is to make operations more efficient and cost effective. This function involves measuring actual with expected standards established during the planning process and effecting necessary corrections if deviations from the standards are found. Feedback is an essential component in the control process. In front office departments, feedback should be sought from guests, employees and other departments of the lodging operation. Figure 1.1 is a sample of the control process, in which standards are set during the planning function, operations take place, feedback is obtained from different sources, an evaluation of results is conducted, and new standards are prescribed.

The need for front office managers to control the activities of their department represents an important management function. Without controls there is no way of evaluating the degree to which the objectives set during the planning function are met. In other words, the actual results need to be compared to desired or anticipated goals and standard of performance. Labor cost percentages are typical standards of control; if the labor cost was set in the budget at 18 percent of revenue and the actual labor cost is running at 22 percent, the results are over budget and some corrective measures must be taken.

THE FRONT OFFICE MANAGER AS DEPARTMENT HEAD

The position of front office manager in the organizational structure of lodging operations is that of **department head** or member of the middle management team. In small properties, front office managers report directly to the general manager of the establishment, while in large properties they report to the **rooms division director.**

Today's successful front office managers require skills beyond those of a person who is just in charge of keeping the place going. An effective manager of this department must be object-, people-, and idea-oriented.

TECHNICAL, PEOPLE, AND CONCEPTUAL SKILLS

Front office managers cannot concentrate their managerial ability on technical skills alone — technology, budgets, controls. They also must concern themselves with people and with the conceptualization of notions about the resolution of management-related issues. Front office managers must have a thorough knowledge of how the job is done and how the equipment works, but also be able to exercise leadership and influence people to have the work done while being sensitive to employees' needs. At the same time, they must be able to analyze situations, implement change, and effect innovative ideas in the workplace.

SUPERVISION

A supervisor is anyone whose responsibility is to oversee operations; therefore every manager is a supervisor. The definition of supervision is quite similar to that of management in that it is concerned with directing, facilitating, and monitoring the work of others in order to have the job done. The front office manager's field of supervision encompasses two major components: employees and guests. Poor supervision of employees may lead to dealing with guests inefficiently, which in turn may create customer disloyalty and an eventual loss of profits.

Front office managers can effect supervision tightly or loosely. Supervision can be exacted by following prescribed rules and regulations or by allowing teamwork and decision making by line employees. In the latter case, workers are expected to exercise initiative and self-coordination. Whether to use one style or the other should depend on the composition of the work force. When there is a substantial turnover of employees and their working skills are weak, supervision should be tighter than when the work force is well trained and reliable.

LEADERSHIP

Providing leadership is one aspect of management. Leadership can be defined as "the ability to lead people to willingly perform in ways which achieve the organization's goals." One commonly encountered problem in the lodging industry is that of indifferent employees. Some of the reasons for this may be inadequate wages, poor benefits, part-time positions, and insufficient training so common to the industry. In spite of these obstacles, it is the task of hospitality managers to create an appropriate environment in which employees willingly display a positive attitude toward guests and fellow workers. This can be achieved through proper leadership.

There are three leadership styles generally used by leaders in professional situations. With the **authoritarian style**, the manager dictates tasks to be performed, ways to accomplish them and assumes the determination of policies; input from subordinates is not sought. **The democratic style** of management takes place when all policies are reached after group discussion and consensus, encouraged and facilitated by the manager. A **laissez-faire style** gives subordinates complete freedom for group or individual decisions while the manager does not take part in matters related to work. A front office manager exerting the same leadership style in all circumstances will most likely fail to achieve optimum results in the workplace. As different problems require different solutions, a flexible approach should be used when leading people. For instance, if a uniformed employee such as a bellperson refuses to perform a task necessary for the normal operation of the department, the manager should compel the worker to do the job. On the other hand, if the same bellperson is performing a job satisfactorily, the manager should not interfere.

Several studies conducted to identify leadership traits of successful leaders have yielded similar results. Successful business managers generally are well educated, self-assured, decisive, risk-takers, power-seekers, problem-solvers, and good in their relationships with people. Besides these attributes, front office managers should be good at motivating, communicating, delegating, and administrating their invested power and authority.

POWER/AUTHORITY

Power is the ability a person has to influence the behavior of others. When power is institutionalized in organizations, the ability to influence the behavior of others becomes a right. This established power is referred to as authority. The use of power should be administered wisely as individuals generally cannot grow and develop in an atmosphere of overwhelming authority.

Some managers may have an innate ability to do or affect something; others may resort to their invested authority to get things accomplished. Managers may exert their authority by coercion, reward, suggestion, persuasion, or emulation. **Coercive** and **reward power** refer to situations in which the manager administers punishment or recompense depending on the employee's behavior. Rewards and punishments should be administered fairly and be based on the behavior modification they may effect when applied to workers. **Suggestion** applies when the leader places an idea or proposition before a worker for consideration and possible action. If suggestion doesn't work, the manager may resort to **persuasion**, that is, advising or urging (rather than forcing) a person to do something. The best source of leader power is **emulation** in which workers want to equal or excel the professional behavior of a superior. Front office managers who are experts in their fields and possess charismatic behavior generally fit this type of leadership.

DELEGATION

No one should attempt to perform the duties of front office manager without delegating to others some of the functions involved in the management of the department. Carrying out the responsibility of managing the front office department requires the completion of numerous tasks, most of which are done by assistants, shift supervisors, and hourly employees.

Delegation can be defined as the process of assigning work with the necessary authority and accountability to accomplish it effectively. In practice, the process of delegation involves the creation of a relationship in which authority and responsibility are shared between manager and employee to get the job done. When delegation takes place effectively, the manager is left free to coordinate the different activities of the department. There are four steps that must be followed when delegating tasks: defining the task, designating who is to perform the job, empowering the employee to do the job, and requiring accountability for it. Figure 1.2 is a diagram showing a simple delegation process.

PROVIDING INFORMATION TO GUESTS

↓

will be accomplished by

↓

THE CONCIERGE

↓

with corresponding

↓

EMPOWERMENT

↓

and adequate

↓

ACCOUNTABILITY

FIGURE 1.2 DELEGATION DIAGRAM

Several methods of delegation can be used in the front office department. The manager may decide to define the results expected after the task is accomplished. For instance, front office clerks will check guests in and out with a minimum number of complaints. The manager may set performance standards to be met after the completion of tasks: for example, using comment cards filled out by guests to critique the performance of employees on duty. The manager may also establish specific procedures to do the job; for instance, breaking down the way clerks take reservations into components to be followed sequentially by the person answering the phone. Some managers find it difficult to delegate authority to others for reasons that may include lack of trust in employees, unwillingness to invest any of their authority in others, and enjoying hands-on work. This management approach usually ends in burnout.

Front office managers must understand that, although authority and responsibility may have been delegated, they are ultimately responsible for the acts of their subordinates. For this very reason, the process of delegation must always be carefully administered. Responsibility ultimately belongs to the superior and cannot be shifted to subordinates. The manager of the front office, employed by the company, cannot avoid total responsibility for the results of the department. If employees are negligent in their duties or upset guests, the front office manager must answer to the rooms division director or general manager (in smaller operations) for these actions. Figure 1.3 is a sample job description for front office managers.

Job title: Front Office Manager

Job responsibility: To directly supervise all services provided by the front office department and oversee the performance of front desk, reservations, switchboard, concierge, and uniformed personnel as stated in the property's operating manual.

Responsible to: Rooms Division Director (or general manager in smaller establishments).

DUTIES AND RESPONSIBILITIES:

1. Understand how all front office operating systems function.
2. Know the property's fire and evacuation procedures.
3. Decide on all matters regarding selecting, hiring, disciplining, and firing of front office employees.
4. Supervise the scheduling of front office staff.

5. Participate in the compilation of room sales projections with the sales department.
6. Prepare weekly room sales forecast.
7. Plan and control productivity and budgetary projections of the front office.
8. Organize the training and cross-training of front office employees.
9. Perform regular evaluations of front office employees.
10. Oversee all reports generated at the front office.
11. Act as liaison between the front office and other departments and maintain a professional relationship with the controller's office, housekeeping, sales, and engineering.
12. Control cash banks and cash/credit from daily operations.
13. Enforce standing check-cashing and credit policies.
14. Resolve guest problems and complaints.
15. Know the house room-status at all times.
16. Control the overbooking of guestrooms to avoid walking guests.
17. Pre-register groups.
18. Relay occupancy projections to other departments on a daily basis.
19. Ensure that all guest folios and city leger accounts are current at all times.
20. Conduct regular meetings of front office employees.
21. Supervise the appearance and grooming of all front office employees.

Management reserves the right to modify this job description and to assign other tasks to front office employees as circumstances require.

Required Job Qualifications: Able to operate the property's PMS system and other equipment at the front office. Possess physical endurance and dexterity to be able to work long hours when necessary.

Preferred qualifications: ***Education:*** A degree in hotel and restaurant management required. Knowledge of a second language preferred. ***Experience:*** over two years previous work in establishments of equivalent category. Good references required. ***Personality:*** pleasant, able to interact with guests and fellow workers.

Appearance: professional.

FIGURE 1.3 SAMPLE FRONT OFFICE MANAGER JOB DESCRIPTION

OTHER MANAGEMENT RESPONSIBILITIES OF THE FRONT OFFICE MANAGER

Besides the planning, organizing, directing, and controlling functions of management listed above there are several other management skills that front office managers must master to effectively fulfill the numerous responsibilities inherent in their positions. Among those, the management of time, the resolution of operational and personnel problems, the achievement of quality, the practice of values, and the ability to make decisions are the most important.

TIME MANAGEMENT

Time must be managed proactively by managers in order to be ready for upcoming events rather than having to react to crises. The tasks to be accomplished in the front office department are so numerous that managers often find, to their dismay that 8, 10, and even 12 hours of work per day are not enough to get the job done. In most cases, too many hours on the job lead to burnout and ultimately even resigning the position.

Job demands in the front office department generally can be categorized into short-run, intermediate-run, or long-run time frames. Short-run demands include day-to-day matters of an operational nature, such as ensuring that room counts are accurate at all times, that the rooming of guests is conducted effectively by uniformed personnel, that guests don't spend too much time checking in, and so on. Short-term demands usually require intense interaction with employees as many activities take place at the same time.

Intermediate-run demands require planning and organizing activities necessary to maintain the cohesiveness and efficiency of the front office department. The training and development of front office employees and the preparation of labor forecasts for upcoming events are typical examples of intermediate-run activities. These activities not only require downward communication but also lateral interaction with other departments of the property. For example, the arrival in the coming month of a large convention would require a review with the sales department of the specific steps necessary to coordinate this event.

Long-range forecasting is another important task for front office managers, specifically in the preparation of annual budgets. This process requires the provision of resources for an upcoming fiscal year. Long-run demands require substantial upward communication with the rooms division director, lateral communication with the controller, and downward communication with department supervisors.

The first step in managing time is to chart it. Having a time log such as a computer program or wall bulletin board where the day's and week's activities are entered helps to plan ahead and to be aware of how much time each activity requires to be completed. Computer software such as Microsoft® Outlook can be equally effective. Tickler file systems and phone call screening are some practices that can save precious time.

PROBLEM SOLVING

A problem in the workplace can be defined as any impediment that interferes with the achievement of goals. Considering the unpredictability and immediacy of situations, the type of employees, and the pace of front office operations, front office managers must possess an extraordinary ability to solve problems swiftly without resorting to a "shoot-from-the-hip" response.

The first step to effective problem solving is to identify the real issue. For instance, if check-in of guests is chronically slow, front desk employees might be blamed for it, although the real cause could be an obsolete computer system. Once problems have been clearly identified, their solution can be attempted individually or collectively. When the problem deals with human aspects, the task becomes more difficult and judgmental and usually needs the involvement of others. In collective problem solving, the manager's role is to foster ideas, then guide the process to its conclusion. Brainstorming is an effective technique aimed at eliciting group input by discussion in order to find solutions to problems.

The solution of problems can be facilitated by **empowering employees** to do whatever is necessary, within reason, to resolve problems for guests rather than to shift the problem upward to management. Some workers may be reluctant to solve problems for fear of making mistakes or assuming too much authority. In these cases, employees need to be given some leeway to make their own decisions in uncomplicated cases.

TOTAL QUALITY MANAGEMENT (TQM)

Quality control has been a major concern of American businesses for a very long time, since companies long ago realized that quality standards for any given product are ultimately established by the customer. However, while manufacturing companies in general concern themselves mainly with the quality of mechanical processes, lodging operations must concern themselves with both product and service quality.

The principles of total quality management that apply to front office operations are having an understanding of customer requirements, measuring customer satisfaction, empowering employees, and focusing on the continuous improvement of the search for quality. Front office managers in lodging operations must be aware of the expectations of the traveling public when staying in their properties. Fast check-ins and check-outs, efficient baggage delivery to rooms, the ability to connect a laptop to an in-room Ethernet plugin without problems, and friendly service are generally ranked high by the American traveler. In locations where the customer base is different from the norm, surveys should be conducted to find out the expectations of guests. For instance, a property that regularly receives large numbers of tourists from Japan may want to know what pleases Japanese guests whose tastes might differ from those of, say, European customers.

Guests' input should be sought regularly to find out if they are pleased with the accommodations and services offered. Electronic surveys, comment cards and personal interaction with guests will provide the information the department needs to measure guest satisfaction. Although the task is routine for desk clerks, guests should be approached often by a front office manager to find out if their stay was satisfactory. These relationships with guests should be the rule in lodging operations rather than the exception.

Empowering employees to take initiative in customer satisfaction is essential to quality management. In order to achieve this, employees should be given decision-making latitude and be given twice the necessary training to enable them to make reasonable decisions. This TQM approach generally results in a streamlined chain of command and in workers taking responsibility for their own work performance.

The concept of TQM also implies that the process of striving for excellence is not finite—it is about constantly improving and innovating. Avoiding errors, not fixing them, should be a never-ending process. Well-implemented TQM programs can also provide tangible savings to front office operations.

ETHICAL VALUES

It is the manager's obligation to follow those lines of action that conform to the values of society. High standards of professional ethics must be observed, especially by anyone in any management position as that sets the example for employees. Among ethical issues which the front desk may encounter are sexual harassment, both with employees or guests; privacy concerns, again in some cases of employees or guests; racial discrimination in hiring and pay; considerate and fair treatment of employees; and outright theft by either guests or employees.

Some guidelines for a front office manager to observe include:

- Obey the law when hiring. Choose employees on the perceived competence for the position they will be filling, not on the basis of race, religion, gender, age or sexual orientation.
- The same is true with pay, bonuses, scheduling, and promotion. Consider the employees' competence, effort and seniority, but not incidental factors such as age or gender which can be perceived as bias.

- At the same time, a good manager must be considerate of employees' particular circumstances and should try to work with their requests, i.e. scheduling around a student's classes, or a mother's need to pick up kids from school, and so on.

The ethical reputation of companies is often determined by the behavior of the managers who work for them. Front office managers should make reasonable efforts to foresee possible negative ethical consequences that would mar the reputation of their companies, their guests, or their subordinates.

DECISION-MAKING

Choosing from among alternatives of a course of action is called decision-making. One of the front office manager's central jobs is to prioritize what needs to be done, who will do it, where, and even how. The process of decision-making involves the identification of what needs to be accomplished, the search for possible alternatives, the evaluation of these alternatives, and the selection and implementation of the best one by which the job can be done. Managers should avoid making rapid-fire decisions as they often fall short of the desired target.

Good managers often decide to get a job done in the most cost-effective way possible in order to maximize profits; however, the needs, attitudes, and prejudices of people must be taken into account. For example, a front office manager may decide to improve the labor cost percentage of the department by laying off two full-time workers and hiring four part-time employees without benefits to do the same job. While the results may be positive in the short run, the reaction of the remaining full-time workers can be quite negative as they might perceive the company as not taking the welfare of its people into account.

One way to improve decision-making is by getting employees involved in the process. This method usually draws on different viewpoints and motivates people to be cooperative in carrying out an idea. Indeed, some companies use the concept of **quality circles**, in which total worker involvement in the decision-making process as well as in matters related to production and quality is sought.

KEY TERMS

Cycle of control
Department head
Empowerment of employees

Emulation
Leadership styles
authoritarian
democratic
laissez-faire
Long-range objectives
Persuasion power
coercive
reward
Quality circles
Short-range objectives
Span of control
Suggestion
Unity of command

DISCUSSION AND REVIEW QUESTIONS

1. Why should front office managers have concern for people as well as for production in the workplace?
2. When planning activities in the front office department, what could be a short-range objective? A long-range objective?
3. Describe the principle of unity of command and explain why it should be adopted in front office operations.
4. Give a practical example of the control process as a management function in front office operations.
5. When managing employees, what is the difference between authoritarian and laissez-faire styles?
6. What are the advantages and disadvantages of empowering hourly employees in the front office department?
7. Explain a practical way of implementing total quality management (TQM) in the front office department.
8. In your opinion, why should front office managers follow an ethical code of professional conduct in the workplace?
9. Describe both an ethical example and an unethical example of the professional conduct of a front office manager.
10. Why would you, as a front office manager, adopt quality circles in your department?

PRACTICAL SITUATIONS

Situation 1.1

Productivity of front office employees

Juan Jones, front office manager at the Embassy Court Hotel, wrote the following memo regarding operations in the front office department of the hotel: "The level of productivity of front desk clerks has been very low lately. On two occasions last week, there have been long lines of guests trying to check in in spite of the fact that the desk was fully manned. Beginning today, the 30-minute mid-morning break will be reduced to 15 minutes in order to increase productivity. I will be checking the front desk often to make sure that everyone is on task. We must avoid long lines of guests at all times!"

(a) How would you evaluate Mr. Jones' attitude regarding his concern for production? (b) How would you evaluate his attitude regarding his concern for people? (c) What would you have done in his place?

Situation 1.2

An ethical decision?

Mary Donaldson is rooms division director of an independent resort in a small town in the Southwest. The establishment has an excellent reputation and no direct competition. As a result, business is good and the average earnings before taxes for the last ten years have been above the industry average. Mary is considered an excellent division director by the general manager and receives substantial bonuses for achieving, and sometimes bettering, the budgeted bottom line. Ms. Donaldson considers herself very lucky to be operating in an area of abundant worker supply because of the lack of other properties in the area. The division has been able to maintain very low expenses for salaries and employee benefits.

The hourly workers in the front office and housekeeping, however, do not consider themselves so fortunate. Most of them receive minimum wage and have difficulties making ends meet on a weekly basis. Last month, they addressed a letter signed by a group of employees asking for a raise in wages of twenty percent over the minimum salary they receive. After making the necessary calculations, Ms. Donaldson figured out that the rooms division's profit would diminish from 74 percent to 69 percent. This would prevent her from receiving the 12 percent bonus from the departmental bottom-line income which had been set at a minimum of 70 percent.

Ms. Donaldson decides not to forward the petition to the general manager after considering that the supply of local workers would guarantee a sufficient number of applicants willing to work for the compensation the division currently offers. She also thought that as a manager, her job was to maximize profit while complying with existing labor laws.

ASSIGNMENT: Discuss the case, and decide whether Mary Donaldson behaved ethically in this case and the potential impact her decision would have on the stakeholders involved and on the resort's operations.

Situation 1.3

Ethical or unlawful decision?

You are a front office manager at a resort in Utah. You have received several complaints about shift supervisor Johnson repeatedly asking female employees of the department for dates after work. After discussing the problem with him, he becomes defensive, saying that he will quit the job if you keep bothering him about his personal relationships with his fellow workers. Because Johnson is a very dedicated, productive employee, you decide not to pay any attention to the complaints lest you end up losing this otherwise excellent supervisor.

(a) Are you behaving responsibly in this particular situation? (b) Why or why not?

CASE STUDY 1.1

The difficult personality of Brittani Brown

Brittani Brown graduated with a 4.0 GPA. At commencement, she was asked to deliver a speech to the graduating class and be the standard bearer at the university ceremony. Everyone who knew Brittani assumed that her success in the hospitality industry was a sure thing. Predictably, she obtained a management-in-training position with Orbit Hotels and Resorts, a lodging management company operating twelve first-rate properties in West Virginia.

After one year with the organization, Ms. Brown was promoted to front office manager and promised a resident manager position within two years. Three years having passed without her being promoted, she decided to discuss the issue with the director of personnel, Mr. Thomas. The meeting did not go well at all; it ended with Ms. Brown accusing management of false promises and lack of integrity. In a fit of fury, she left the room shutting the door with a loud bang. Two hours later, having cleaned up her office, she threw her working keys on Mr. Thomas' desk and left the hotel for good.

It was not difficult for her to find a new job. The new company, although small, was acquiring properties at a steady pace. She was hired to manage the front office of a busy 350-room hotel near Sacramento. Ms. Brown's performance in the organization was so efficient that soon after she was selected for promotion as resident manager of the company's flagship property in Tucson, AZ.

At that time, the board of directors of the organization approved the takeover of the company by Orbit Hotels and Resorts where Emmet Thomas had been promoted to CEO. By executive order, Ms. Brown's promotion to resident manager was swiftly rescinded. Confidentially, Mr. Thomas explained to the board that he found the personal behavior of Brittani Brown to be dysfunctional.

ASSIGNMENT:

What political mistake did Brittani Brown make?
In your opinion, how could Brittani have avoided her blunders?

CHAPTER 2

DESIGN OF THE FRONT OFFICE DEPARTMENT

CHAPTER OBJECTIVES

- Discuss the main functions of the front office in lodging operations.
- Explain the elements of the rooms division.
- Describe the departments included in the rooms division of large lodging establishments.
- Define the design and typical classification of guestrooms by bed structure.
- Understand how the front office is staffed and the scheduling of employees
- Explain the guestroom room entry control systems.
- Discuss the interaction between the front office and other departments.

OVERVIEW

This chapter explains the functions of the front office and describes the composition of the rooms division of which the front office is an integral part. As the nerve center of the operation, the front office is the hub from where most guest-related activities are coordinated. In large lodging operations, the front office includes the sub-departments of front desk, reservations, and uniformed services. It is the responsibility of the front office manager to plan, coordinate, and control the functions of the department under the direct supervision of the rooms division director.

The design and classification of guestrooms and the card room entry systems used in lodging properties are concisely covered in this chapter. It emphasizes the fact that hard-keys are ineffective in maintaining the operation secure while electronic equipment is a known deterrent of theft by employees and intruders. The chapter ends with a discussion of the interaction necessary between the front office and the property's operational and support units.

THE ROLE OF THE FRONT OFFICE IN LODGING OPERATIONS

The main functions of the front office are to provide services directly to guests, to maintain a detailed up-to-the-minute inventory of guestrooms, and to keep accurate records of business transactions. In other words, the front office deals with reservations, room allocation, registration, billings and payments. The overall goal is to sell as many guestrooms as possible at the highest feasible rate. The standards for front office positions depend on the size and category of each establishment but, in all cases, a well-structured organization of the department, including work shifts, job descriptions, and job specifications, are necessary to achieve a high level of productivity and guest satisfaction.

Large establishments are generally organized to include the **front desk** where guests are registered and checked out, room availability is maintained, and accounts are kept; the **bell staff** or uniformed personnel who attend to transportation, luggage handling, escorting, information, and other services provided to guests; and the **reservation department** which deals with booking requests.

THE ROOMS DIVISION

The task of providing hospitality and services to guests in a friendly and efficient manner falls mainly on the property's **rooms division**. The overall success of a lodging establishment depends on the profitability of the rooms division, which generally accounts for a large share of a property's sales while generating a gross profit percentage from 70 to 80 percent of the division's revenue. Besides providing lodging and professional services, rooms division personnel must provide the "home-away-from-home" feeling so cherished by those travelers who are temporarily separated from their families. Offering tastefully decorated guestrooms and public areas and impeccable cleanliness in a subdued, relaxing atmosphere is also of the utmost importance.

Large properties are divided into operational units called divisions. Two of these divisions—rooms, and food and beverage— are **revenue-generating centers**, while the remaining departments are considered to be **support centers**. The executive in charge of the rooms division is the **rooms division director**, who in some properties may be called resident manager, executive manager, or senior assistant manager. Figure 2.1 shows the breakdown of divisions in a large property. The rooms division director reports directly to the property's general manager. As a member of the **executive committee**, he/she takes an active part in policy-making decisions related to operations. Other members of this committee generally include the food and beverage director, in charge of the food and beverage division; the sales director, who deals with sales, marketing, and public relations; the controller or chief financial officer; the human resources director, in charge of personnel matters; and the plant manager, responsible for the engineering and maintenance needs of the property.

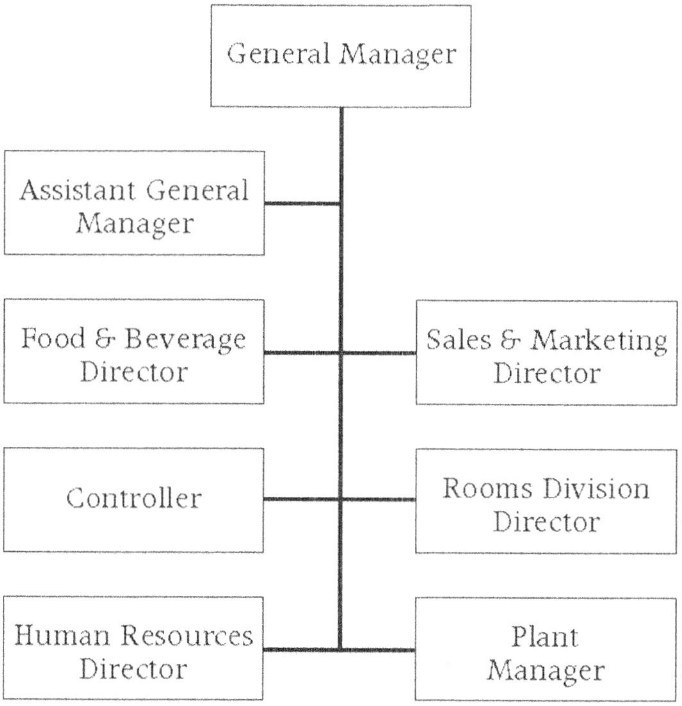

FIGURE 2.1 SAMPLE DIVISION CHART OF LARGE PROPERTY

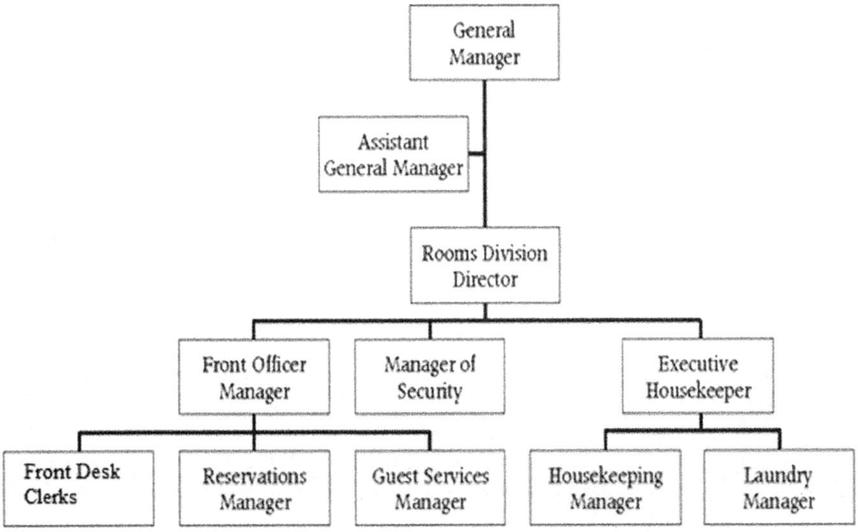

FIGURE 2.2 SAMPLE DEPARTMENT CHART OF THE ROOMS DIVISION

Figure 2.2 shows the rooms division divided into departments. Of these, the front office is of critical importance to the property. The front office manager is the head of the department and is, therefore, directly responsible for managing this nerve center of the property. The position of front office manager in the organizational chart is that of **department head**, equal in rank to the executive housekeeper, the security manager, and the remaining managers in charge of departments in other divisions. In smaller properties, division directors do not exist; instead, department heads manage the different units, reporting directly to the general manager or assistant.

In large lodging properties the front office manager oversees operations at the front desk, reservations, and services provided by uniformed personnel. The front desk is open 24 hours a day, usually divided into three 8-hour shifts: morning, evening, and night. The **morning shift** usually covers 8 AM to 4 PM; the **evening shift** from 4 PM to midnight, and the **night** or **graveyard shift** from midnight to 8 AM. The morning and evening shifts generally include a shift supervisor; the night shift is usually managed by the property's night auditor.

The basic duties of the front desk clerks, also called **desk attendants** and **receptionists,** are to welcome and register arriving travelers, check out departing customers, collect payments, and represent the property to its guests. Although most telephone functions are fully automated and can be handled directly by guests, large properties use telephone operators to answer calls coming from outside or in-house calls activated when guests dial "0" for the operator or a dedicated number to reach the front desk. Telephone operators or the desk clerks are responsible for the all-important **wakeup calls** that are activated by punching the room number and the wake-up time into an automated device.

If something goes wrong with their stay, guests usually complain first to the front desk. Although shift duties overlap, the morning shift deals mainly with most guest departures, the evening shift with arrivals, and the night shift with accounting procedures. In smaller properties where reservations are taken at the front desk, clerks must be trained in upselling techniques and in keeping the availability status of rooms at all times to avoid overbooking.

The reservations department's main responsibility is to achieve 100 percent occupancy by combining reservations booked in advance with the up-to-the-moment call-in and walk-in sales. Very large properties, where the number of daily check-outs is significant, offer **cashier** services at the front desk to expedite cash and credit-card transactions, exchange foreign currency, provide safe-deposit box service, and control the shift banks of the property's outlets, such as restaurants, lounges and cash bars.

Guest services, supervised by the **bell captain** or **head porter,** are provided by uniformed personnel which include the **bell staff, transportation drivers, valet parking** and **door attendants,** and the property's **concierge.** The main responsibilities of bell attendants are to greet, welcome, escort guests to their rooms if they request this type of service, to deliver packages and valet linen to guests, and to provide information on the establishment's services and guestroom features. Transportation drivers are in charge of the property's limousine or shuttle van service that is provided by most establishments located near an airport. Some of these vehicles are equipped with cell phones so that drivers can relay the arriving guests' information to the front desk to allow the clerk on duty to anticipate the check-in. Courtesy vans can also provide transportation service to guests to local businesses, entertainment, sporting and dining establishments. The job of valet parking and door attendants is to assist guests with their luggage and to park their vehicles so that they don't have to worry about finding a parking space, walking to the hotel in inclement weather, or locating their cars in the parking lot. Valet parking attendants are also responsible for the security of guests' vehicles.

Located in the lobby or beside the front desk, the concierge provides assistance with information about the property's services, the city and surrounding area, entertainment, local tours and activities, church services, purchasing theater or concert tickets, and other miscellaneous queries. It is desirable that the person hired for this position speak a second language, particularly in areas frequented by travelers from abroad. In smaller properties where there is no concierge, this service is provided by the front desk clerks and bell personnel.

By offering a professional concierge, the establishment can provide direct information to guests as, often, the front desk can only be reached by waiting in line. Most luxury properties offer **concierge floors** where special services and security to guests lodging in that section of guestrooms are provided. Access to the floor is limited to guests with special elevator cards. The services offered by the concierge, besides information, can range from providing continental breakfast, shoeshine, and an evening cocktail hour. Certified concierges are identified by the display of gold-crossed keys on their uniform lapels. To earn this distinction, a concierge must be certified by the international association of concierges which sets the standards for its members. Some lodging properties have the position of **manager-on-duty (MOD)** to ensure that there is a person available at all times to solve operational problems and to take care of guest requests. Job descriptions for these positions are listed in chapter six.

FRONT OFFICE STAFFING AND SCHEDULING

To provide an effective service at the front desk, management must select the right staff, train them well, and provide them with state-of-the-art equipment. Front office managers should always aim at recruiting the best person for the job based on each position's job description. Employees working at the front desk should be proficient in:

- Operating computers and other technology-based equipment.
- Taking advanced bookings.
- Understanding billing procedures.
- Handling cash.
- Balancing accounts.
- Interacting with guests, sometimes in languages other than English.

Ideally, each front desk position should have some personal specifications guidelines which could consist of these features:

- Physical appearance
- Prior work experience
- Education
- Technical skills
- Pleasant disposition

Physical appearance is important as front desk clerks are the first representatives of the property to guests. The hiring criteria must not be discriminatory in any way but attention should be paid to appropriate grooming and a pleasant disposition. Because of the complexity of front office operations, previous work experience would help the applicant adapt to the needs of the position. The level of education should conform to the job's requirement for guest service agents, including being good with numbers and attentive to details. The knowledge of lodging computer systems and equipment should be considered highly desirable, together with linguistic ability to understand what people with different accents (or languages) are saying and to respond appropriately. Awareness of intercultural differences can also be helpful. Not less important is the disposition of the applicant to being hospitable; that is, having a tendency to empathize with others. Front desk clerks should also be efficient sellers, for which they have to show signs of enthusiasm and persuasiveness, necessary qualities at the time of closing transactions with travelers.

Scheduling front office employees can be difficult because fluctuations in occupancy, the number of transient check-ins and outs, the arrival of groups, and high and low seasons. For example, a downtown business property may be very busy on weekdays and quiet on weekends; guest arrivals may be heavy on Mondays during the evening shift and departures strong on Friday mornings, or groups can arrive by bus requiring the delivery of a large number of luggage pieces in a very short period of time. While scheduling too many employees could negatively affect payroll costs and employee productivity, forecasting a lower-than-needed number of workers may generate guest complaints and dissatisfaction.

Another complexity faced by the front office manager is the necessity to accommodate employee needs, such as the request by college students to avoid working hours that conflict with their classes. At the same time, the scheduler has to keep up with the needs of the property at all times. The following basic guidelines can help schedule employees at the front office:

- Schedules should cover at least a full workweek in order to provide employees with enough warning so they can plan for their out-of-work activities.
- The posted schedules should be updated daily to adjust for arrival or departure fluctuations.
- Schedules should be made available to employees with sufficient anticipation, usually at least three days before the beginning of the next workweek.

In large establishments, separate sections, each with their own supervisors, are required while in smaller properties most duties may be the responsibility of one or two clerks, who may have to take bookings, register and check out guests, answer the phone, post charges, handle cash, and deal with guests' requests and, unfortunately, complaints.

Typically, new clerks start in the back office so that they learn about the layout of the house and the operating systems. When they feel ready, they are scheduled to work behind the counter to face real live guests. The number of clerks that need to be scheduled at any given time depends on several factors, particularly on these:

- The number of occupied rooms at the time of the shift and the predicted arrivals/departures.
- The level of automation of the property; for example, establishments with self-check-in and check-out options require fewer employees.
- The amount of personal contact with guests required; for instance, if a hotel has or has not concierge services.
- The level of service the establishment hopes to provide; for example, ensuring that guests don't have to line up for more than a few minutes.

Front office managers will have the task of evaluating what is to be done and how fast, keeping in mind that guests want to be checked in promptly on arrival and checked out efficiently when they leave. Some considerations for the manager to keep in mind may be that the telephone is answered within, say, three rings 24 hours a day; that cashiering peaks occur mostly during the morning shift; and that heavy registering happens generally in the evening hours. Planning for group arrivals and departures must also be considered.

Usually, medium and large hotels schedule employees in three distinct shifts: the morning shift that may run from 8 AM until 4 PM; the evening shift, from 4 to midnight; and the night or graveyard shift, from 12 to 8 AM. The latter shift typically requires a reduced staff supervised by the night auditor whose job is to balance the day's accounts. Often, the busiest days of business hotels are Monday through Friday while resorts and vacation establishments have higher occupancy on week-ends.

In most cases, preparing the weekly roster is the job of the manager who has to juggle the ups and downs of occupancy with special requests from employees asking for unexpected days off. In all cases, the filling of positions by shift must be fair to all and should avoid any employee to working the evening and morning shifts back to back. A very schematic example of a day's work could be as follows:

8 AM to 4 PM The morning shift takes over the night shift. Activities include checking the cash bank, printing scheduled departures, checking out guests, printing the day's arrivals, checking in early arrivals, determining number of rooms available today, checking credit limits of stay-over rooms, checking housekeeping occupied-room report and accounting for discrepancies, reconciling cash and balancing the cash bank.

4 PM to 12 AM The evening shift takes over from the morning shift. Activities include checking the cash bank, checking guest arrival list, checking VIP arrivals and special accommodation requests, determining room availability (rooms to sell), checking in guests, checking 6 PM releases and adding no-shows to room availability list, if overbooked arranging for alternative accommodations in other properties, posting charges to guest folios (in a property not fully automated), reconciling cash and balancing the cash bank.

12 AM TO 8 AM The night shift takes over the evening shift. Activities include checking the cash bank, checking in late scheduled arrivals and transients, checking today's room status, performing night audit (printing all reports), printing tomorrow's expected departures list, printing tentative room availability for tomorrow, reconciling cash and balancing the cash bank.

The main goal when scheduling should be to assign workloads for a maximum of a 40-hour workweek to avoid overtime. Obviously, front office employees should be given their days off during the slowest part of the week. The overall goal should be to minimize payroll costs while providing the best service possible.

GUESTROOM DESIGN AND CLASSIFICATION

The guestroom is the lodging industry's most important product. Regardless of their types of service, properties must maintain interior design consistency standards throughout the building and in particular in their guestrooms. Color patterns, fabric and upholstery quality, and overall appearance must befit the category it represents. Colors, for instance, must be coordinated and match the furniture and fixtures, such as lamp bases, vases, and wall pictures.

The bed size of rooms provides a basic classification by which guestrooms are identified. Today, rooms with single beds (38 x 74 inches) are rare. **Twin rooms** are fitted with two twin-size beds (42 x 76), **double rooms** with one (or two) double-size bed(s) (54 x 76), **queen rooms** with one (or two) queen-size bed(s) (60 x 80), and **king rooms** with one (or two) king-size bed(s) (76 x 84 inches). There are rooms with **murphy beds**, a wall-bed concealed during the day behind a wall panel, called **parlor rooms**. The advantage of having parlor rooms is that they can be used as a living room when the bed is up. Some properties offer **suites** that consist of a bedroom plus a living room, usually with a **sofa bed** and kitchenette. Some chains specialize in an **all-suite** concept, such as Embassy Suites, where all rooms offered to the public are suites. These properties appeal to families travelling with children and to business guests wanting to use a living room to conduct interviews or meetings in a space separate from the bedroom. Luxury hotels boast special living quarters usually known as **presidential suites** for which affluent guests are willing to pay exorbitant rates in exchange for extraordinary accommodations consisting of very special furnishings and amenities.

In the age of technology, today's traveler is putting a new spin on the concept of guest-room equipment. Examples of guestroom technological equipment are:

- High-speed wireless Ethernet offering isolation between users (private VLAN).
- TV with access to movies on demand and video games for kids.
- TV with Internet access for guests who have not brought their own laptop but would like to browse from their rooms.
- Sufficient outlets for charging cell phones, cameras, and laptops.

Guestrooms are often equipped with multi-line telephones; some hotels provide cellular phones and 24-hour access to translators plus information in other languages. Office centers are fitted with high-tech office support equipment, such as computers with desktop publishing, a printer, a fax machine, a scanner, a video room, and a drafting center.

Refrigerators and microwave ovens are common in suite hotels, and coffee makers, together with a selection of coffee and tea blends, are now available in the rooms of most properties. Wide-screen television sets and high-quality clock radios are a must in four- and five- diamond properties, as are in-room safes. In-room strongboxes are seen as a last-ditch defense for guests' personal belongings, including items as large as laptop computers. The locking systems of in-room safes range from ordinary keys to digital programmable push buttons, magnetic-lock devices, and the guest's credit card. Besides being a great convenience for guests who don't want to line up for safety deposit boxes, in-room safes are effective against thieves and even employees who may use stolen keys to burglarize a room. Some safes have built-in memory, which enables the front office personnel to read the date and time of the most recent safe openings and closings. This can provide convincing evidence in case of a loss claim against the property.

Some upscale lodging properties offer minibars in their guestrooms and suites. Fully automated minibars can electronically sense when an item is removed, sending the corresponding charge to the guest's room account. The interface with the front office system provides check-in and check-out information, allowing the minibar to be automatically locked when the room is vacant. Upon check-out the guest cannot go back to the room and use the minibar. Additionally, the minibar can remain locked for certain categories of guests, such as those who pay cash at check-in, tour groups, and aircrews. Staff will also have no access when the room is vacant. Current technology provides comprehensive reports to allow control of store issues. Only items will be issued which have been consumed by guests, avoiding oversupply by the minibar attendants and, therefore, pilferage opportunities. Non-automated units must rely on the honesty of the guest to notify the front desk just before checking out if goods have been consumed. Some brands provide for a courtesy shelf allowing guests to use the minibar to refrigerate their own items such as fruit, milk bottles, and baby food.

New technology allows minibar attendants to use a hand-held device to display and refill requirements electronically. This system helps to speed up replenishments and reduce labor costs. Automated minibars decrease labor costs as only one minibar attendant for every 400 rooms is needed instead of one for 100 rooms with manual machines. Brantas International offers a computerized energy saving system that allows for management of temperature and cooling cycles of the minibar. Cooling can be set according to electricity rate periods and room status, thus allowing management to enhance cooling efficiency reducing energy costs significantly. Brantas' Bartech uses remotely controlled electronic thermostats.

GUESTROOM ENTRY CONTROL SYSTEMS

Mechanical locks are not effective to deter crime from occurring; as a matter of fact, lodging properties using traditional guestroom keys are considered to be at a competitive disadvantage. Today most, if not all, lodging establishments in the United States use electronic lock systems rather than the traditional hard keys of the past. Card entry systems are designed so that every guest checking into the property receives a card with a combination different from the one used the previous night. In fact, the computer terminal issuing cards at the front desk is capable of providing millions of combinations for entrance to a room. Card entry systems can also register a specific card and the time guests and staff used it during the day or night to enter the room. Also, if a master card is lost, the entire floor or floors can be reset very quickly.

Some entry card systems are designed to encode two different tracks, enabling the property to control access not only to guestrooms, but to other designated areas such as pools, health clubs, elevators, concierge floors, and in-room safes. The cards can also be used to activate electric circuits when they are inserted in a slot on the wall in guestrooms, allowing the property to save energy when the guests take the card back on leaving the room. State-of-the-art cellular control systems can be programmed to issue cards that can limit employee access to rooms by name, time, and date. For example, a section housekeeper card can be programmed to access her section of rooms at certain times during the day and on specific days of the week only. Likewise, cards provided to guests will only work for the duration of the guest's stay.

Besides the individual card keys provided to guests, master card keys are issued to room attendants, room inspectors, housekeeping and engineering managers, and **managers on duty (MODs).** The keys provided to housekeepers usually are designed to open one section of rooms, those keys assigned to inspectors several sections, and the keys given to managers may open all the guestrooms in the house. The control center of property guestroom entry cards is at the front office which is where the issuing system is located. For security control, **master cards** should be re-coded and re-issued to employees every month or so for security reasons.

There are two common versions of electronic locking systems: **hard wired** and those equipped with **microprocessors.** The hard-wired system works through a console at the front desk that is interfaced with all key locks. At check-in, the front desk punches a code that is transmitted to the guestroom lock by way of wires, allowing access to the new guest. The installation of this system is expensive because of the extensive wiring network necessary to connect the console to all the rooms. Most common is the stand-alone system which consists of a battery-powered microprocessor and card reader installed in every lock. Hoteliers should make sure that the electronic systems chosen are hack-proof as there are devices that thieves can buy at low cost which permit them to break into individual guestrooms if the locking mechanisms are not secure.

INTERACTION BETWEEN THE FRONT OFFICE AND OTHER DEPARTMENTS

Because the front office department is an integral part of all the areas into which a lodging operation is divided, a strong relationship must exist with all other units of the property as well. For instance, the sales department, which often must have access to ready rooms to show to meeting planners or tour operator representatives, must communicate this need to the front office department to ensure that the rooms are not occupied. There are many relevant software programs that graduates will find when they join the lodging industry. These user-friendly programs can be learned on site with just basic computer knowledge by new employees.

COMMUNICATION WITH HOUSEKEEPING

Guestrooms in lodging properties are sold by the front office. The front desk must know at any given moment which rooms have been cleaned and are available for occupancy. Housekeeping must provide the front desk with a list of rooms that are ready for occupancy so guests can be checked in. If communication between the two departments is poor or breaks down, delays in guest check-in will occur or people will be checked into rooms that are thought to be ready but that in fact are occupied or not ready. If this happens often, the property's reputation will suffer.

The cycle of communication begins early each day when the front desk provides the housekeeping department with a computer-generated or written report called the **night clerk's room report**. The purpose of this report is to inform the housekeeping department very early in the morning of the status of all guestrooms on the property as it appears on the front desk records. Figure 2.3 shows a sample of this report. The nomenclature used varies from property to property, but the most commonly used definitions are these:

SO = occupied (stay over)
OOO = out-of-order
V = vacant (on change)
C/O = guest has (or will) check out today
EA = early arrival today
R = Ready room

NIGHT CLERK'S REPORT

Date: ________________ Prepared By: __________________________
Total Rooms Occupied: ____
Check Outs: ____
Stay Overs: ____
Out of Order: ____

	Status		Status		Status		Status
101	SO	201	OOO	301	SO	401	V
102	SO	202	SO	302	SO	402	OOO
103	C/O	203	SO	303	R	403	SO
104	V	204	C/O-EA	304	R	404	R
105	SO	205	V	305	C/O	405	R

The report indicates that rooms 101, 102, 105, 202, 203, 301, 302 and 403 are occupied and staying over. Rooms 103, 204 and 305 are checkouts. Rooms 201 and 402 are out of order. Rooms 104, 205 and 401 are vacant and not ready. Rooms 303, 304, 404 and 405 are ready to be sold. There is a scheduled early arrival in room 204.

FIGURE 2.3 SAMPLE OF NIGHT CLERK'S REPORT TO HOUSEKEEPING

As soon as it is possible, an **AM guestroom check** is performed by housekeeping to ascertain whether the information provided in the night clerk's report was accurate. When discrepancies are found between the status of rooms received from the night clerk and the physical inspection of the rooms, the front desk is immediately notified. For instance, if the front desk reports that a certain room is vacant and housekeeping finds it occupied, a discrepancy exists and the front desk should be notified. There are several reasons why discrepancies may occur. The most common are:

- A guest switches from one room to another and the front desk fails to change its records.
- An error is made by the night clerk when filling out the night clerk's report.
- A guest is given the wrong room key by mistake.
- The room has been or is being used by an unauthorized employee.
- The room is sold by the front desk without being recorded, and the money is pocketed by the clerk.
- A guest checks in or out between the time the report is made and the room check is conducted.

The **PM guestroom check** is conducted by the housekeeping department just before the end of the morning shift. This check consists of entering every room in the house at approximately the same time in order to generate a report showing the status of all guestrooms. The report is made available to the front desk and compared with front desk records. As with the AM report, if discrepancies are found, they are immediately investigated and the records corrected. Besides reporting whether rooms are occupied, vacant, out of order, or ready, the report should provide the front desk with information that can help the department better control guest records. The most common symbols used are:

- B = slept out (guest did not use the room but baggage is still in the room)
- NB = occupied, no baggage
- DND = do-not-disturb sign on door
- LO = lock out (room has been locked by management so that guest cannot re-enter)

As the evening progresses and the room attendants on the evening shift continue to clean rooms from late check-outs and day-rate occupancy, the front desk is notified of the rooms available for sale.

Other communications between the front office and the housekeeping department involve information about the arrival of VIPs, the early check-in of groups, the closing of certain sections for deep-cleaning or repairs, lost and found items, special guest requests, etc. The communication between the front desk and the housekeeping department is greatly improved when the property uses a computerized system. For instance, when a guest checks out, the front desk clerk enters the departure in the computer and it appears instantly on the housekeeping monitor. When housekeeping has rooms ready to be sold, the information is entered in the system and it too shows up quickly at the front desk terminal.

There is an increasing number of digital programs that can help the two departments communicate very effectively. For example, OPTii offers a hand-held device which can instantly modify the status of guestrooms. The touch-screen interface can send and receive timely communications and generate reports on rooms cleaned without the need to use computer screens or make telephone calls between the front desk and the housekeeping department. OPTii URL is www.optiisolutions.com.

The front desk routinely provides housekeeping advanced reports on room sales projections, usually weekly, to assist the department in scheduling employees and in planning personnel vacation days. The communication between the two departments is especially important as guests usually call the operator or the front desk to request amenities or guestroom supplies.

COMMUNICATION WITH ENGINEERING

The relationship between the front office and the engineering department must be as close as that with housekeeping, as maintenance employees must know the occupancy status of rooms before conducting repairs or scheduling preventive maintenance. Requests for fixing in-room equipment, fixtures, and furniture while guests have already checked in are usually channeled through the front office which follows up with the generation of a work order that is sent to the maintenance department. The number of items that may be in need of repairs in a single guestroom can be substantial: beds, chairs, desks, TV, radio, lights, doors, toilets, faucets, walls, heating, air conditioning, and so on. It is therefore imperative that good communication between the two departments exists at all times. For instance, if a guestroom lock is found to be broken, maintenance must be notified, the room must be put out of order, the work performed, the area cleaned, and the room put back in vacant-ready status. As with housekeeping, a computerized system or hand-held electronic device should be used for instant message delivery.

There are two types of maintenance performed by the engineering department in hospitality lodging properties. **Regular maintenance** is performed when an item is broken and needs to be repaired. In this case, a **work order** is generated. If the repair needs to be done in order to be able to sell the room that day, an urgent request is sent to engineering so that the work is given priority over other nonessential jobs.

MAINTENANCE REQUEST

By ____ Date ____________

Location ____

Problem ____

Assigned to____

Date completed. ________________________________ Time Spent ___________

Completed By____

Remarks ____

Original: Originator Canary: Maintenance: Manila: Maintenance

FIGURE 2.4 SAMPLE MAINTENANCE REQUEST FORM

Figure 2.4 is a standard form used for requesting repair and maintenance services from the engineering department. **Preventive maintenance** consists of inspecting guestrooms and other areas on a regular basis to identify repair and maintenance needs. In most properties, the front office manager cooperates in blocking off sections of rooms for preventive maintenance as this involves conducting a thorough maintenance inspection of the rooms two or three times a year. Figure 2.5 is a sample **maintenance checklist** used to perform maintenance inspections. The form should list every item that could be in need of repair. After the preventive maintenance inspection has been completed, a check mark will indicate that the standards of operations have been met, while an "x" will indicate that the item in question is in need of repair. Preventive maintenance programs are essential to ensure that guests staying at the property find the rooms in perfect working order.

Room Number:___________________

Guestroom:

Doors	Lights	Electrical
A/C Units	Walls	Ceiling
Floor	Furniture	Windows
Television	Telephone	Mirrors
Drapes	Closet	Bed

Remarks:__________________

Bathroom:

Lights	Paint	Air vent
Tub	Vanity	Shower
Caulking	Drains	Toilet

Remarks________________

FIGURE 2.5 SAMPLE MAINTENANCE CHECKLIST

COMMUNICATION WITH HUMAN RESOURCES

Communication between the front office and human resources departments is necessary when considering personnel staffing. When an employee is needed, an **employee requisition** is filled out and sent to human resources to initiate the process. Most properties have software linking the two departments. Figure 2.6 is a sample employee requisition that provides human resources with the necessary information for the job in question. After receiving the request, human resources advertises for the position, pre-screens the candidates, conducts the first interview, and checks references. The final candidates are then sent to the front office for a second interview and hiring selection.

HOLIDAY INN GWINNETT CENTER
COURTESY OF INTERCONTINENTAL HOTELS GROUP

SAMPLE EMPLOYEE REQUISITION

Date: ______________ Department: ______________________________________

Position: ____

New: _________ Replacement: _________ Number required: _________

Classification: ____

(Full-time, Part-time, Temporary, Pool)

Working hours: ______________ Estimated no. of hours/week: ________

Desired starting date: ____

Starting rate of pay: ______________ Base rate: ________________________

Specification (General description of duties): __________________________

Special Qualifications (Desired or required): __________________________

FIGURE 2.6 SAMPLE EMPLOYEE REQUISITION

Human resources is usually also involved in the orientation of new front office employees at which time the company's philosophy, compensation package, pay schedule, and rules and regulations are explained in detail to the new worker. This department also ensures that the new employee fills out all necessary forms related to legal residency, income tax, and personal information. Good communication with human resources will help result in hiring the right employees to fill front office vacancies.

COMMUNICATION WITH FOOD AND BEVERAGE (F&B)

Food and beverage is the second major revenue center in the property after the rooms division. The food and beverage division in large hotels is comprised of the property's kitchens, restaurants, coffee shops, cafeterias, bars, lounges, banquets, catering services, clubs, and room service. Communication between the front office and the F & B points of sale usually involves the posting of charges to go into the individual guests' accounts. Often, charges are posted incorrectly and the discrepancies must be ironed out, or they are posted late at the time a guest is checking out, in which case the front desk must telephone the outlet to find out the amount to be billed before the guest departs.

As with housekeeping, the front desk must provide advanced reports on room sales projections to assist the kitchen and the different outlets in scheduling employees and in purchasing food and beverage supplies with anticipation. Besides, large numbers of guests checking in and out should be predicted in order to increase food production and man the restaurants and bars for an increased number of breakfasts or dinners to be served.

Communication with the banquet department involves the expedient charging of function costs to the appropriate account and the daily posting of events on the marquee and bulletin boards in the lobby.

COMMUNICATION WITH SALES AND MARKETING

The primary goal of the sales and marketing division is to sell the products and services offered by the property. There must be good communication between sales and the front office if customer satisfaction is to be achieved. For instance, if sales and marketing has guaranteed an early check-in to a large group of guests attending a convention without notifying the front office, room assignments may not be ready, causing an unnecessary delay at the arrival of a tour bus or shuttle vans from the airport. The sales and marketing office should provide a list of convention participants so that the front office can prepare a **rooming list,** a record of the names of a group of travelers checking into the property, in order to pre-register guests before their arrival at the property. The pre-registration of a large number of people is appreciated by the organizers of a convention as it prevents unnecessary delays at check-in.

The front office manager usually prepares sales projection reports for budgetary purposes together with the sales and marketing director based on historical occupancy data and on bookings on hand. The reservations section of the front office must inform sales and marketing of the availability of rooms for the booking of potential meetings or conventions. This is achieved by keeping the reservations database up to date which can eliminate the possibility of a simultaneous booking of a large number of rooms by both departments.

Communication between sales and the front office is also necessary when specific rooms or suites must be available for inspection by meeting planners who are considering the property for a possible convention. The rooms are blocked off in the system to avoid selling them to regular guests when the visit of the convention representative is scheduled.

The front office should keep an accurate database of registration information, such as guest profiles, zip codes of origin, company affiliation, and stay frequency, and make it available to the sales and marketing department which will use the information for marketing campaigns or special offers. By the same token, the sales department should provide the front desk with complete information of functions that take place at the property, such as dates, times, venues, and so on, so that employees on duty can answer questions and provide directions to in-house guests and outside visitors.

COMMUNICATION WITH THE ACCOUNTING OFFICE

Because the financial control of front office operations is conducted by the accounting office, communication between the two departments is substantial. The property's controller (or comptroller) monitors all business transactions that take place at the front office, especially those involving cash. The front office must provide a series of reports detailing all debit and credit operations that take place daily, both of in-house guests and of city leger accounts. This is conducted by the night auditor who categorizes the day's business transactions, summarizes them, and provides the results using a series of reports to the accounting office for auditing. The accounting office receives the cash and credit totals collected during the day and monitors the money float (banks) that are provided to the morning, evening, and night front office shifts that are necessary to provide change to guests and cover possible paid-out expenses. In some establishments, the cashiers working in the front office area are employees of the accounting department and report directly to the controller. In addition, the front office must provide accounting with all information regarding wages and salaries of its employees such as pay increases, hours worked per week, overtime, and bonuses awarded to workers.

KEY TERMS

All-suite property
AM guestroom check
Bell captain
Bell staff
Cashier (Front Office)
Concierge
Concierge floor
Department head
Desk attendant
Door attendant
Double room
Employee requisition
Evening shift (Front Office)
Executive committee
Graveyard shift (Front Office)
Hard-wired locking system
Head porter
King room
Maintenance checklist
Manager on duty (MOD)

Master card
Microprocessor-based locking system
Morning shift (Front Office)
Murphy bed
Night clerk's room report
Night shift (Front Office)
Parlor room
PM guestroom check
Presidential suite
Preventive maintenance
Queen room
Receptionist
Regular maintenance
Revenue-generating center
Rooming list
Rooms division
Rooms division director
Sofa bed
Support center
Transportation drivers
Twin room
Valet parking
Wakeup call
Work order

DISCUSSION AND REVIEW QUESTIONS

1. Explain why the rooms division is considered a revenue center rather than a support center.
2. Indicate the purpose of the AM guestroom check report conducted by housekeeping.
3. Give two reasons why there must be efficient communication between the front office and the maintenance departments.
4. As a front office manager, which department would you contact to solve a problem arising from a missing rooming list for a convention?
5. In a **large** lodging operations, whom does the front office manager report to?
6. Into how many shifts is a 24-hour period divided at the front office?
7. What is(are) the purpose(s) of concierge floors?
8. What is the purpose of having guestrooms fitted with Murphy beds?

9. Which department compiles the PM guestroom report?
10. What is the purpose of a rooming list? Which department provides the front office with rooming lists?

PRACTICAL SITUATIONS

Situation 2.1

Evening shift action at the front desk

It is 10:00 PM. As supervisor of the evening shift at the front desk, you receive a computer message from the engineering department indicating that the problem with the toilet in the out-of-order room 125 has been solved. The plumber on duty tells you that he has done the best he could but that the floor in the bathroom is still a mess. The hotel is fully booked and the front desk keeps receiving requests for accommodations. What actions would you take in this situation?

Situation 2.2

Report discrepancy

As front office supervisor, you receive the AM guestroom check report from housekeeping and discover that room 2004 is occupied, although the computer shows that the room is vacant.

(a) What do you think could have happened for the discrepancy to exist? (b) What do you do from there?

Situation 2.3

Communication with F & B

You are on duty at the front desk at 8:30 AM. A guest is checking out and tells you that he just had breakfast in the Atrium restaurant. You print a copy of the guest's bill and find out that the charge has not been posted yet. How do you solve the problem?

CASE STUDY 2.1

Communication Lost

Annelise Bloomquist is the front office manager of a four-star hotel located near Dallas international airport. The property has 350 guestrooms and meeting space for conventions and corporate seminars. The Belfour Corporation uses the hotel regularly and has recommended the hotel to its customers as a good place to meet. This year, the Belfour's meeting planner, Mr. Bolivar, has planned to book the company's board of director's meeting at the hotel.

John Bolivar contacted the hotel's sales office on Monday, February 6, indicating that he is traveling to Dallas on February 15 to organize this very important gathering. The flight is scheduled to land at 1:05 PM Dallas's time. The sales director, Ms. Kurtz, assures John that a suite will be reserved for him for this date and suggests that the following day they meet for lunch to discuss the details of the board reunion at the hotel. After talking to the meeting planner, Ms. Kurtz goes personally to the front office to arrange with Annelise the accommodation of Mr. Bolivar on February 15. The booking is recorded with a special note to treat this visit as extremely important.

On Mr. Bolivar's arrival, he is welcomed by Ms. Bloomquist and given a key to room 1005, on the tenth floor of the building. Five minutes later, the meeting planner returns to the front desk to announce that suite 1005, originally reserved by Annelise for Mr. Bolivar, is occupied by someone else. To Annelise's horror she quickly realizes that there was no other suite left in the house to accommodate Mr. Bolivar.

After checking the system, room 1005 appeared as vacant and ready. The records showed that the suite had been occupied the night before by Mr. and Mrs. Brown who were checked out that morning at 11:30 AM by front desk clerk Robin. Annelise asked Robin if she had completed the departure and notified housekeeping that the room was to be made. Robin's answer was, "Yes, I checked Mr. Brown out but gave him permission to stay until 2 PM because his flight out of Dallas is scheduled for 3 o'clock. As you know, Mr. Brown is a regular guest with us."

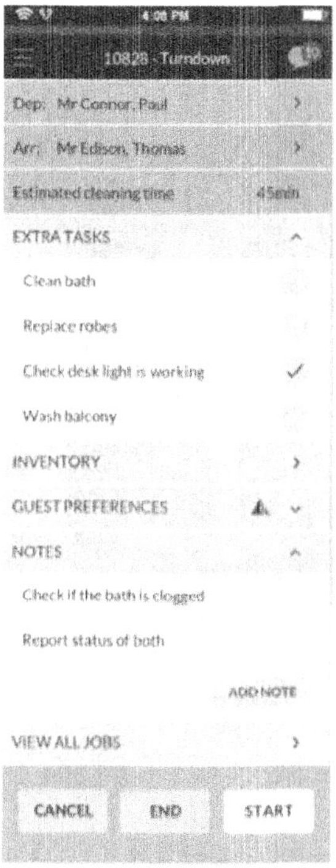

Hand-held housekeeper device screen

Courtesy of Optiisolutions

ASSIGNMENT:

Analyze the case and discuss with a class member whether there were any breaks in communication among the sales, housekeeping, and front office departments.

BARTECH FULLY-AUTOMATED MINIBAR
COURTESY OF BARTECH TECHNOLOGY & DESIGN

CHAPTER 3

FRONT OFFICE TECHNOLOGY

CHAPTER OBJECTIVES

- Present a synopsis of technology as it pertains to the front office in lodging operations.
- Provide a brief account of digital technology.
- Explain how the Internet and World Wide Web work.
- Discuss the importance of the presence of the lodging industry on the Web.
- Describe the property management systems available for use at the front office.
- Explain the need to adopt and update in-room technologies in lodging establishments.
- Explore how mobile technology is being adopted by the lodging industry.

OVERVIEW

This chapter focuses on technology available to automate lodging properties. It begins with a brief history of digital technology as it applies to front office operations and explores the systems that are available in today's market. It describes the Internet and its interconnection between network providers and lodging-industry users.

The World Wide Web and its application to lodging are discussed, and the relevance of social media to communicate and share information about the industry is stressed. The chapter describes some PMSs on the market and their technical applications that can be used to automate the front office while interfacing with other property systems.

The chapter ends commenting on the expectations guests have of finding in-room technology services regarding information, connectivity and entertainment. The need for the lodging industry to endlessly update its technology as it continues to develop is emphasized.

SYNOPSIS OF FRONT OFFICE AUTOMATION

The era we are in is unique in that the scope of tasks that can be automated is increasing rapidly. Looking back in time, there was no technology associated with front office operations since the modern origins of the lodging industry decades ago. Until the 1960s, all operations were performed by hand, including keeping guests' accounts. Accounting in both front and back of the house was done using huge paper ledgers where every transaction was entered one at a time using black ink for debits and red ink when a credit was posted. Because additions and subtractions had to be made without calculators, the job of keeping and balancing accounts at the front office was very labor intensive. The first automated machines to be used at the front desk were manufactured by NCR in the United States and by the German company Anker in Europe although postings still had to be punched one at a time on the machine's keyboard. At the beginning of the 1960s, the first semiconductor transistor-based machines appeared and in the 1970s, integrated circuit technology and microprocessors paved the way to today's generation of state-of-the-art technology. The repetitive clerical tasks of the past can now be eliminated, resulting in substantial labor savings. Formerly, several employees were necessary behind the desk, while today, it is common to see just a few clerks processing the same amount of work at a large lodging property.

Communication between the front office and other departments has also been improved by having interfaced terminals which send and receive information instantaneously. For example, in the past a telephone call was necessary to inform the front desk of a charge in a restaurant incurred by a departing guest. Today, the charge is automatically posted in the guest's folio.

Computing and digital technologies now impact nearly every aspect of life, including the lodging industry. But what does it mean to be digital? A basic knowledge is needed to understand how digital technology is applied to business information systems.

DIGITAL TECHNOLOGY

Digital technology includes all forms of computers that provide information expressed through words, numbers, sound, and images. The information can be effectively stored, transmitted, shared, and managed in many different ways. Students need to understand not only how to handle computers but also the basic concepts underlying them and the digital technology they are to find when working in front office settings.

A **computer** is an electronic device that combines **hardware** and **software** components to process the data inputted into it; this is comparable to the old NCR or Anker machines in which information was entered by punching numbers using keys (input), the difference being that computers can process these data and generate useful results (output) in a fraction of the time it took with antiquated methods. In addition, a computer can store enough data in its hard drive component at the stroke of a key to capture all of the volumes stacked on the shelves in the back office. Examples of customized software that has direct applicability to front office operations are accounting, room reservations, word processing, and revenue and yield management.

A computer's hardware consists of the physical parts that we can actually see when we look at it while the software contains electronic instructions that tell the computer what to do with the data. Manufacturers of hardware and software include HP, Motorola, Dell, and Apple while the best-known software company is Microsoft. Data can be stored in a computer until we command it to process the information displayed on the screen or printed on paper.

The primary uses of computers at a front office of lodging operations are to manage information related to guests and the operation itself, and to process databases that may include thousands of records. Surprisingly, computers work using just two digits: 1 and 0. These binary units are called **bits** while a group of eight bits is a **byte.** In practice, bits can be encoded to represent a value of, say, 1 for black and 0 for white. After processing several bytes of this value, a black and white picture can be constructed. Software is used to encode and decode the bytes. In fact, the process is quite simple although it may take some thinking to understand the whole systematic sequence of actions.

All computers contain the same basic components although different ones are used for different purposes. For example, smart phones and laptops are computers, as are our desk tops. A computer you may not be as familiar with is a **server**. A server is a computer that generally does not have a single user. Rather, servers are often powerful computers that service a number of other computers called clients. As a simple example, think of an online service, such as Google. Google runs a number of servers in a building called a data center. These computers are what your computer talks to when you do a Google search over the Internet. Servers are used by lodging corporations for many purposes such as providing basic IT services, and compiling inputs and data from different properties.

Server **virtualization** allows for multiple operating systems to run on the same hardware. Traditionally, one operating system would be paired with an individual server; however, if the operating system is not fully using the hardware, it sits idle. Virtualization also allows for consolidation of multiple operating systems onto the same server, thus potentially increasing efficiency. Specialized control software lets the physical resources of a single computer server-memory, disk space and computing power, to be divided between several software applications. **Cloud computing** takes virtual server tools one stage further, using them to allocate the resources of vast numbers of servers quickly and flexibly to accommodate different companies' needs. Cloud resources are less expensive than those at a single property and hoteliers don't need to worry about installing additional hardware resources as their businesses grow; they just call up the cloud vendor and ask for it to be allocated. Operators can choose from three different ways of payment for using servers:

1. A flat fee per room per month for the software, interfaces, and support.
2. A flat fee per occupied room night, tying the property's costs directly to occupancy, and thus to room revenue.
3. A one-time up-front license fee plus a monthly hosting/support fee.

All in all, systems managed off-property offer substantial maintenance savings, simpler ways to interface, and better security. The core value propositions of the cloud are:

- Economies of scale.
- The systems are managed by domain experts so no in-house expertise is needed.
- Billing is based on consumption.

Some technical drawbacks include security and regulatory compliance considerations, and the lack of availability if the connection to the cloud is down. The operating costs for high-speed networks and for monthly hosting fees need also be evaluated before adopting the system. The larger hotel chains may find it appropriate to set up and manage their own server cloud, but individual hotels and smaller companies need to do some research on the pros and cons of making the change.

THE INTERNET

The Internet is a global system of interconnected computer networks serving billions of users; it is in fact a network of networks that provides services to individuals, businesses and organizations around the world. Among other functions, the Internet is used to communicate, learn, entertain and share information. Businesses invest in the Internet to leverage competitive advantage. Some of the technologies the Internet offers are the World-Wide-Web, instant messaging, social networks, maps, and so on. Large corporations such as Google or Amazon have the ability to run hundreds of thousands of computers in large datacenters to provide online services such as searches, shopping, or social interaction while you browse the Web.

The first web browser was launched on the Internet in 1993. With consumers flocking to this global network, businesses found a powerful new sales and marketing tool. Today, the Internet consists of a colossal number of pathways such as those provided via fiber-optic cables to supply connections to users. These national and international communication networks are owned by giant telecommunication companies, such as AT&T, Verizon and British

Telecom. **Network Service Providers (NSPs)**, in turn, enable Internet users to connect to their networks through stations called **points of presence (POPs).** Individuals, companies, and service providers are connected to the Web using these POPs. A company that provides individuals and organizations with access to the Internet, usually via modems, is called an **Internet service provider (ISP),** such as Century Link in Arizona. The ISP charges monthly fees to serve as liaison between users and network service providers.

The simplified flow can be visualized as:

The Web
↕
NSP
↕
POP
↕
ISP
↕
User (Client)

As the telephone network uses a phone book with users' names and addresses, the Internet uses the **Domain Name System (DNS)** to identify the names of clients. Domain names are managed by the Internet Corporation for Assigned Names and Numbers and can be purchased from accredited registrars such as www.enameco.com. Registering a domain name does not provide you with a website but with ownership of the name you have registered.

A domain name consists of one or more parts called labels which are delimited by dots, such as in *nau.edu*. The right-most labels convey the top-level domains. Common top level domains are *.com*, *.org*, or *.edu*. Most countries use top level domains associated with the countries' names; for example *.es* for Spain, *.it* for Italy or *.uk* for United Kingdom.

Because most travelers use the Internet to make reservations in lodging properties the importance of this technology to operators is paramount. Typically, a potential guest goes online, does a search of establishments in an area, selects one, and proceeds to reserve a room or series of rooms. The system provides the person involved with a confirmation number and a printout with the details of the reservation. Lodging properties' operators should have a **direct website**, especially if they are independent establishments. If the property belongs to a lodging chain (either franchised or corporate-owned), it will be featured in the **Chain's website.** In addition, lodging properties should be part of interfaced **Online Travel Agencies** such as Orbitz, Expedia or Travelocity which act as vendors on behalf of the establishments.

THE WORLD WIDE WEB

The Web can be defined as a service that provides access to information and services through Internet. By relating documents to each other using **hyperlinks**, a network of interrelated information is formed that is easy to navigate. A hyperlink is a word, phrase, or image that when clicked opens a related document. Protocols allow different computers to communicate; the protocol of the Web is called **HTTP** which controls communication between **web browsers** and users. A web browser is a form of software offered by clients such as Internet Explorer, Safari, and Firefox. These web browsers provide access to millions of resources available on the Internet using desktop and notebook computers, smart and cell phones, and netbooks. The location of a webpage on the server can be identified by using a **URL**. A URL is actually a webpage address; for example, www.createspace.com.

THE LODGING INDUSTRY ON THE WEB

The Web has had an important effect on the travel industry and the way potential guests select lodging establishments. **Global Distribution System (GDS)** is a worldwide computerized reservation network structured as a single point of access for reserving airline seats and other travel features as well as lodging accommodations. It is used by travel agents, online reservation sites and large corporations. The premier global distribution systems are Amadeus, Galileo, Sabre, Apollo and Worldspan. They are owned and operated as joint ventures by major airlines, car rental companies and hotel groups. Intermediary marketing companies such as Xotels and LuxuryRes offer hotel GDS services to avail lodging properties to travel agents and consortia worldwide.

Travel websites such as Travelocity, Expedia, Priceline, and Hotels.com help travelers find the best deals in lodging properties in practically any place in the world. It is, therefore, critical to be present in the travel market by having a website and by contracting with intermediary travel websites. For example, a traveler wanting to find a room in Flagstaff, Arizona, may contact Expedia or conduct a google search simply by typing "hotels flagstaff" to see a list of choices. On searching for Marriott Flagstaff the results for him/her to choose from would be the Courtyard Flagstaff, SpringHill Suites Flagstaff, and Flagstaff Fairfield Inn, all belonging to the Marriott family of lodging properties. A search for a place to stay in Flagstaff with Expedia would provide 74 lodging options ranging in price from 40 to 120 dollars in low season. Operators of lodging establishments have the option of being present in travel companies by negotiating special deals or packages from which travelers can choose. If potential guests have an Iphone, they can download apps that help them almost instantaneously to locate a lodging establishment anywhere in the world.

SOCIAL MEDIA

Social media provide ways to communicate and share information with users through social networking sites such as Facebook, LinkedIn and Twitter. Customers are increasing their reliance on social networking sites and blogs to gain insight into lodging properties before they book. An increasing number of lodging companies are present and active in these networks at corporate and individual-property levels offering information and appealing tidbits for people to get interested in patronizing their establishments. Although members of these social sites access postings through an invitation process, the potential that a piece of news originated by a lodging property can be read by a large number of people is real.

Lodging properties can engage new and existing customers in a variety of ways by linking up with social media online platforms to share information and even use them as booking channels. Facebook, for example, offers a software mobile application **(mAPP)** to reserve and book rooms online. Twitter can also be used as a free tool for guests and lodging properties to interact with each other.

WIRELESS FIDELITY (WI-FI)

Wi-Fi is a type of networking technology that uses access points to wirelessly connect users to networks within a range of around 250 to 1000 feet. This technology works by sending and receiving data using radio frequencies to and from computers and other digital devices equipped with Wi-Fi adapters. Most lodging properties offer wireless Internet as a service in order to attract more guests.

FRONT OFFICE INFORMATION TECHNOLOGY

Typically, a network in lodging properties links computers together to allow users to share data and communication channels. A **local area network (LAN)** links components together in the same building by interfacing computer systems that operate independently, for example, between the front office and a point of sale located in the property's restaurant. **Wide area networks (WAN)** are designed to connect computers in a certain geographic area, for instance a company's central reservation system located in Dallas, Texas, with properties across the country. The host computer and the system points can be linked by way of telephone lines, cable, or wireless networks using radiofrequency channels.

THE PROPERTY MANAGEMENT SYSTEM (PMS)

Property management systems are computerized applications designed to manage different aspects of lodging operations, such as guest bookings, online reservations, points of sale, accounting, and telephone call billing. Individual properties usually determine the type of PMS they require based on the number of guestrooms and services offered. In some cases, the PMS system is determined by management or the franchising company that runs the operation. There are several PMS systems on the market that operate with different types of software. Essential to a PMS software configuration is that it interface with other in-house and external systems. Examples of property management systems are IBM's Guest 360 by Agilysys, Front Desk & Audit System – Hotel Reservation Software by Resort Data Processing Inc, and Opera by Micros.

FRONT OFFICE COMPUTER APPLICATIONS

Property management systems consist of a series of computer software packages capable of supporting the various activities that take place at the front office. The principal areas serviced by software packages are concerned with the management of reservations, guestroom inventory, and guest accounting.

Typically, the PMS of a medium-size lodging property can manage the interface of 20 to 30 systems while in a large establishment the number is much higher. These systems are integrated in the PMS of a lodging property:

- Individual guest and group check-in and check-out
- Self-check-in and check-out
- Telephone call accounting
- Credit card authorization
- Sales and marketing
- In-room entertainment
- Room reservations
- Room rates and packages
- Room inventory and sales forecast
- F & B point of sale
- Guest wake-up
- In-room energy control, safe, minibar

- Guest accounting
- Yield and revenue management
- Guest profile and history
- Key management

Besides integrating other software systems and automating several aspects of a lodging operation, a state-of-the-art PMS, such as Agilysys Guest 360, can gather guest intelligence to gain a competitive advantage. For instance, the system can be programmed to provide a room upgrade process defining guestroom attributes grouped into categories. From this definition, pricing and basis of rating for each category can be established to match guests' requests. This procedure allows for the optimization of room availability.

As the market becomes more competitive, lodging properties must become savvier in finding and retaining guests. A profile containing the data of guests' preferences can help maximize occupancy and at the same time retain corporate and business travelers. By storing profiles, reservationists can identify trends to help the front desk staff upsell based on past stays at the property. Guest 360, for example, uses a flexible screen design that enables the operator to access various subsystems to easily integrate preferred options, such as managing guest folios and reservation confirmations simultaneously. Its reservations portal offers room inventory online displaying accurate room availability at all times. This PMS also provides record keeping for guest accounting and accounts receivable to ensure that charges are billed correctly.

Property management systems can also be contracted via Internet without the need to use in-house software. For example, innRoad, a company that provides PMS by remote, offers the ease of integrating front and back-office operations using a web-based system. A lodging property using innRoad online services can have access to global distribution systems of hundreds of travel agents and websites specializing in room reservations, in addition to the capacity for travel agents and individual travelers being able to make reservations online through the property's website. Besides other functions, the central reservation system allows booking rooms across multiple properties while its front office capability provides the necessary tools to check guests in and out, assign rooms, handle billings and perform accounting functions.

Micros Opera Property Management System includes the following specific features:

<u>Reservations:</u> The features are integrated with other functions such as guest profiles, cashiering, and deposits. The software module offers options for making and updating individual, group, and business block reservations, including deposit handling, cancellations, confirmations, wait listing, room blocking and sharing.

Rate management: The system can set and control rates for rate quotations and interface with revenue and yield management applications.

Profiles: Opera's property management software provides profiles of guest demographics and records of business accounts, contacts, groups, travel agents, and reservation sources.

Front office: This software module handles individual guests, groups and walk-ins, and has features for room blocking, managing guest messages and wakeup calls.

Back office: Revenue, market statistics, daily statistics, and city ledger transfers can be made from Micros Opera PMS to a back office system.

Rooms management: The Opera system can handle all facets of room supervision including availability, housekeeping, maintenance, and facility management. The Queue Rooms feature coordinates front office and housekeeping efforts when guests are waiting for rooms that are not available for assignment.

Cashiering: This module allows for posting guest and city-ledger customers, managing advance deposits, checking guests out and folio printing. This feature can manage multiple payments including cash, check, credit card, and direct billing, allowing for cross-posting of guest charges.

Accounts receivable: The system integrates accounts receivable including direct billing, invoicing, account aging, bill payments, statement generation, and account history.

Commissions: Opera's property management software can calculate, process, and follow up on all types of commission payments, either by check or via electronic funds transfer (EFT).

The software offered by Resort Data Processing includes integrated modules to manage reservations, e-mail, statements, packages, travel agents, frequent guest awards, front office and audit procedures, and work orders.

Specifically, this company's advertised technology can perform these procedures:

- Integrating front desk and reservations operations by assigning a number to every reservation. The number can be used as confirmation and guest folio for easy tracking. Reservations made directly by guests with the Internet reservation module are also fully integrated.

- Speedy guest registration and check-out. The module allows for registration cards to be pre-printed and gives the location of vacant-and-ready rooms. Available rooms of a given type can be quickly displayed to accommodate walk-in business.
- Integrating scanners that make it possible to read the guest name and credit card number by swiping the credit card. The system automatically pre-authorizes credit on the guest's card or accepts a credit card payment at check-in.
- Customizing audit procedures depending on the needs of individual properties.
- Providing an automated room key encoder that issues room key cards at check-in as well as for room re-allocation.
- An advance-deposit ledger allowing for deposits to be automatically transferred to the in-house guest ledger and to the guest folio as a credit.
- A yield management system helping to increase average daily rates and occupancy by showing the best available rates by date.
- The PMS posting charges to guest folios while assigning the amounts to revenue centers, such as room revenue, room service, phone, and bar.
- Storing forever and reprinting every transaction in guest folios any time after the guest has checked out.
- Assigning each guest credit limit with the system notifying the clerk when charges incurred by a guest place him/her over the allowed amount.
- RDP offers a check-out module in which a credit card scanner automatically calls the credit card company for authorization and deposits the balance into the property's bank account.
- Issuing cashier-balancing reports ensuring accurate cash drawer balancing procedure which deters fraud and theft. The reports help to balance cash drawers quickly and close the day's shifts.
- The night audit module automatically interfacing with the travel agent payable system, allowing for all commissionable transactions to be paid to the travel agent that has generated the reservation.
- The front office system integrating to the city ledger. Transfers from the guest to city ledgers can be made automatically.

SELF-CHECK-IN AND CHECK-OUT SYSTEMS

Self-serve kiosks increase the speed of the check-in and check-out process, allowing guests to bypass front desk lines. Some consumers rate self-service as a differentiator; especially travelers accustomed to the kiosks used in airline terminals appreciate the self-service machines installed in lodging properties' registration areas. Hyatt International has introduced NCR kiosks at the New York Hyatt, the Hyatt Regency O'Hare in Chicago and in other locations to respond to increasing demand from guests. These machines, which can print reservation cards and folios, can perform check-in and check-out operations in about 15 seconds, reducing lines and time spent waiting.

As an example, IBM advertises self-service, PMS-interfaced kiosks that can yield significant savings with reduced front desk staffing needs. Guests can quickly and easily check in, input their loyalty card number, change their room selection, and receive their room keys. On check-out, they can review their folios, get updated printouts, and print their boarding passes for their return flight home. This automatic service allows for the property's staff to have more time to provide the human touch for those waiting for one-on-one service.

TELEPHONE CALL ACCOUNTING

Call Accounting Systems (CAS) are generally integrated into the property's PMS. When an external number is dialed from a guestroom, the CAS identifies the extension from which the call is made and the cost of the call plus a surcharge to be determined by the property is posted in the guest's folio. The CAS has the capability of choosing a provider of service, such as AT&T or Verizon, through which to route the call, selecting the best rate available at that particular time. Most lodging properties offer free local and toll-free calls to guests.

Voice over Internet Protocol (VoIP) refers to communication services that are transported via the Internet rather than by telephone networks. The system works by converting analog audio signals, the kind one hears when talking on the phone, into digital data that can be transmitted over the Internet. In order to use this technology, a broadband, a high-speed Internet connection, and VoIP handsets in guestrooms are necessary. Instead of using digital handsets there is the option of installing adaptors on each telephone set to convert the analog signal into digital.

VOICE-MAIL AND WAKE-UP SYSTEMS

Most voice-mail and wake-up systems are interfaced with the property's PMS. Guests can personalize a greeting message, choose their own language for instructions, and have the option to cancel, save, or forward messages to another room extension. With a few keystrokes, guests can schedule their own wakeup calls on their room phones. Front desk staff can also schedule wakeup calls for the guests using touch-tone commands on the console. Some systems play a customized wakeup greeting when the guest answers. The brand DuVoice, for instance, offers a system in which the front desk staff has access to detailed reports on wake-up activity. For example, the pending wakeup report shows all scheduled calls; the failed wakeup shows all rooms where wake-up calls were not answered by the guest; the wakeup report shows all wakeup activity for a specific room, including when calls were scheduled, who scheduled the calls and the result of completed calls.

IN-ROOM TECHNOLOGY

In a rapidly changing technology environment, guests continue to expect increasing added values and operational efficiencies when they patronize lodging properties. Hoteliers are compelled to resort to specialized companies for the installation of network services that provide state-of-the-art information, entertainment, and connectivity systems. A technology company devoted to creating solutions and products that meet ever evolving customer demands is Quadriga. The top ten bits of technology recommended by Quadriga that every lodging room should have, ranging from the most obvious to the more unusual, are listed here:

- High definition television (HDTV) providing a range of high quality channels.
- High speed Internet access (wired and Wi-Fi) to accommodate the needs of business travelers. Although most rooms now are fitted with Internet access, the challenge is to offer guests the same level of broadband service as they receive in their offices and residences in terms of speed, reliability, and security. One way of doing this is by offering a tiered bandwidth service, i.e. pricing it according to usage, where those who use less bandwidth pay a smaller fee than those who require more. Some lodging companies offer this service free to all and/or preferred guests as a marketing tool.
- MP3 docking stations. Millions of iPods are in use and many travelers utilize them to listen to favorite songs, watch movies, or view family photos.
- Convenient and plentiful power sources to prevent guests from having to dive under pieces of furniture to access power sockets to connect their laptop, mobile, and chargers. One option is to provide a connectivity panel which enables plug-ins for a laptop, digital camera, or MP# to be viewed/listened to via the television so they don't have to keep recharging their batteries.
- Mirror televisions installed in bathrooms that are equipped with high definition technology, digital tuners, and touch screen functionality.
- Lighting and climate control allowing guests to set them remotely.
- Radio Frequency Identification (RFID) door locks for keyless entry to rooms and other areas of the property. In addition to this, new technology has been developed

to allow guests to use any brand of mobile phone to gain access to their guestrooms, so they don't have to worry about their keys at all.

- Energy management systems which adjust the temperature and lighting in guestrooms upon detection that the room is empty. Infrared signals can also be used so housekeeping staff can tell if the room is occupied by pressing a button.
- Ipads that are made available to guests to use in rooms can enhance the services offered in-house, such as room-service ordering. The Ipad can be fully interfaced with the room service point of sale, the order sent directly to the kitchen for processing and the total posted to the guest's folio. The property's services can also be accessed on the device without the need to call the concierge desk. The same Ipad can have a software package installed on it so that the guest can operate lights, air conditioning, and TV. Another advantage of in-room Ipads is the elimination of guest services information packages as they can be accessed directly on the device.

Other in-room interfaced systems include personalized welcome messages on the TV; merchandising of hotel services, such as restaurants, spas or athletic clubs; video on demand; a pictorial list of dishes available for ordering through room service; accessibility to updated folios; and self-checkout.

THE FUTURE

The most advanced technology available focuses on turning millions of computers into single clouds of supermachines managing the flow between PCs. These global systems work because of virtualization, a software that commands a server into doing the tasks of several systems. This technology will allow PMS vendors to release cloud versions of their systems where lodging properties will have the ability to access their software applications on a web browser. Cloud computing is set to offer hoteliers a more cost effective way to use technology without having to invest in cumbersome hardware on premises.

Front Office managers can keep updated with the advances of lodging technology by following information provided by the **Hotel Technology Next Generation (HTNG)** association, a global trade organization dedicated to enhancing the deployment of technology in hotels and to finding next-generation solutions that will enable hoteliers to do business globally in the 21st Century. HTNG is run by and for the benefit of hotel executives, with active support from technology providers and other industry participants. It is governed by a board of directors consisting of senior executives from more than a dozen leading hotel companies with participation by advisors from the hotel, consulting, and academic community.

HTNG operates a branding and certification program for hotel technology. The "HTNG-certified" logo on a technology product represents a commitment by the vendor to the buyer that the product meets the highest industry standards for interoperability, backed up by specific conformance to industry-defined norms. The association holds annual conferences where experts' views on the latest technological advancements can be learned.

The Hotel Business Review is also an excellent online resource to stay abreast of ever-changing technology. The journal provides information on best practices in hotel management, including current advancements in technology applications for front office operations.

MOBILE TECHNOLOGY

As this book goes to print, searches from mobile devices account for about 20% of Google's traffic. Because 50% of web interactions via a mobile phone start with a search query, the importance of hoteliers having a marketing strategy pinned on mobile technology is obvious. It is already a fact that combined shipments of smartphones and tablets are outperforming those of PCs. Many business travelers use their devices to find local lodging, and it is estimated that by 2014 the number of mobile technology users will exceed 100 million in the U.S. alone. The new technology has changed the way that the world is functioning. For travelers, for instance, visiting countries where foreign languages are spoken, the use of mobile devices makes it possible for them to communicate in a language they don't know with front desk employees using the translator option. Guests, via their mobile APPs, can update a booking, add or cancel a night, check in or out while they are not at the property, and even ask for a pickup wherever they are. Within the property, mAPPs can be used to increase efficiency in daily operations such as obtaining instant information on guestroom status updates.

An increasing number of travelers are replacing the laptop, telephone, and PC by this emerging mobile technology. Because the mobile Web is an important travel planning and booking channel worldwide, lodging properties will necessarily have to adopt this consumer technology to gain a competitive advantage. At the same time, lodging companies will have to invest in resources necessary to keep up with the succession of changes that will inevitably take place as this technology advances. For example, Ipads require a broader bandwidth than other devices, placing a larger capacity demand on Wi-Fi systems. To the Ipad, mobile technology such as Kindle Fire, Android, Galaxy and other tablet devices have to be added, causing overloads that may result in guest complaints about deficient download experiences. As mobile devices have created a challenge for lodging properties to catch up with technological advances, it is a fact that the industry must be ready to embrace this shift to stay competitive in the twenty-first century.

KEY TERMS

Bit
Byte
Call accounting system (CAS)
Chain website
Cloud (the)
Computer
Direct website
Domain name system (DNS)
Global distribution system (GDS)
Hardware
Hotel technology next generation (HTNG)
HTTP
Hyperlink
Internet Service Provider (ISP)
Local Area Network (LAN)
Mobile application (mAPP)
Network Service Provider (NSP)
On-line travel agency
Point of Presence (POP)
Property Management System (PMS)
Random Access Memory (RAM)
Server
Software
Uniform Resource Locator (URL)
Voice over internet protocol (VoIP)
Web browser
Wide Area Network (WAN)
Wireless Fidelity (Wi-Fi)

DISCUSSION AND REVIEW QUESTIONS

1. Describe the Voice over Internet Protocol system.
2. Name three in-property systems that can be interfaced with the PMS.
3. What is the difference between LAN and WAN?
4. What is the Global Distribution System?
5. How many bits are there in a byte? In a kilobyte?
6. What is the name of the primary storage area in a computer for programs and data?

7. Explain the meaning of Internet service provider.
8. Which organization manages the Internet's domain name system?
9. Explain how an online travel agency conducts business with a lodging property.
10. What communication controls the HTTP?

PRACTICAL SITUATIONS

Situation 1

Exploring the Web

Pretend that you have been asked to travel to Dallas, Texas, for a second interview with a lodging company offering a front office assistant management position. The date of your meeting is June 15. The company's personnel director has promised to pay $950 to cover your airfare, two nights stay at a local hotel and meals. The least expensive airline ticket that you can get is offered by United Airlines for $450 round trip which leaves $500 to pay for lodging and meals. Go to the website www.expedia.com and find a hotel near the Dallas airport that you can afford for the nights of June 14 and 15.

Situation 2

Domain Name System Report

Conduct a Google.com search using "domain name system." Enter the Wikipedia page under domain name systems and compile a report responding to the following:

1. What is the Domain Name System?
2. What is the structure of the DNS?
3. Write a synopsis of the history of DNS.
4. How does DNS operate?

Situation 3

Synopsis of Mobile Technology

Your front office management class instructor has asked students to compile a synopsis of current mobile technology.

1. Enter Webopedia.org, Wikipedia.org, on-line technology magazines or Google 'technology blogs' and prepare the written report.

CASE STUDY 3.1

Selecting a PMS

Elizabeth Krahn has been hired as front office manager of a 150-room ski lodge near Pierre, South Dakota. The owners, knowing that she holds a degree from a hotel and restaurant management program, have chosen her for the position hoping that she is familiar with the new technology on the market for this type of establishment. The resort's front office uses an antiquated PC program for reservations and doesn't have any check-in and check-out system. The place has a room rack and a bucket where the day's reservations are kept. All communication with the housekeeping and engineering departments are carried out by phone.

Pretend that you are Elizabeth Krahn. Conduct a google search entering "PMS hotels" and explore the systems offered by three companies that sell front office systems. Compile the features of the systems offered by the three companies and decide which one you recommend purchasing. Present a report to your instructor indicating the rational for your decision.

Hotel Indigo San Diego

Courtesy of InterContinental Hotels Group

PART 2

PROFESSIONAL ASPECTS OF FRONT OFFICE MANAGEMENT

CHAPTER 4

EFFECTIVE COMMUNICATION AT THE FRONT OFFICE

CHAPTER OBJECTIVES

- Emphasize the importance of communication in the front office department.
- Describe the aspects of good communication.
- Define the components of formal presentations.
- Explain the importance of impromptu speaking for front office employees.
- Learn about written and face-to-face communication.
- Discuss examples of communication between the front office and other departments.
- State the need to practice good communication within the front office department.

OVERVIEW

Proficiency in oral communication is critical in a department where interaction with guests is constant. Most hospitality companies believe that there is a direct link between good communication skills of front office employees and high occupancy. Therefore, they emphasize that the front office staff be excellent communicators. In this chapter we look at scenarios that will illustrate to students the need for good verbal and written communication skills at the front office and how to develop them.

THE COMMUNICATION PROCESS

Front desk, reservations, and guest services personnel spend a considerable part of their work time communicating with others; as a matter of fact, communication is at the very heart of front office operations. In day-to-day activities, these employees must be capable of interacting professionally with guests and other employees and with the community at large. Every time an employee makes contact with a guest, there is a direct effect on the success of the property as customers usually make an instant judgment about the business. Some people are better with certain types of communication situations than others; that is, a front desk clerk who is excellent at one-to-one communication with a customer may be a lackluster speaker when he/she has to address a group of incoming guests in the lobby. Or the reverse, a guest service agent who is an engaging public speaker may be very poor in situations that call for a two-way exchange. In addition, a front office manager may be a good writer but may falter with oral communication. Because the front office is the hub of interdepartmental operations, it is also imperative that front office employees be competent in communicating with other areas of the operation. Ideally, only people-centered individuals concerned with the well-being of others should be hired for front-of-the-house positions.

The main purpose of communicating with others is to exchange information, views and attitudes. Many procedures at the front desk are based on oral, written, and technological communication. For example, a guest communicates his desire to book a room in a lodging property and the front office informs him of booking availability; the front desk communicates the guest's arrival to other departments so that they can prepare for his arrival with information for registration; the guest's charges while at the property are communicated to the front office so they can be posted to the account, and so the process continues until his departure.

The basic objectives of professional communication can be summarized as follows:

Informational:	To provide facts requested or needed by guests and other employees.
Motivational:	To reinforce or modify behavior of subordinates.
Emotional:	To express acceptance, praise or role definition.
Controlling:	To clarify accountability, tasks or authority

TABLE 4.1: BASIC PURPOSES OF COMMUNICATION

An example of informational communication would be giving driving directions to a guest. Praising a bellperson for a job well done would be an instance of motivational interaction. An example of negative emotional communication would be to admonish a reservation clerk in front of others while a positive case would be to tell a guest how delighted one is to see him back again at the property. Formal controlling communication attempts to direct the activities of individuals: for instance, explaining to a guest service agent the necessary steps to balance the cash register.

Often, the most important components of one-on-one communication is **listening**, a skill that is critical to determine the needs, problems, and moods of the person who is speaking. Listening is crucial for front office employees communicating with a guest who is angry or upset. The mere fact that we are listening indicates concern and empathy for the speaker about the problem as well as showing a desire to fix it. Calm and interested listening is the best tool for dissipating the anxiety of the speaker and a perfect opportunity to gauge the guests' state of mind. Are they in a hurry to check in or out? Do they look overtired after a long trip? Do they appear to be upset because the room they were assigned is not to their liking? Some common listening flaws include interrupting the other person, not paying attention to the conversation (day dreaming), changing the subject, and rushing the speaker.

A helpful listening skill is **paraphrasing** which is used to make sure that the listener understands the ideas and information presented by the speaker. To paraphrase is to state the other's ideas in our own words, giving an example of what we think the other person is talking about. A poor paraphrased response to a guest complaining about his room, because it doesn't deal with the unhappiness of the guest nor clarifies the reasons for his not being happy, is

Would you like to be moved to another room?

A better paraphrase would be:

I understand that you are not happy with the room, Sir. What would you like me to do about it?

This answer shifts the issue into a problem-solving mode.

Oral communication is both verbal and nonverbal. **Verbal factors** are the words spoken and the tone of voice used. Because words can lead to many situations—from misunderstanding and false accusations to trust and loyalty—good communicators must be careful to measure what they say. In most situations, a message will be taken literally by a guest or employee and may be repeated many times. The **voice rate** is also important because it sets the pace of the communication. Voice conveys many feelings—from anxiety and urgency to enthusiasm, serenity, and confidence. The use of words and phrases that dilute the message should be minimized, such as "like," "you know," "he goes," (to mean "he says"), and "you know what I mean." The **voice tone** used when communicating with others can sometimes emphasize the meaning more than the words that are used. For example, a front desk clerk may say, "You are too early. We usually start checking guests in after two o'clock," using a blaming, critical tone of voice making the traveler feel uneasy. The same statement said pleasantly has the opposite effect and at the same time gives a reasonable explanation.

Nonverbal behavior also sends signals to guests and employees. Gestures serve as expressions of emotion and eye contact is used to establish trust in our culture. Guests and employees from different cultural backgrounds, however, may display other nonverbal behaviors. For example, Hispanics and Native Americans may avoid eye contact, not because they are untrustworthy but because that is their way of showing respect.

Front office employees should strive to build **rapport** with guests with whom they are to communicate. Rapport is the ability to communicate effectively while making others comfortable. In this way, front office supervisors and managers should adopt pleasant behaviors to establish good communication with guests and employees. Another way to establish good rapport is through **empathy**—the appreciative perception or understanding of another person, in other words, putting yourself in the other person's shoes.

A typical example of lack of empathy can be expressed in the following dialogue:

Guest checking out:	*"I didn't sleep well last night. The air conditioning was really noisy."*
Front desk clerk:	*"I am sorry to hear that. Will you be paying by credit card?"*

A well-trained guest service agent should have answered:

"I am sorry to hear that. Can you tell me more about that so I can have the problem fixed? I hope that you were not too much inconvenienced."

Here are some useful tips regarding communication:

- Weigh your answers. Think before speaking.
- Keep an open-door policy for guests and employees.
- Chat informally with guests and employees whenever possible.
- Listen carefully before you answer.
- Avoid being critical; be factual instead.

FORMAL PRESENTATIONS

Sooner or later, a front office manager or **guest service agent** will be asked to present a subject to a formal gathering. In fact, part of the hiring strategy of some recruiters is to ask students interviewing for a job to make a formal presentation on a topic of their choice.

Formal presentations require sufficient preparation. Rather than memorizing a speech word for word, speakers should simply assemble and arrange ideas beforehand. A good way is for the presenter to prepare a visual aid listing the main points or facts of the presentation. This approach serves two purposes: one is to divert the focus of attention of the audience to a point away from the speaker; the second is as a prompt for the presenter to be able to talk about the topics listed on the screen in an orderly manner.

A formal presentation should be divided into three parts: (1) a short introduction, (2) the main body of the speech, and (3) a brief summary of the main points presented. Here are a few useful tips on delivering a presentation:

- Emphasize the main points of the presentation.
- Maintain eye contact with the audience.
- Bring the main ideas home using appropriate gestures.
- Keep an even, steady pace throughout the presentation.
- Pause briefly between topics.
- Relate topics to listeners' interests.
- Provide illustrations and examples.
- Convey trust that you are speaking in earnest.
- Make the audience feel like a partner in the presentation.

IMPROMPTU/EXTEMPORANEOUS SPEAKING

Giving prepared speeches can be relatively easy because the speaker can gather and organize information ahead of time. However, success at **impromptu speaking**—speaking without preparation—sometimes may be more difficult because you may be caught off guard and not sure what to say.

The demands of a front office operation make it indispensable for its staff to be capable of putting together thoughts quickly and verbalizing fluently. To acquire this ability, it is best to practice **extemporaneous speaking**—speaking on the spur of the moment without preparation or notes. Students can do this by becoming members of **Toastmasters International**—an organization with branches throughout the United States that teaches speaking skills. Students can also learn by volunteering impromptu speaking in class or later at formal or informal gatherings in the workplace. An example of impromptu speaking would be to explain the layout of the property and the different services offered to a group of tourists at check-in.

WRITTEN COMMUNICATION

As potential front office managers, students should have developed the ability to communicate well in writing. Because written statements are permanent, they become lasting records that may reflect positively or negatively on the writer in future situations. Therefore, all such communication must be carefully written and made accurate. Front office managers are expected to be able to write correctly, observing the rules of grammar, spelling, and punctuation.

As with formal presentations, written statements should be, if possible, divided into three sections: (1) introduction, (2) main body, and (3) conclusion. The most common forms of written communication are e-mails and memorandums, reports and, less frequently, business letters. Memos to employees and other departments, and reports to management should be written in a crisp, clear style.

FACE-TO-FACE COMMUNICATION

The amount of verbal communication that takes place at the front office is substantial. The department can be described as the hub of a wheel with spokes going out in every direction. Most of the communicating consists of one-on-one verbal interaction. Besides the typical questions when checking in or out, a guest at the front desk might ask questions like these:

- Where is City Hall?
- How do I get to the university?
- When is check-out time?
- Where is a good restaurant?
- Is there a path for jogging nearby?
- How do I get to the nearest bank?
- How do I get to I-25?
- Where is the nearest mall?
- Can you get me a taxi?
- Where is a Catholic church?

Face-to-face discussions, formal and informal, take place with guests and employees throughout the day, such as providing information to guests asking for directions in the property or the area. With this type of direct communication, managers, supervisors and employees of the front office have the opportunity to listen, express thanks, and, most important, gather and disseminate information. By listening attentively to guests, they can obtain information needed to improve operations.

Face-to-face communication, on occasion, can have very negative results. Bored or disinterested front desk clerks or guest services employees can convey to the guest the message that they don't really care very much about helping them. Sometimes, it is not so much what is said, but how it is said that matters. Ideally, front office employees should be motivated to communicate with a genuine desire of making guests feel welcome by offering a smile and a warm greeting. Good service depends on personal interactions, meaning that the communicative behavior of front-of-the-house employees plays an important role in determining the property's quality as perceived by the guest. In fact, it wouldn't be farfetched to assume that front office employees are often responsible for making or breaking an operation's reputation.

Regarding face-to-face communication, often you can establish empathy by sensing guests' moods and adapting accordingly. If they are anxious, you in turn want to be serious to reflect your concern. If they are cheerful, be cheerful, and rarely does a little joke hurt. If they are angry, give them time to vent. Listening well lets them know that you take their problems seriously and intend to address them.

It is difficult for young professionals to assert themselves with confidence when conducting business as they are trained to recognize and accept that "guests are always right." As a matter of fact, the main job of the front office staff is to ensure that each guest is looked after in the best possible way. However, there are times when a clerk or uniformed employee must take a position contrary to the guest's wishes. For example, denying an unreasonable demand for a discount, having to walk a traveler who holds a confirmed reservation when the property is overbooked, or dealing with someone using rude language. Communicating assertively is necessary in some cases to safeguard the interests of the company or to state a fact in a professional way. Future front office employees must learn to overcome shyness and become outgoing individuals capable of being confident in all types of situations. Assertive skills should be developed to enable graduates to act confidently even in challenging cases. For instance, if a guest points out to a clerk that she forgot to apply a discount, the best response would be to acknowledge the fact with a brief apology. A confident acknowledgement accepts the criticism while maintaining the conversation on a professional level. By answering assertively while concentrating on the facts, a criticism can be played down without falling in the trap of defending oneself. For example, a troublesome guest can say: "This total is wrong. Don't you know how to multiply?" A good answer to that unjust comment could be simply, "Could you show me where I went wrong?"

Two techniques to say "no" to someone who doesn't want to take it for an answer can be:

- Letting your body language support you by remaining calm and maintaining direct eye contact with the guest.
- Repeating a statement as many times as it takes for the guest to understand that you are not willing to budge.

Language can also become a barrier between front office personnel and guests who don't speak English well. Hiring employees who know a foreign language is advantageous for meeting the needs of non-English-speaking guests. It is highly recommended that hospitality students take foreign language courses, especially Spanish if the property is located in areas where most workers are Hispanic, to improve their communication skills before joining the industry.

Some basic Spanish greetings to be used at the front office are:

Buenos días	boo-éh-nohs dée-ahs	Good morning
Buenas tardes	boo-éh-nahs táhr-dehs	Good afternoon
Bienvenido	bee-éhn-veh-née-doh	Welcome
Gracias	gráh-see-ahs	Thank you
Por favor	pohr fah-vóhr	Please
Hablo español un poco	áh-bloh ehs-pah-nyóhl oon póh-coh	I speak a little Spanish
Sí, señor	see seh-nyóhr	Yes, Sir
No, señora	noh she-nyó-rah	No, madam
Me llamo...	meh yáh-moh	My name is...

A few basic terms related to the front desk are:

Cuarto	coo-áhr-toh	Room
Doble	dóh-bleh	Double
Suite	soo-éet	Suite
Cuarto de fumador	coo-áhr-toh deh foo-mah-dóhr	Smoking room
Cuarto de no fumador	coo-áhr-toh deh noh foo-mah-dóhr	Non-smoking room
Firme aquí	féer-meh ah-kée	Sign here
Su número es...	soo nóo-meh-roh ehs	Your number is....
Tiene equipaje?	Tee-éh-neh eh-kee-páh-heh?	Do you have any bags?
Ascensor	ahs-sehn-sóhr	Elevator
Botones	boh-tóh-nehs	Bellhop
Máquina de hielo	máh-kee-nah deh ee-éh-loh	Ice-making machine
Aparcamiento	ah-pahr-kah-mee-éhn-toh	Parking
Baño	báh-nyoh	Restroom

BODY LANGUAGE

Besides verbal communication, the way a message is supported through non-verbal behavior affects the reactions of people toward the speaker. Nonverbal communication applies to what can be *seen* by the other person, such as gestures, facial expressions, eye contact, and positioning. For example, movement towards a guest standing on the other side of the counter may indicate interest, or mirroring of nods or smiles could indicate acceptance. Research indicates that a high percentage of our communication is conveyed through facial expressions and tone of voice, determining to a large extent the impact of our message.

The use of personal space is important when communicating with people from other cultures. Hispanics, for instance, prefer to communicate positioning themselves quite close to the person they are talking to. Hugging as an introduction or touching each other's arms is common. On the other hand, people from Asia consider any personal contact beyond an initial handshake too much.

It is often said that some recruiters may decide to reject a candidate in an interview after only a few minutes of interaction. This can be caused by a negative feeling that is conveyed by a candidate's nonverbal behavior. For example, smiling is considered very important in the hospitality industry; a person who does not smile may be perceived by potential employers as overly introverted or even unfriendly, traits seen as negative by hospitality professionals.

Besides smiling, there is other positive body language that is considered important; maintaining eye contact, listening attentively (without appearing to be distracted), minimizing nervous movements (like tapping the counter or fumbling with the computer), and maintaining a relaxed body posture.

Some examples of non-verbal signals associated with attitudes observed by people communicating with others are:

- Avoiding eye contact or turning away from the speaker can be associated with suspicion.
- Leaning back or crossing arms can be seen as defensiveness.
- Assuming a relaxed facial expression or opening hands signals openness.

COMMUNICATION EXAMPLES BETWEEN THE FRONT OFFICE AND OTHER DEPARTMENTS

In chapter 2, we discussed the specific ways used at the front office to communicate with the housekeeping, engineering, human resources, food and beverage, sales and marketing, and accounting departments. The front office has the critical function of acting as the center for gathering and disseminating information throughout the property.

Here are some typical communication breakdowns between these departments and the front office:

Housekeeping Department: *Late on a Saturday afternoon, the front desk of the Royal Hotel receives a call from Swift Organized Tours wanting to lodge ninety passengers traveling in two buses that same evening. One of the vehicles has developed engine problems and is in need of immediate repair. Guest service agent Jim Mckenzie accepts the reservation of 54 rooms for one night's stay. The weekly occupancy forecast for Saturday issued to all departments by the front office was very low; only 80 of the property's 350 rooms were predicted to be occupied. However, a convention is due to check in early on Sunday that will fill the hotel for the following three days. Executive housekeeper manager Eileen Jenkins wisely scheduled five section housekeepers to work to service the 80 rooms predicted (at the rate of 16 rooms each).*

The front desk manager is off duty Saturday but has standing procedures in place to notify the housekeeping department of any substantial changes in room occupancy if they happen. About 9 PM, Mckenzie calls the housekeeping office but no one answers. He leaves a voice message indicating that 54 rooms were picked up unexpectedly that evening.

On opening the department Sunday morning, Jenkins realizes that she is shorthanded and begins calling around asking off-duty room attendants to report to work. Being Sunday, none of the crew off-duty is able to report to work. The rooms to be cleaned are now 161, including the tour group and several unpredicted walk-ins. With only half of the workforce present, Jenkins asks the three public area attendants and all housemen on duty to help clean the rooms needed for the incoming group. Most of the convention guests begin arriving at noon. Several of them have to wait in the lobby until five PM before they are checked into their rooms. The convention director complains bitterly to the general manager that he was promised an early check-in for the participants.

Analyze the communication in this scenario and be ready to discuss in class how this situation could have been prevented.

Engineering Department: *The Royal Hotel has recently installed maintenance software allowing operational departments to call in requests directly to the work order system. A morning-shift front desk clerk has received a call at 3 PM from room 310 about a clogged toilet in need of urgent attention. He punches the request immediately after receiving the call and notifies engineering that the room guests have already checked out and that there is a scheduled check-in for four o'clock that afternoon, making the repair very urgent.*

Jason Duran is assigned to conduct the necessary work and decides that the job won't take more than thirty minutes. Knowing that from room 310 he will have to go all the way up to the flat roof to repair a condenser in the cooling tower, he enters the room into the software system as work completed. While preparing to unclog the toilet, Duran receives a call on his pager from the chief engineer ordering him to report immediately to elevator # 3 where some guests are trapped between floors 6 and 7. A call is placed to Otis to send help as soon as possible and the chief engineer decides to attempt to rescue the guests in the elevator by lowering the car by hand to floor 6. He tells Duran to go up to the motor with him to begin the rescue. After considerable tries and with the help of the Otis' employee who arrives half an hour after the call, the door of the elevator is opened to the relief of everyone involved. The time is 4:30.

Meanwhile, Mr. and Mrs. Vasquez were checked in room 310 to find that the toilet is clogged and that the floor in the bathroom is covered with tools left behind by Duran.

Analyze the communication in this scenario and be ready to discuss in class how this situation could have been prevented.

Human Resources: *Elliott Douglas is a graduate of a hospitality program and front office manager of a resort in Colorado Springs. Douglas receives a call from a friend from college who graduated from the same program asking him to consider hiring his cousin Tom who has considerable experience in front office operations. Coincidentally, Mr. Douglas is looking for a front desk clerk to work the graveyard shift with the property's night auditor.*

He calls the human resources department to tell them to stop the search and arrange an appointment with Tom to conduct the initial interview. The second interview with the front office manager goes very well and he decides that Tom is to start the day after. The following day, a call from human resources confirms that Tom provided all documentation and that the only procedure left is to check his references, a process that would take a couple days.

Mr. Douglas, pressed by the need to cover the graveyard shift, calls human resources insisting that he needs the new employee to start working immediately, that Tom is the cousin of a good friend of his, and that there is no need to waste time checking references. Human resources accepts Elliott's request and hires the new employee without checking his past-work history. Two months later, Tom doesn't show up for his Wednesday shift while at the same time the front desk cash bank of $1,500 could not be accounted for.

Analyze the communication in this scenario and be ready to discuss in class how this situation could have been prevented.

Food and Beverage: *The restaurant of the Zephyr Lodge at Big Sur is usually busy on weekends but quiet Monday through Thursday. Ralph Scott is an affluent resident in the area who likes to invite his close friends for a relaxed evening meal at the Zephyr. He often books a table on weekdays to avoid the weekend rush.*

On a Monday morning, Mr. Scott drives his Jaguar to the lodge and reserves a table for ten for that evening, indicating that they would be ordering a la carte as usual. His request is taken by the guest service agent on duty who rings the restaurant to pass on the reservation. The person who answers is Robert, a busser who is alone and in the process of wiping down the tables in preparation for the lunch service. Robert decides that there is no need to warn the restaurant manager as the place is always quiet Monday evenings.

Coincidentally, a tour director traveling by bus with sixty wealthy Italians en route from San Francisco to San Diego decides to surprise the group by having an unscheduled dinner overlooking the Pacific Ocean at the Zephyr. He calls from Santa Barbara to give ample warning to the restaurant manager before their arrival that evening.

Mr. Scott's party arrives on time to find that there is no table available and that they would have to wait one hour before they could be served. He is upset with the situation, particularly after having reserved the table earlier in the day. He takes his friends to a nearby restaurant and decides not to patronize the Zephyr for a while.

Analyze the facts of this scenario from a communication perspective and be ready to discuss in class how this situation could have been prevented.

Sales and Marketing: *As gateway to the Grand Canyon, Flagstaff has several hospitality establishments which market themselves as the ideal rest stop for bus tours on the way to and from the National Park. Gabbie Reiner, sales manager of one of the Flagstaff hotels, has received an email from Dragon Tours located in Beijing. The reservation is for 25 twin-size and 5 single rooms for one night. The company indicated that the tour director would use a voucher as a method of payment. Ms. Reiner answers that the hotel would be glad to book the rooms but that only cash, traveler checks or credit card as payment would be accepted. Dragon Tours promptly answers that they will be using a major credit card and the booking is confirmed. A copy of the reservation, including the method of payment, is sent to the front office and the 30 rooms are entered in the reservation system for the scheduled stay.*

The morning after the arrival the tour director approaches the front desk, asks for the invoice and fills out a Dragon Tours company check for the total due. The guest service agent on duty accepts it and proceeds to check out the rooms in the system. One month later, the check is returned by the bank for lack of sufficient funds.

Analyze the communication in this scenario and be ready to discuss in class how this situation could have been prevented.

Accounting Office: *A second-hand car company opens an outlet near a mall in Boca Raton, Florida. Manager John Collins, a suave gentleman from Chicago, contacts in person the rooms director of a local downtown hotel with the purpose of opening a city ledger account to be used by company representatives when conducting business in the area. The account is set up with the proviso that bills should be paid not later than thirty days from the day of the transactions.*

The manager occasionally books rooms for out-of-town visitors to be paid by his company and, more often, uses the hotel restaurant, lounge, and spa for him, his family and guests. For *the first three months, checks are received on time after the accounting office bills the monthly statements. Payments become more sporadic as time goes by and after one year Collins' company is $9,300 in arrears. Soon thereafter, the second-hand car enterprise goes into chapter 11 and out of business the following month. John Collins and his family leave town for an unknown destination.*

Analyze the communication in this scenario and be ready to discuss in class how this situation could have been prevented.

INTRA-DEPARTMENTAL COMMUNICATION

An important task to be performed by the front office manager is that of keeping employees informed about what is going on in the department and the property. Everyone should be aware of events taking place: front desk, service personnel and, obviously, the concierge. Some tools to open and maintain clear lines of communication are memoranda, bulletin boards, departmental briefings, and one-on-one information.

Because the front office operation is open 24 hours a day, there must be an efficient method in place to communicate information from shift to shift. This can be done using a **log book** where notes are written and passed on to the new crew taking over from those going off duty.

The more front office employees understand other departments' procedures, the smoother the relationship among departments will be. This information can be imparted to new staff members at orientation or by cross training, assigning front office personnel to spend some time familiarizing themselves with other departments. The knowledge can provide front office employees with insights useful in dealing with guests staying at the property.

Supervisors should give feedback to employees in a positive, caring way. The statement, "May I give you some feedback on entering charges on guest folios," is better than saying "This is the correct way to enter charges on guest folios." A clerk who is having difficulties working with the computer would rather hear the statement "With a bit more practice you will be able to handle the desk by yourself" than "You are still slow checking guests out." In fact, instead of providing feedback about what is wrong, managers should try to tell subordinates how they can improve their performance and emphasize what they are doing right.

KEY TERMS

Empathy
Extemporaneous speaking
Impromptu speaking
Kinesthetic listener
Listening skills
Nonverbal behavior
Paraphrasing
Rapport
Toastmasters International
Verbal factors
Visual listener
Voice tone

DISCUSSION AND REVIEW QUESTIONS

1. Give three reasons why communication is particularly important at the front desk of lodging operations.
2. What type of personality should front office employees have?
3. What are three components of the listening skill in communication?
4. What is the purpose of paraphrasing a speaker's statement?
5. What do you understand by rapport?
6. Give three examples of positive body language.
7. Give one example of negative body language.
8. What is the difference between an impromptu and a planned presentation?
9. What are the three parts in which formal presentations should be divided?
10. Why is effective communication necessary within the front office department? Give an example of a fact that should be passed on from one front office shift to the next.
11. Why is it particularly difficult to comply with the premise that "guests are always right?"

PRACTICAL SITUATIONS

Situation 4.1

Addressing a Group of Guests on the Spur of the Moment

As front desk manager of a resort in Florida, you have just checked in a large Elderhostel group on their way to South Carolina. As the guests gather in the lobby, waiting to be escorted to their rooms, the group guide raises her voice and signals for you to come forward to welcome the group and to explain the services the resort offers. "I'd like to introduce the front office manager," she begins. "He has a few words for you on behalf of the resort."

ASSIGNMENT:

Stand in front of the class, pretend that the students are the Elderhostel travelers and address the group.

Situation 4.2

Communication by e-mail: A Tour guide complaint

Paola Corsi is the front office manager of a hotel in Las Vegas, Nevada. Massimo Natali, the corporate public relations manager of the company, sent Paola the following e-mail.

Dear Paola,

We have received a letter from the manager of Iberotours regarding the visit of one of their groups to your hotel on June 20. According to the tour guide, they had to wait two hours before they could be checked in. Although they found the accommodations to be excellent, they really resent the fact that nobody at the front desk cared very much while they were waiting in the lobby. Could you please look into the matter and respond by e-mail, copying me all the facts so I can answer the letter knowledgeably. As you know, Iberotours represents a good chunk of our overall business and we don't want to lose them for any reason.

Massimo

Hotel Suite
Courtesy of InterContinental Hotels Group

ASSIGNMENT:

Answer Massimo's e-mail, explaining how this incident may have occurred.

Situation 4.3

Exceeding Budget Expectations

The fiscal year is almost over. All indications point to your front office department having exceeded budget expectations for the year, for which you receive a letter of commendation from the regional office of your company. As manager, you believe that the success is mainly due to the stellar performance of your employees who have strived to upsell rooms and minimize refunds and rebates.

You decide to let the good news be known to your entire staff by writing an internal memo and posting it on the bulletin board of the department.

ASSIGNMENT:

Write a memo on the subject as if you were the front office manager.

CASE STUDY 4.1

Formal Presentation

You are currently working as rooms division director of a hotel in Santa Fe, New Mexico. You are also serving as president of the local Hotel/Motel Association. The city council has been announcing for some time that increasing the current lodging tax is necessary. The raise, they argue, will provide the city with extra funds to improve beautification efforts of downtown historical areas.

The Hotel/Motel Association believes that the tax is unfair because most lodging properties in Santa Fe are not located in the downtown area. Besides, the group is convinced that the increase would serve as a deterrent to attract people to Santa Fe, negatively affecting the convention business.

In the last association meeting, you were chosen unanimously by the attending members to defend the position of the Hotel/Motel Association regarding the tax increase at next week's open forum that has been scheduled by the city.

ASSIGNMENT:

Prepare the report that you will bring before the council, including overhead material, emphasizing the reasons against raising the lodging tax. When you present the argument, stand in front of the room, away from any table, chair or lectern. Be aware of your body language.

CASE STUDY 4.2

Communication by Business Letter

As a rooms division director of a hotel in downtown Toledo, Ohio, you receive the following letter:

May 20, 20__
Chamber of Commerce
267 Agassiz Street,
Toledo, Ohio 43551

Dear Sir,

The Ohio Chamber of Commerce plans to have its annual convention in Toledo on July 20-23. We anticipate that between 60 and 70 members and spouses from out of town will be attending the event. We are asking all lodging properties in the area to provide us with a proposal to accommodate this number of people. We are looking to reserve 55 rooms for double and 10 for single occupancy at this time.

If you are interested in hosting the delegates, please let us know the best rates you can offer us at your earliest convenience.

Sincerely,

Jake Pistolesi,
President

ASSIGNMENT:

Answer this letter, using the appropriate format for business letter writing.

CHAPTER 5

THE FRONT OFFICE AND CUSTOMER SERVICE

CHAPTER OBJECTIVES

- Explain the importance of quality control and customer service in lodging properties.
- Define the four customer service basic principles that apply to front office operations.
- Discuss the need of benchmarking in an effort to perform customer service effectively.
- Describe how to service the guest at the front office.
- Discuss the handling of guest complaints.
- Learn about automated customer service programs.
- Understand that customers may have unrealistic expectations.

OVERVIEW

One of the persistent challenges in the hospitality industry is providing and maintaining customer satisfaction. The philosophy of quality control and customer service focuses on managing a set of business practices that emphasizes continuous improvement in all aspects of operations, competence in performing activities, involvement and empowering employees and, especially, fully satisfying customer expectations. Often, instituting excellent customer service in lodging properties involves re-structuring the corporate culture and shifting to total quality and an emphasis on improvement in continuous customer service in all departments.

This chapter discusses the importance of customer service from a front office perspective and provides ideas to implement good practices and to motivate employees to commit themselves to providing quality service. A list of commitments towards consistent improvement of quality and services is also provided.

QUALITY CONTROL AND CUSTOMER SERVICE

Quality control has been a major concern in American businesses for a very long time since companies long ago realized that standards for any given product are ultimately established by the customer. However, while manufacturing companies in general concern themselves mainly with the quality of mechanical processes, lodging operations must concern themselves with both product and service. Managing quality in lodging operations involves hiring and training employees who, not only are good with their technical skills, but can also interact well with guests to deliver excellent customer service. In addition, managing for quality must include criteria established by the guests themselves.

Providing services that customers want is the starting point for providing customer satisfaction. Lodging companies are designed to deliver a tangible product along with an intangible service. The physical product by itself, such as a bed to sleep on, no matter how comfortable or luxurious it may be cannot provide for the needs of guests without the active participation of the property's staff. In other words, both physical facilities and employees' services are essential to the guest. As any seasoned hotelier will tell you, guest service is critical to a property's success. To compete, lodging properties must be aggressive in their ability to provide services as it is good customer relations which differentiates one establishment from another and successful from unsuccessful properties. By achieving customer satisfaction lodging properties can increase their options to maximize revenue and, therefore, to augment their income. Customer service includes a series of activities aimed at enhancing the level of guest satisfaction to ensure that customer expectation has been met.

From this perspective, personal interaction should be a component of an overall approach to systematic service improvement. How is service measured? Because of its intangibility, service is difficult to quantify. For instance, a bellperson can carry luggage to a guest's room promptly but the guest's evaluation of the service may depend as much on the bellperson's attitude as on the speed with which the luggage was delivered. It is not only how efficiently the service is rendered but also the manner in which it is performed that makes the difference.

The basic principles of customer service that apply to front office operations are *understanding customer requirements, empowering employees, measuring customer satisfaction,* and *focusing on continuous improvement.* Front office managers in lodging operations must be aware of the expectations of the traveling public when staying at their properties. Efficient, friendly reservation systems, fast check-in and check-out, and accurate records of guests' accounts are generally ranked as top requirements for the American traveler. In locations where the customer base is different from the norm, surveys should be conducted to find out guests' expectations. For instance, a property that regularly receives tourists from China may want to know what pleases Chinese guests, whose tastes probably differ from those of customers from Iowa.

Guests' input should be sought regularly to find out whether they are satisfied with the services offered. **Comment cards, online comment questionnaires, shop audits,** and personal interaction with guests will provide the information the department needs to measure guest satisfaction. Good relationships with guests should be the rule in lodging operations rather than the exception. Guest feedback surveys should be quantified by individual lodging properties in monthly or bimonthly reports detailing the comments gathered in different service areas as well as the number of incidences. Typical negative comments about service received at the front office include slow airport pick up by the shuttle van, poor handling of luggage, slow check-in or check-out, delay getting into room, being refused accommodation because of overbooking, too restrictive check-out hours, and unsympathetic employees.

Empowering employees to take initiative in customer satisfaction is essential to quality management. In order to achieve this, employees should be given greater decision-making latitude and provided with twice the necessary training to enable them to make reasonable decisions. Desk clerks should be empowered to determine the best way to satisfy customers; for example, by being given the authority to write off, within reason, charges for items that a guest is unhappy with.

The concept of customer service implies that the process of striving for excellence is not finite—it is about constantly improving and innovating. Avoiding errors, not fixing them, should be a never-ending process.

UNDERSTANDING CUSTOMER REQUIREMENTS.

Front office employees must be trained to perceive the meaning guests are trying to convey. This can be done by listening carefully and allowing speakers to fully express themselves. Once the communication is understood, a good technique is to summarize the statement to make sure that both parties are addressing the same issue. Satisfying the guests' desires or solving the problem should be the next step, avoiding passing the buck or offering excuses. For instance, if a guest at the front desk asks a question such as "Can I pay with a traveler check in the restaurant?" the clerk should not answer "Please ask the cashier at the restaurant," but reply instead "Just a moment, let me call the restaurant and find out for you." Here, the clerk is being helpful. Customer service improvement processes have become part of the strategy for implementing guidelines aimed at achieving total customer satisfaction.

EMPOWERING EMPLOYEES.

Management should empower line workers to take initiative in customer satisfaction and to make decisions conducive to pleasing guests. Front office employees should be given enough decision-making latitude to make reasonable decisions. Otherwise, a typical scenario is for a clerk to tell a waiting guest that she has to ask her supervisor about the resolution of a simple problem only to find out that the person in charge has left the office. In this case, either the guest must wait until the supervisor is found or be told that he cannot be helped because the clerk has no authority to decide the matter. Empowering employees streamlines chain of command and makes employees responsible for their own performance.

MEASURING CUSTOMER SATISFACTION.

One of the key strategies for customer-focused operations is to measure and monitor service quality and customer satisfaction. Customer satisfaction can be defined as "a post consumption evaluative judgment concerning a specific product or service." Guests' input should be sought regularly to find out whether they are pleased with the accommodations and services provided to them. Personal interaction, comment cards and in-house, post-stay on-line questionnaires or **secret shopper** audits will provide information to quantify customer feedback the department needs to measure guest satisfaction.

Personal interaction with departing travelers by front office employees is also very important to gather input from guests. Nothing can be more revealing than the comments of a guest checking out of the property when asked by a front desk clerk about his stay. Comment cards have the advantage of easy distribution and collection to get information about the attributes that have an impact on guests' satisfaction while on-line questionnaires seem to become more popular every day because of the increasing popularity of the Internet. Secret shoppers are experts hired by hospitality companies to conduct service audits of individual properties. Posing as guests, they are able to observe the behavior of employees on the job during the process of making a reservation, checking in and out, and so on. The report, sent to the company by mystery customers after their stay, helps management correct service deficiencies and improve product quality. The appearance of the property and its standards of service are also measured by inspectors from **Forbes Travel Guide** and **AAA** who anonymously evaluate properties against set standards.

Formerly known as the *Mobil Travel Guide*, Forbes has assisted travelers for over 50 years in making smart decisions about where to stay when traveling. Representatives conduct rigorous inspections of the lodging properties they visit and test more than 500 standards before they award a rating of stars according to what they find. Some properties awarded a 5-star rating by Forbes are

The Mandarin Oriental Hotel, Singapore
The Beverly Hill Hotel, Beverly Hills, CA
The Broadmoor, Colorado Springs, CO
The Four Seasons Hotel, Washington, DC

AAA professional inspectors get an in-depth, inside view of every AAA-approved property. They strive to avoid any treatment or services not extended to every guest to experience properties the same way AAA members do. Inspectors use published guidelines to evaluate, approve and rate lodgings on a scale of one to five diamonds. Examples of 5-diamond lodging properties are these:

The Four Seasons Hotel, Mexico City
Tortuga Bay Punta Cana, Punta Cana, Dominican Republic
The Ritz-Carlton Resort, Rose Hall, Jamaica
The Grand Del Mar, San Diego, CA

FOCUSING ON CONTINUOUS IMPROVEMENT

Striving for excellence in customer service is about constantly improving - avoiding errors, not fixing them. All guest feedback should be analyzed and actions taken to ensure that negative experiences are not repeated. All complaints should be investigated and addressed by management until they are resolved. Some of the actions to be implemented could involve changes in standard operating procedures, improving equipment, or retraining employees. The ability to continuously improve customer service is a valuable competitive asset and resource strength.

Rewarding front office employees who distinguish themselves providing excellent customer service helps encourage them to go that extra mile to help guests. Commendation memos, complimentary stays in a sister establishment, or monetary bonuses provide incentives for employees to do their best. Most lodging companies have in place programs to enhance customer service and thus achieve the loyalty of their guests by providing them with the facilities, amenities and service they expect.

For customer service practices to be performed well, lodging companies should **benchmark** how they perform these activities against best-of-the-industry performers. Benchmarking is the practice that allows a company to determine whether its business performance compares favorably with the competition. It entails doing cross-company comparisons and inquiring about internal procedures. Benchmarking must be conducted within ethical frameworks of business behavior because, in some cases, benchmarking can lead to organizations colluding to implement unfair trading practices. **Business collusion**—a secret business agreement with a competitor to fix prices—undermines free market competition and is against the law. Seeking out and adopting best customer service practices is essential to implementing the necessary strategies to improve a company's performance, however, the best practices of other lodging companies should be adapted to a property's own specific situation. Here are some of the questions to be posed before benchmarking a property:

- How well are we performing compared to our competitors?
- What are the best customer service practices and how well does our company perform these practices?
- What customer service performance should we focus on?

Companies that benchmark their customer service performance report the following benefits:

- Identifying specific problem areas.
- Focusing employees on the areas of the customer service cycle which need attention.
- Making it easier to raise the customer service bar.
- Creating a genuine desire to improve current customer service levels.
- Increasing customer satisfaction which, in turn, positively impacts customer loyalty and retention.

Ritz-Carlton, for instance, is a lodging company committed to customer service and continuous service improvement based on the following four doctrines:

1. The company credo
2. The employee promise
3. The three steps to service
4. The business premise

Credo: *The Ritz-Carlton Hotel is a place where the genuine care and comfort of our guests is our highest mission. We pledge to provide the finest personal service and facilities for our guests who will always enjoy a warm, relaxed yet refined ambience. The Ritz-Carlton experience enlivens the senses, instills well-being, and fulfills even the unexpressed wishes and needs of our guests.*

The Employee Promise: *At the Ritz-Carlton, our Ladies and Gentlemen are the most important resource in our service commitment to our guests. By applying the principles of trust, honesty, respect, integrity and commitment, we nurture and maximize talent to the benefit of each individual and the company. The Ritz-Carlton fosters a work environment where diversity is valued, quality of life is enhanced, individual aspirations are fulfilled, and the Ritz-Carlton mystique is strengthened.*

The motto: *"We are Ladies and Gentlemen serving Ladies and Gentlemen."*

Ritz-Carlton's Three Steps to Service: *1) a warm and sincere greeting. Use the guest name, if and when possible. 2) Anticipation and compliance with guest needs. 3) Fond farewell. Give them a warm good-bye and use their names, if and when possible.*

Every employee is expected to embrace these service-oriented qualities, find new ways to interpret them, and put them into practice during every moment of their working shift. Using benchmarking to provide all stakeholders with the latest best practices can help speed the diffusion and adaptation of practices throughout lodging companies and properties.

A DECALOGUE FOR CONSISTENT IMPROVEMENT OF PRODUCTS AND SERVICES

Lodging properties could apply the following series of commitments, adopted from William Edwards Deming's philosophy of management, towards achieving quality and customer service in their front office departments:

1. Offering a quality product and satisfying customer needs at an affordable price.
2. Adopting a commitment at the top and throughout the department so employees understand the purpose of the unit towards quality and service.
3. Accepting that the improvement of the product and services must be continuous.
4. Realizing that, essentially, the job of the front office manager, supervisors, and uniformed employees is not that of fixing problems; instead, the product must be good to begin with.
5. Acknowledging that training and re-training is necessary to achieve quality and excellent customer service.
6. Believing that the empowerment of employees is critical to achieve quality and service.
7. Agreeing that the job of every front office employee must be defined clearly in order to achieve quality and service.
8. Accepting that individual employees must not be blamed for lack of quality or poor service; the entire system should be made responsible.
9. Seeing the managers as facilitators for employees to achieve a quality product and effective services.
10. Understanding that managers and supervisors should not micromanage front office operations.

THE USE OF CUSTOMER EXPERIENCE ANALYTICS

The overall goal of all business should be to have customers who won't even consider switching to another company or brand. A consistently satisfying customer experience is the only way to create a sustainable competitive advantage because loyal customers are more profitable as new ones are more expensive to acquire. The best method of establishing long term loyalty is by deserving it. Customer loyalty can be purchased, for example by offering a more advantageous program than the competition, but this approach can have unintended consequences by conditioning customers to expect deals, discounts, and rewards.

Instead, true customer loyalty can be secured by measuring the levels of customer satisfaction experienced by the people who patronize our establishments and improving where necessary. In other words, customer satisfaction breeds loyalty. When customers' needs and expectations are consistently met, they do not think of changing brands.

SERVICING THE GUEST

Because of its people-serving-people orientation, service is the cornerstone of the hospitality industry. The basic purpose behind servicing the guest can be summarized as ensuring customer satisfaction leading to retention in order to create guest loyalty towards the operation. The two elements involved in this process are the guests, who are the reason-for-being in business and for making the operation worthwhile, and the employees who provide the product and services to fulfill the needs of the customers. Guest satisfaction is important in the lodging business to create loyalty; that is, to make guests feel that they want to come back and visit the property over and over again. Travelers develop loyalty towards a hotel chain or independent establishments for different reasons. Some may find the property's location to be convenient, others may consider the rates affordable, still others may like the food served in the restaurant; but the majority of travelers decide to return to a specific property because they find the employees friendly, because they are recognized when checking in and during their stay or because they are provided with courteous, competent service at the front desk.

One of the first hotels where I worked when I started my career in lodging was the 5-star Meliá Don Pepe in Marbella, Spain. In that pre-computerized era keys were left at the concierge's desk, and guests were very impressed when the clerks addressed them by their names when requesting the keys to go to their rooms. The guests' names were written in very small letters under each room's pigeon hole where the keys were kept. Today, this can be done by installing caller ID programs which show the guests' names when they call the front desk from any extension in the house. In this era of technology, the human element is still needed; nothing is more comforting to travelers than being addressed by name. Conversely, guests like to know the name and title of the employee they are interacting with. It is a simple matter to provide employees with name tags that can be easily read.

Although top-management of most lodging chains has developed a culture of service, service mission statements, and guest- service standards, the crucial task of creating customer service is up to each department. It is the genuine desire on the part of the employees to want to please the guest that differentiates one establishment from another. Nevertheless, each property must have clear service guidelines broken down by department to provide employees with basic guidelines aimed at providing good customer service. Here are basic rules:

- Establish eye contact.
- Smile.
- Greet the guest.
- Address the guest by last name.
- Listen carefully.
- Thank the guest.

In a typical scenario at the front desk, the clerk should look the guest in the eye, smile genuinely, use a friendly greeting, such as "good morning, Mr. Robard" and listen carefully to what the person has to say. After the transaction has been completed, an authentic thank you to the guest is indispensable.

Every lodging company should develop its own service strategy, with statements such as 'We are committed to providing excellent customer service by listening to our guests and fulfilling their expectations.' Starwood, for instance, offers a webpage where customers can contact the company's corporate customer service by phone, email or letter regarding billing issues, preferred guest-related questions or any specific complaint. The customer service department is also available through Starwood's Social Media online services, such as Spg.com, Twitter, Facebook, and FaceTime. That is customer service!

Starwood puts forth its customer service-related values in this way:

- Go the Extra Step by taking actions that build lasting connections and loyalty.
- Play as a Team by working globally and across all teams in the company.
- Do the Right thing by using good judgment, respecting our communities, associates, owners, partners and the environment.

SETTING SERVICE STANDARDS AT THE FRONT DESK

Service can be defined as the process of satisfying the guests' needs. In most cases, it is not just what is done for the guest but how it is done that is important. Although service is intangible, service standards must be set, particularly those related to the time required for their delivery. Nevertheless, to determine how long it should take to check in a guest, several variables should be considered, such as the number of clerks on duty at a specific time, the front office equipment, and the information that clerks are supposed to gather from registering guests, but in all cases service levels must be realistic and standards must be in place to compensate when something goes wrong. A standard of service could be to relocate front office workers from other functions to help out when check-in or check-out lines are, say, four or more guests deep. Other service standards could involve answering the phone before the fourth ring or responding to email messages the same working day they are received.

Service standards must be realistic and responsive to the department's budget. It could be desirable to have three clerks behind the front desk counter at all times to speed up operations but this approach may be financially unviable. Front office managers should strive to provide consistent service at all times although this is not always possible because services are performed by people not machines, and people are not as consistent as machines. A good approach to providing consistent service is to vary staffing levels with anticipated occupancy.

It is important to keep in mind that the main goal of setting service standards should be to provide a level of service that exceeds that provided by the competition as service is what differentiates one property from another in the minds of customers; in other words, service must be regarded as a competitive strategy. If it is true that good service costs money, it is also true that improved services make for more satisfied guests, which leads to repeat business, higher revenues, and greater profits.

HANDLING GUEST COMPLAINTS

Unfortunately, despite best efforts on the part of the front office staff to maximize customer attention, guests will occasionally be disappointed with one or more of the services the property provides. Because of this, complaints should be anticipated and guidelines developed to instruct employees on how to resolve them.

As most complaints are directed to the front office, that department must be instructed how to handle them. Nothing irritates guests more than having their discontent ignored. Complaints should be welcomed by the front office staff as an opportunity to correct something that might have gone wrong. Guests who decide not to express their annoyance often will not return and will tell relatives, friends or business associates about the problem they had, discouraging them also from visiting the property. The fact is that after a complaint has been registered, management learns of a deficiency and has the opportunity to resolve it so it doesn't happen again. For their part, complaining guests then often feel that the property cares about their needs.

Most complaints arise from mechanical, service-related or situational incidents. **Mechanical complaints** are mostly related to equipment malfunctions, such as with lighting, climate control, door-opening devices, television sets and surges in the bathroom water supply.

Even having a good preventive maintenance program doesn't eliminate potential equipment malfunction. Mechanical problems are resolved by notifying the engineering or housekeeping departments about the problem. **Service-related complaints** are related to poor service, particularly lack of friendliness on the part of the staff. Other service-related problems occur because of lengthy waits for service, lack of assistance with luggage, and missed wake-up calls. Service-related problems are difficult to address as, usually, the opportunity for fixing them has already passed. In all cases, the incident must be reported in detail to a supervisor or manager for the appropriate follow-up so that it doesn't happen again. **Situational complaints** may happen when guests feel uneasy due to rude or tactless employees interacting with other workers; for example, customers overhearing employees arguing among themselves or who witness members of the staff disputing internal operational matters.

Guest complaints deserve attention in all cases, especially if the customer is loudly voicing his opinion at the front desk when other people are present. All observations should be recorded in an **incidence log book** or computer program to bring them to the attention of management. Follow up complaints taking these measures:

- Respond immediately to correct the deficiency.
- Never make a promise that might not be fulfilled about fixing the problem (for example, assuring the guest that the deficiency will be corrected in "five" minutes).
- Admit when a problem cannot be solved at the time, and offer the guest a reasonable alternative.

Helpful guidelines to deal with complaints are these:

- Apologize for the inconvenience caused.
- Listen with empathy.
- Avoid arguing or adopting a defensive position.
- Always tell guests the truth about the situation at hand.
- Offer a possible solution to the problem.
- Monitor the completion of the corrective action.
- Contact the guest after the problem has been addressed to ascertain if it has been satisfactorily solved.

AUTOMATED CUSTOMER SERVICE

The customer service function is best provided by a person, rather than a device, particularly in the hospitality industry. There are, however, automated means that lodging companies can use to complement the service provided by employees. For example, small properties can offer automated 24-hour customer service when departments operate with limited staff. These services include the Internet and touch-tone phones. The challenge is centered on maintaining the personal touch by creating a sense of personal connection online or with automated devices.

One advantage technology offers is getting instant feedback from guests using programs that analyze community blogs and forums where customers can log positive or negative experiences they have when visiting a lodging property. **Customer Relationship Management (CRM)** is a model that can be used to manage a property's interaction with guests and potential customers. It involves adopting technology to automate and organize customer service and sales activities to attract and retain travelers. For example, CRM software can be used to identify the preferences of a particular guest, from a specific room to a type of pillow or tea brand. **The International Customer Service Institute (TICSI)** recommends the adoption of a site assessment program to assist organizations with monitoring their changing business environment and customer needs. Regular assessment would ensure that companies remain competitive and up to date regarding its customers' expectations.

Companies like Synthesio offer their expertise to monitor online social media globally. By analyzing pools of data, they advertise that they can provide lodging chains with reports which help find the right balance of technology and human service. The French lodging company, Accor, decided to have monitored its over 5,000 comments each month on social travel sites such as Booking.com and TripAdvisor as a means to focus on customer satisfaction and quality of service. The company wanted to learn what customers were saying about the Accor brand and about approximately 12,000 competitor hotels. By combining the data obtained with its own internal findings they hoped to provide their individual establishments with guidelines for taking action on the social media content obtained. The project was divided into short, intermediate, and long term phases. The short term phase consisted of running a pilot program on a few hotels to raise awareness of the importance of social media data. The first step was to identify customized **key performance indicators (KPIs)** to measure customer satisfaction. During the intermediate phase they used the data gathered to identify which hotels were faring better than others while the long term effort aimed at identifying specific problems and focusing on improving Accor's online image. Individual properties were also provided with guidelines to respond online and to increase customer satisfaction and brand awareness. According to the report, the online reputation of the company was improved by 55%; Accor's Novotel brand saw double-digit growth in online sales over a year. At the same time, properties with a reputation for poor service were identified and their management alerted so that customer satisfaction could be improved. Synthesio's URL is http://synthesio.com.

UNREALISTIC CUSTOMER EXPECTATIONS

When a complaint is insoluble, an admission of the fact should be made by the employee involved, and if the time needed to correct a problem is unknown, no rash promises should be made to guests. There are occasions in which guests may have requests impossible to fulfill. The typical case is that of a customer refusing to pay for a steak that was too tough, *after having eating it.* At the front desk, a departing guest may demand a discount for an innocuous happening, in which case the best technique for dealing with the unreasonable request is to be assertive while defending the company's interests. A scenario about a guest expecting inappropriate compensation could be this:

Front desk clerk Lee:	*Good morning, sir, how can I help you?*
Guest:	*My name is James. I am checking out of room 3005.*
Clerk Lee:	*Just a moment Mr. James while I pull your account. Did you have a good stay with us?*
Mr. James:	*Yes, but your pool service is not the best.*
Clerk Lee:	*Our pool service, sir? Can you describe to me what happened?*
Mr. James:	*My wife and I went down to the pool and couldn't find any towels. I had to go up to my room on the tenth floor to get towels.*
Clerk Lee:	*I am sorry about that, Mr. James. At what time of the day did that happen?*
Mr. James:	*It was about 10 o'clock in the morning.*
Clerk Lee:	*Did you look in the container marked "TOWELS" at the entrance of the pool? It is replenished every day by 9 AM. Was the pool very busy at the time?*
Mr. James:	*No. As a matter of fact we were alone. We didn't see any container. Anyway, I feel that you should award us a discount because of the inconvenience of having to go to our room to get our towels.*
Clerk Lee:	*I am sorry, Sir. I cannot allow for a discount for the incident, but I am truly sorry that you had to go to your room when the towels where right there.*

KEY TERMS

American Automobile Association (AAA)
Benchmarking
Business collusion
Comment cards

Customer Relationship Management (CRM)
Forbes Travel Guide
Incidence logbook
Key performance indicators (KPIs)
Mechanical complaint
Online comment questionnaire
Secret shopper
Service-related complaint
Shop audits
Situational complaint
The International Customer Service Institute (TICSI)

DISCUSSION AND REVIEW QUESTIONS

1. Explain why quality standards are ultimately established by customers in lodging operations.
2. Why is service intangible? Name a tangible product in a lodging property.
3. What are three ways to elicit input from guests who are or have been staying in a resort?
4. Which are four negative comments that guests may make in surveys about front office service?
5. Think of and share with the class an instance in which a front desk clerk could speed up service because he/she has been empowered to make decisions.
6. In order to understand customer requirements well, what is the first step a bellperson should take?
7. Why should customer service be benchmarked with other competing establishments?
8. Compose a brief mission statement that a lodging company could use as its philosophy on customer service.
9. As a front desk clerk, how would you react to a mechanical complaint reported to you by a guest from a guestroom?
10. What is the purpose of the incidence log book at the front office?

PRACTICAL SITUATIONS

Situation 5.1

Customer service at the front desk

The check-in standing policy at a 4-star business hotel in downtown Albuquerque, New Mexico, is that guests cannot be guaranteed registering into a room prior to 2 PM. It is Sunday morning and Mr. Procopio, a very-tired looking traveler, approaches the front desk and tells front desk clerk Ann Lucero that his connecting flight to Minneapolis has been delayed by ten hours and that he needs a day room where he can rest for the next eight hours. Ann knows that the hotel was sold out last night but wants to provide service to the traveler whom she recognizes as a regular guest of the hotel.

Lucero calls housekeeping and requests a clean room for the waiting guest. The supervisor in housekeeping notifies Ann that, being Sunday, she is short of help but that she would do her best to have a vacant-and-ready room as soon as possible. Eager to please, Lucero registers the traveler and tells him that the room is being made up and that it will take about 15 minutes to have it ready for him. Mr. Procopio accommodates himself in the lobby and starts working on his laptop. Time passes, and 30 minutes later the customer asks Ann for the room, indicating that he is really tired and needs to rest. Lucero calls housekeeping and she is told that it will be another 50 minutes before the room can be made ready as the section housekeepers are all busy making up the stay-over rooms first. On hearing the news, Mr. Procopio decides to leave, but not before handing Ann a note addressed to management, which reads: "I have been a guest in this hotel for years. Your front desk employee has kept me waiting in the lobby for almost an hour when I was dead tired and in need of rest. And this happened after having been promised by her that a room would be ready for me 15 minutes after my arrival. Needless to say, I am most disappointed about your service to regular guests."

ASSIGNMENT:

Discuss this incidence with another student and determine if this was a case of poor customer service. After all, wasn't Ann trying to fulfill the request of a regular guest of the hotel?

Situation 5.2

Business collusion

There are two business hotels in downtown Pleasantville, the Regency and the Baymont. Both hotels are independently owned by local business leaders who, although competitors, have been friends for years. The Regency is relatively old, offering guests rooms that are comfortable but with simple décor. The Baymont is a newer property, with bright, elegantly outfitted guest rooms. This establishment, however, is perceived as being poorly cleaned and maintained.

Hoping to improve business still more, the owners of the two hotels decide to meet and exchange information about each other's methods of operation. After trading operational procedures for some months, it seems to everyone that both establishments are improving in quality and service. Just before the two weeks in April when Pleasantville fair and rodeo celebrations take place and because the two hotels were always booked solid at that time, the owners decide to set room rates of both hotels at $150 per night. The regular rates, outside of the fair weeks, are $ 75 at the Regency and $ 85 at the Baymont.

ASSIGNMENT:

What was constructive in the relationship between the two properties?
What was against the law?

Situation 5.3

Poor front office customer service ratings

Ted Tomlison accepted a job as front office assistant manager at a convention hotel in Las Vegas. After his orientation and initial training, his was given the task of analyzing the comment cards and online questionnaires used by the hotel to gage customer satisfaction. The primary targets of negative comments were the front desk and the bell department. The highest guest dissatisfaction originated from the arrival and departure of convention groups, when customers had to wait a long time registering before they were given the keys to their rooms. There were also several complaints about the congestion at the front door and the lack of bellpersons to handle the customers' luggage. Guests also complained about persistent inaccuracies found on accounts which caused unnecessary delays when checking out.

InterContinental The Barclay, New York
Courtesy of InterContinental Hotels Group

ASSIGNMENT:

What seems to be the underlying problems with the front office? What should Ted be doing to turn the situation around and lower the number of negative comments?

CASE STUDY CASE 5.1

Analysis of Service in a Downtown Hotel

The Oxford Hotel was inaugurated in Lincoln, Nebraska, in 1944. For years, the establishment was the indisputable headquarters for visitors from the surrounding area and the center of activity for the community, patronized by the most prominent local families and business leaders. The Oxford, which in the past offered fine dining and banquet services unmatched by the competition, was listed on the National Register of Historic Places. For the last 5 years, however, the return on investment to owners had been less than desirable. The reason, according to the hotel's management, was competition created by two newly opened chain-operated establishments located within walking distance of the Oxford. The new hotels benefited from strong nationwide marketing campaigns and from belonging to a central reservation system network.

Many of the formerly staunch community supporters of the Oxford were torn between patronizing the nostalgic, historic landmark and enjoying the modern amenities offered by the new properties. The owners, of necessity, decided to hire an industry consultant to find out what could be done to return the Oxford to acceptable profitability levels. The first step proposed by the secret shopper consisted of conducting a shop audit, followed by an interview with the current general manager. The following is a copy of the report sent to the owners by the consultant that concerned front office operations:

I started the shop audit by telephoning the hotel directly to reserve a room a 11 AM on Monday. The operator answered the call after five rings and connected me with reservations. The clerk, very courteously, took down the information and confirmed that she was giving me a "special rate for a standard room." I had not asked for a special rate; in fact, I would have preferred a junior suite or similar accommodation as I was travelling with my 10-year-old son.

When we arrived at the hotel by cab, there was no doorman at the entrance of the hotel. We carried our luggage into the lobby where a bellperson offered to take out suitcases. The lobby was impressive, with dark oak paneling and furniture. The elevator doors were finished in laminated burnished copper. The décor conveyed a formal elegance. There were two clerks at the front desk; one was busy entering data into a computer terminal and the other was speaking to a guest at the counter. It might have been 4 minutes before the person at the computer greeted me and offered help.

At checkout, there was a line of guests with only one clerk visible. After several minutes, the clerk opened a side door and asked for help. The front desk supervisor came out and the line split in two. My bill had a phone charge that was not mine. The clerk disappeared into the back office and reappeared with a bundle of vouchers that backed up the charge on the folio. After some discussion, the clerk agreed that the amount had been posted to my account by mistake. We were not asked whether or not our stay at the hotel had been a pleasant one, although the employee wished us a happy trip and said that he hoped to see us back again at the property. There were no bellpersons on site and we had to carry on our own luggage to a waiting taxi at the curbside.

ASSIGNMENT:

Analyze the report and list the positive and negative examples of customer service noted by the consultant. How would you correct the negative experiences?

CHAPTER 6

FRONT OFFICE HUMAN RESOURCE MANAGEMENT

CHAPTER OBJECTIVES

- Understand the need to minimize employee turnover and absenteeism in the front office department in order to maximize departmental income.
- Explain the process of selecting, hiring, and evaluating front office employees.
- List some considerations to be followed when interviewing employees.
- Discuss procedures for testing and inducting workers.
- Describe the four major areas involved in front office employee training.
- Discuss motivation theories applicable to front office workers.
- Describe the concept of employee evaluation and compensation.
- Learn how to effect worker satisfaction.
- Discuss the necessity of implementing guidelines for disciplining employees.
- Acquire awareness of cultural diversity, racial discrimination, and sexual harassment.

OVERVIEW

Front office managers should develop a strategy of gaining competitive advantage through an effective use of people; that is, by making efficient use of their labor force in order to attain higher quality service and productivity, and lower labor costs. Employee turnover and absenteeism rates in the lodging industry are very high, substantially increasing the labor cost associated with constant recruiting and employee training. Successful front office managers, however, can minimize turnover by following sound techniques for recruiting, hiring, and training employees. Practicing motivational methods and having in place adequate evaluation and compensation techniques can also create worker satisfaction and reduce turnover. Just as important as creating worker satisfaction is having in place fair, clear guidelines for disciplining those employees who do not perform within company regulations.

As the number of minority workers in lodging companies is very large, this chapter addresses the issue of cultural diversity and provides procedures to avoid racial discrimination and sexual harassment in the workplace.

THE NEED TO CURB HIGH EMPLOYEE TURNOVER AND ABSENTEEISM

The management of personnel in the lodging industry is complex. The business requires a large number of workers because most of the functions performed need one-on-one interactions with guests. The industry is notorious for offering demanding jobs and for paying minimum wage, particularly at entry-level positions. Many people enter the field when they cannot find work elsewhere, perceiving their employment as a last resort rather than a career. This creates a chronic shortage of personnel as employees come and go in great numbers. It is not uncommon for lodging properties to experience employee turnover rates of over 100 percent per year. It is therefore critical that front office managers strive to maintain low levels of employee turnover and absenteeism.

There are two basic means to reduce turnover and absenteeism: one is to follow the common technical rules of adequately recruiting, selecting, training, and evaluating personnel; the other consists of practicing effective methods of employee motivation, compensation, and the creation of an environment conducive to employee satisfaction.

PERSONNEL ACQUISITION

Lodging property employers are often torn between seeing workers as their most important assets and investing in them or seeing employees as an expense and reducing their payrolls as much as possible. Some companies emphasize putting money into **human capital** to produce economic value while others opt for hiring a minimum of full-time employees and rely on **contingency workers** who are not guaranteed a number of hours large enough to warrant benefits such as dental, vision or even medical insurance. In recessionary times, employers look both for labor cost savings and a reduced ongoing commitment to their workforce. Some resort to **outsourcing** their work force to save money on labor costs. In all cases, the costs and benefits of the labor strategies to be adopted should be weighed before deciding what to do.

In medium and large-size properties the human resource department deals with the functions of recruiting, screening, training, evaluating, disciplining, compensating, and rewarding workers. Ideally, a lodging property should employ only cheerful, good-natured people who smile easily and often, particularly in front-of-the-house departments such as the front office. Conversely, grouchy people, those who cannot keep their tempers, and who feel sorry for themselves should not be hired at all. In all cases, the success of the operation depends on attracting applicants and placing them in the positions most appropriate to their skills and personalities.

Hiring applicants "off the street" may have a very negative outcome. If the wrong person is initially placed in the wrong position, turnover will result, as the person will inevitably leave the company, voluntarily or otherwise. Trial-and-error methods of employing personnel must be avoided; instead, sound recruiting and hiring policies should be adopted.

RECRUITING FRONT OFFICE EMPLOYEES

Employee recruitment is the process by which applicants are screened to fill vacant positions. The process involves selecting, interviewing, and evaluating the qualifications of applicants to find the best person for the job. In large lodging properties, the human resources department assists the front office manager in finding and hiring qualified individuals while in smaller operations, the individual in charge of the front office is in charge of the entire process. The front office hires most of the department's employees **full-time** for the positions of reservationist, front office clerk, concierge, night auditor, and bell staff. Occasionally, such as in high season, **part-time** employees are contracted to work usually less than 30 hours per week, generally receiving no major benefits other than wages. In most cases, part-time workers have an additional source of income, as they may be retirees or college students. Often, because of cost and fear of overstaffing, businesses turn to staffing companies for **temporary help**. One advantage of hiring temporaries is that it allows the employer to evaluate their qualifications and suitability for the job before offering them a full-time permanent position. Lodging properties usually also have a number of people **on-call**, who are asked to report to work when extra help is needed, such as when regular employees are ill or on vacation. Union contracts, however, may have a significant impact on the composition of the company's work force. For example, a union contract may stipulate that all front office workers must be guaranteed a 40-hour work week; in this case, no part-time employees can be hired. In all cases recruiting new employees is a special concern of both organization and newcomer.

In all instances, management expects good performance and cooperation, while the new employee wants fair compensation, to be understood and recognized and, above all, to be helped during the induction process. In large properties, the order to recruit is initiated in the front office department by filling an **employee requisition form** (Figure 6.1). This form indicates the position that needs to be filled and describes the specification of the job and the required qualifications of the applicant. The **job description** is a detailed statement of the tasks required to get the job done. At the front office, job descriptions should be customized to the operational procedures of each lodging property. Each newly hired employee should be given a copy of the job description detailing the job's specific requirements. Figure 6.2 is a sample job descriptions for front desk clerk (guest service agent). Each job description should include the minimum **employee qualifications** required and desired to ensure that applicants will be capable of doing the job for which they are applying. For example, the job description for front desk clerk may require that the applicant has knowledge of basic Spanish if the property is located in a region near the Mexico border and receives many Spanish-speaking travelers. Specific skills needed by front office employees are mathematical ability, knowledge of principles of accounting, and computer literacy.

After receiving the employee requisition, the human resources department usually advertises the position internally (**internal recruiting**) and externally (**external recruiting**). An organization that develops its personnel exclusively from within may be limiting itself by having to promote employees who may not be qualified for the position. On the other hand, capable employees already working for the company should be given a fair option to advance or change positions, and even departments, if they so desire.

Date:________________ Department:________________________________

Position Requested: ____

New:__________ Replacement:__________ Number Required: __________

Classification: ____

(Full-time, Part-time, Temporary)

Working Hours: ____

Desired Starting Date: ____

Starting Rate of Pay: ____

Specification (general description of duties): ________________________

____

____

Special Qualifications (desired or required):________________________

____

____

Department Manager: ____

FIGURE 6.1 SAMPLE EMPLOYEE REQUISITION FORM

Thus, the first step is to inform everyone in the department of the job opening. If no one is interested in applying for the position, employees may have friends or acquaintances who are looking for work. Usually, lodging companies reward workers with bonuses for their referral of potential employees if these are hired and stay employed for a minimum of, say, 6 months. Friends and relatives are usually well accepted by current employees, who are more likely to help the newcomers adjust to their new jobs. Another advantage of recruitment from within is that it avoids incurring recruitment costs. When the new opening is for a supervisory position, special efforts should be made to promote from within as a matter of fairness and to provide opportunities for advancement to the employees already with the company. Charts showing the various opportunities for career progression should be displayed for employees to see. In the front office department, the career path for a front office clerk could lead from an entry-level position to shift supervisor, assistant to the front office manager and, possibly, to rooms division director.

The most common external recruitment method is online advertising. These ads are particularly successful in attracting young people looking for part-time and temporary employment. Internet advertising reaches users who are already capable of using computers and navigating the net. The advantage of this is that young, under-skilled people can usually be adequately trained to perform the requirements of the job; the disadvantage is that once they have been trained, they may decide to change jobs and leave the department.

When a supervisory or management position needs to be filled, private employment agencies often provide a valuable source of recruits, but in most cases the property must pay a substantial fee for their services. Public employment agencies may be sources of good employees in some cases. The state employment services are non-fee referral agencies for workers, and so are organizations for the physically impaired. Most physically impaired individuals are very dependable and efficient in the performance of simple, repetitive jobs. In some cases, companies may benefit from tax credits by hiring workers from federally-supported programs.

Schools and colleges are good sources of recruits with special skills. Local community colleges may offer vocational courses in front office or accounting. Most hotel/restaurant management programs require students to complete hundreds of hours in pre-graduation employment in the industry. Bulletin board advertising in colleges usually results in applications for employment. Some colleges and universities have summer internship programs that allow undergraduate students to practice in hotels and resorts prior to graduation. The students can be used as supervisors or management assistants or they can be put in charge of special projects, such as gathering historical data from former guests' records, developing job descriptions, or getting involved in clerical work. Figure 6.2 is a sample job description of a front office clerk.

Job title: Guest service agent (front desk clerk)

Job responsibility: To perform front desk duties as stated in the hotel's operating manual, fulfill all office-related functions in an efficient, courteous, and professional manner, and provide guests with high standards of service and hospitality.

Responsible to: Front office manager

DUTIES AND RESPONSIBILITIES:

1. Acquire a thorough knowledge of all front office systems.
2. Use proper telephone etiquette.
3. Maintain a high standard of personal grooming.
4. Assign and pre-register rooms, accommodating special requests whenever possible.
5. Welcome, register and check out guests as laid down in the front office operating manual.
6. Adhere to guest credit and check-cashing policies and procedures.
7. Understand how to perform room counts and be aware of room availability at all times.
8. Stay up-to-date on transient, government and corporate room rates, discounts and packages.
9. Know the location of all rooms in the house and their internal structure.
10. Select and block rooms for arriving customers.
11. Know how to exchange foreign currency (if there is no cashier).
12. Maximize revenue and guest satisfaction with upselling techniques.
13. Prepare all necessary reports as laid down in the hotel's operating manual.
14. Verify room status updates with the housekeeping department by communicating promptly all check-outs, late check-outs, early check-ins, and room changes.
15. Check any discrepancies between the AM and PM reports received from housekeeping and the front desk records.
16. Know room reservations and cancellation procedures.
17. Reconcile all payment transactions and cash banks.
18. Ensure that security is maintained in respect to all cash banks.
19. Keep strict security of room-opening cards, guest property and company equipment.
20. Post charges to guest, master, and city-ledger accounts.
21. Enter any problems, complaints and unusual occurrences on the department's log book.
22. Attend departmental meetings.
23. Coordinate repairs and maintenance work with the engineering department.

24. Have full knowledge of the property's fire plan, emergency and evacuation procedures.
25. Perform any reasonable duty required by management besides the normal front desk tasks.

Management reserves the right to modify this job description and to assign other tasks to front office employees as circumstances require.

Required Job Qualifications: Able to operate the property's PMS system and other equipment at the front office. Possess agility and dexterity to service many guests simultaneously. Show a friendly and professional demeanor in all dealings with guests and other employees. Understand that it is often necessary in the hospitality business to change employees from their accustomed shifts to other shifts.

Preferred qualifications: Education: Able to understand basic math and accounting principles. Knowledge of Japanese preferred (for this particular property).

Experience: over six months previous work as front desk clerk in a four-star establishment (for this particular property).

Personality: pleasant, able to interact with guests and fellow workers.

Appearance: well groomed.

FIGURE 6.2 SAMPLE FRONT DESK EMPLOYΔ121EE JOB DESCRIPTION

SELECTING FRONT OFFICE EMPLOYEES

The initial contact with prospective employees begins with their filling out, usually online, an **application form**. This form is a means of securing standard information about applicants. No person can be denied the opportunity to submit an application for employment; questions to be included in application forms depend on the company but, in all cases, every question asked should serve a purpose. No question should be asked that is not useful for research purposes or for determining the applicant's eligibility for the job. The U.S. Equal Employment Opportunity Commission has been set up to enforce the Civil Rights Act which protects against discrimination on the basis of race, color, religion, sex, or national origin. Because of increased emphasis by state and federal governments to avoid discrimination in employment, application forms must be carefully worded to avoid requesting any pre-employment information that could be considered discriminatory.

Questions such as those listed in the left column that follows are considered unlawful and should not be part of an application form. Questions in the right column are acceptable.

Unlawful application form questions	***May ask or require at time of interview***
What race are you?	
Name of your spouse	Names of relatives employed by company
Marital status	
Where does your spouse work?	
Please attach a photograph of yourself	A photo may be required *after* hiring for identification.
Place of birth	
What is your native language?	(If job related), what foreign languages do you speak?
Which country do you originate from?	
Of what country are you a citizen?	Are you a U.S. Citizen?
Are you a native-born U.S, citizen?	Do you have a permanent immigration visa? Can you prove that you can legally work in the U.S.?
Are your parents naturalized U.S. citizens?	
What is your religion of preference?	
Do you have any disabilities?	Have you any physical, medical, or mental impairments that would restrict your ability to do the work?
Date of birth	Are you over 18? Are you over 21? (for serving alcoholic beverages)
Have you ever been treated for AIDS?	
	Military service; dates, branches of service, job-related education and experience.
Do you observe religious holidays?	Can you observe regularly the required days and hours of work?
Have you ever been arrested?	Have you ever been convicted of a crime? (If crime is job-related, hiring may be refused.)
Do you own a car?	Do you have reliable means of getting to work?

The property's human resources department usually conducts the **prescreening interview.** The purpose of this initial interview is to screen out those applicants who do not meet the criteria for the job advertised as specified in the company's job description. For example, a person who is incapable of lifting 50 pounds will be automatically disqualified for the job of bellperson, who have to handle luggage. Figures 6.3 and 6.4 are sample job descriptions for uniformed service personnel and concierges.

Predictors for the capacity of the applicant to fulfill the job include test scores, educational credentials, prior work experience, reference letters and interviews. The employee in charge of pre-employment screening must be well trained in interviewing techniques, as many people applying for jobs exaggerate their skills and abilities, misrepresent their backgrounds, and conceal or minimize their weakest qualities. Applicants who are not selected should be notified as soon as possible of the company's decision and their applications kept on file for future reference, mainly for a different job in the company for which they may be qualified.

The personnel department should immediately check the references of those candidates selected for the interview. Checking references may reveal issues such as extreme absenteeism, irresponsibility, and not giving adequate notice, or may detect a person who always wants to work in a new property and quit as soon as a new establishment opens. References may be checked in writing, although in most cases previous employers will be reluctant to put on paper their honest opinion about the worker. In practice, written reference checking is usually limited to a verification-of-employment statement. Telephone conversations can often reveal much more about the applicant, particularly if the person contacted is an industry colleague. Although in most cases it is impractical, the best way to obtain accurate information about applicants is to have a personal meeting with their former boss.

Applicants who are working at the time of the interview may request that their current employer not be contacted for a reference check. This request should be honored to avoid putting workers in an antagonistic position with their current boss.

Job title: Uniformed Service Personnel

Job responsibility: To perform guest services, in conjunction with the desk staff, related to luggage, transportation, messaging, escorting and miscellaneous assistance.

Responsible to: Bell Captain

DUTIES AND RESPONSIBILITIES:

1. Wear and keep clean the standard uniform and name tag.
2. Handle arriving and departing baggage and other guests' property.

3. Drive guests to and from the airport (mainly for airport-located properties) or other locations as requested.
4. Help door attendant keep the porte-cochere or entrance free from not-authorized vehicles to facilitate the loading and unloading of guests.
5. Maintain a secure checkroom for guests' possessions.
6. Escort guests to rooms when requested, checking that everything is in working order.
7. Explain to guests the functioning of all in-room features and equipment.
8. Transfer guests' luggage when room change is required.
9. Ensure that security is maintained in the lobby and approaches to the property's entrance.
10. Work in conjunction with the front desk and concierge in carrying out guest requests.
11. Deliver messages from the front desk, switchboard, and management to guests or staff.
12. Know the layout of the property and the times of opening and closing of the different outlets and services.
13. Provide information on the town where the property is located and the road pattern to and from local and regional destinations.
14. Park and deliver guests' vehicles if required.

Management reserves the right to modify this job description and to assign other tasks to front office employees as circumstances require.

Required Job Qualifications: Able to drive. Outgoing personality and ability to interact with guests in a courteous way. Capable of lifting heavy waits.

Preferred qualifications: Education: High school diploma or higher.

Experience: Over six months previous work experience preferred.

Personality: Pleasant, able to interact with guests and fellow workers.

Appearance: Well groomed.

Figure 6.3 Sample Bell Attendant (bellman – bellhop) Job Description

Job title: Concierge

Job responsibility: To provide accurate information to guests on in-house facilities, activities and services, off-premises attractions, and directions to local and regional destinations.

Responsible to: Front Office Manager

DUTIES AND RESPONSIBILITIES:

1. Have a thorough knowledge of the property's facilities and services and of the local and regional areas.
2. Keep a list of all events on the property, including current and future functions, and meetings.
3. Know of current local shows, athletic games, tours, special attractions, activities, airline schedules and ground transportation.
4. Provide guests with directions to in-house or outside locations and with onward travel arrangements.
5. Act as liaison between guests and secretarial services or business office.
6. Make reservations and acquire tickets for guests.
7. Keep active the function displays in the lobby in coordination with the sales department.
8. Report positive and negative guest comments to management.

Management reserves the right to modify this job description and to assign other tasks to front office employees as circumstances require.

Required Job Qualifications: Knowledge of a foreign language (at some locations). Outgoing personality and capable of interacting with guests in a courteous way. Attentive to detail.

Preferred qualifications: Education: High school diploma or higher.

Experience: Over six months previous work experience preferred.

Personality: Pleasant, organized, able to interact with guests and fellow workers.

Appearance: well groomed.

FIGURE 6.4 SAMPLE CONCIERGE JOB DESCRIPTION

THE INTERVIEW

Those employees who have cleared the reference check are invited to a personal interview. The goal of an interview is to find the best match between the person and the position to be filled. The interview also allows the candidate and the department head to meet face to face to explore the possibility of a mutual agreement for employment. In the front office department, interviews should be conducted by the front office manager or by the bell captain or head porter for uniformed-service applicants.

Interviewers should evaluate the applicant's technical skills, general temperament, and emotional traits. By asking technical questions related to the job opening, the interviewer should attempt to find out if the applicant is (or will be after training) qualified to perform the job in question. By asking personal questions, the interviewer should try to ascertain the candidate's attitude toward the job and the first impression that the applicant will give in meeting customers and fellow workers. Some of the technical characteristics may be ascertained from factors such as previous work experience and training, knowledge of the job, stamina, and alertness. Some of the personal traits to be sought after are stability, reliability, initiative, and good personal appearance. In essence, the interview is a two-way communication effort in which the interviewer states the nature of the job opening and the applicant presents his or her own qualifications to fill the job. Interviews should be conducted in a private, quiet place where the candidate can be made to feel at ease.

Here are some points to be considered in employment interviewing:

- A checklist can be helpful to avoid overlooking important information. Questions should be prepared from the job description of the position to be filled.
- The interviewer should allow at least half of the interview time to listen to the applicant's statements about himself or herself. To this effect, questions eliciting only "yes" or "no" answers should be avoided. Create open ended questions by making frequent use of "why?" and "how?"
- Most front office tasks are complex and require much of the worker's commitment and dedication. Interviewers should not sugarcoat the job to convince the applicant to accept the position, only to find later that the worker finds it unbearable.
- Interviewers may be swayed in their decision to hire by the neat appearance and smooth talk of candidates (the **halo effect**), only to discover that they are not capable of performing front office work.
- Avoid hiring someone who is overqualified. These candidates often become bored with tasks below their ability level, and eventually quit.

The result of the interview should be communicated to the candidate as soon as possible. If the decision is positive, applicants should know immediately so they can give appropriate notice to their current employers and get ready to start work in the new job. If the decision is negative, applicants should be notified so that they can restart their search for a job in other establishments. In this case, the candidate should also be thanked for the time taken in interviewing with the company.

Some lodging companies regularly use tests given to prospective employees as instruments of selection, particularly to those seeking supervisory and managerial positions. However, because tests are only an indirect method of measurement, they are not as valid as the direct measurement of people's abilities. Tests should never be given in lieu of interviews or direct performance observations. Psychological testing, nevertheless, can be a helpful tool to avoid hiring unqualified candidates. **Intelligence tests** used in the industry measure vocabulary and arithmetic skills; some are designed for supervisory and managerial positions and a few for workers at an entry level. Some **aptitude tests** applicable to the front office measure the applicant's ability to understand how a computer program works; these are suitable for workers involved in entering data or making reservations at a fast pace; others test clerical aptitude and are recommended for bookkeeping, cashier, and clerical jobs. **Interest tests** provide some measure of an applicant's relative interest for certain fields of work. The lodging industry could use interest tests to examine the candidate's interest in people, as this is a people industry.

When using a test as a method of selecting employees, keep in mind that tests have been found to be inherently discriminatory to anyone who has not had the full advantage of free exposure to American culture. For instance, the scores achieved by a candidate belonging to a minority group should not be compared with people in general but only to the scores of other members of the same minority group. In all cases, questions asked during the interview must be appropriate and related to the open position. Some information must be obtained after an applicant is hired and not during the initial interview such as proof of age.

HIRING

Hiring involves taking all the necessary steps to prepare the new employee for a successful working relationship with the company. The hiring period lasts through the initial adjustment to the job and ends when the new-hire begins working on his/her own.

Induction: After being accepted for employment, workers are usually asked to report to the human resources department for their induction into the company. The purpose of the induction process is to fill the necessary paperwork about the new employee, to answer questions, and to make the newcomer feel welcome. All documentation regarding the new worker should be completed. This procedure includes filling out the W-4 (tax withholding statement), I-9 (proof of residence), and health and welfare insurance forms. At this time newcomers are provided with the **employee handbook**. Properties that hire large numbers of employees should use **employment checklist forms** (Figure 6.5) to ensure that no part of the induction process has been overlooked. The employment checklist includes all prerequisites that need to be completed before employees are sent to their respective departments to begin work.

Name: ________________________ Social Security Number: ____________

Address: ____

City: ____________________________ State: ______________ Zip: ________

Item **Complete**

Application . . . .

Resume . . . .

Proof of residency (I-9) . . . .

Health and welfare documents . . . .

W-4 form. . . . .

Deductions from pay (if any) . . . .

Hotel employee handbook issued . . . .

Company orientation . . . .

Payroll number assigned. . . . .

Name tag issued. . . . .

Employee has been turned over to _____________________ in the _________________ department for training and department orientation.

Figure 6.5 Sample Employment Checklist

The induction process continues with the **orientation** of the new employee. During orientation, the philosophy of the company is explained, the benefits, pay rate, and deductions are discussed, and the dos and don'ts that the job entails, or general house policies as stated in the employee handbook, are described in detail. The initial orientation session should be followed with a second meeting after the new employee has had a chance to become familiar with the job—anywhere between two and four weeks later. At this time, any questions that the worker may have are answered. Specifically, the orientation phase includes information about the company in general and the property in particular; the benefits (wages, insurance, vacations, paid holidays and perks); what the job entails (schedules, breaks, meal times, overtime, performance standards, security, safety); and the rules to be observed (smoking, entrance and exit to the property, disciplinary actions, and parking).

After the orientation process has been completed at the personnel department, the new employee is escorted to the front office where a departmental orientation takes place. Here, the hours of work and the necessity for calling in as soon as possible in case of illness or emergency are explained, as well as where to check in and out, uniform procedures, grooming standards, and when breaks and meal periods are scheduled. The employee is then given a tour of the property and is introduced to his or her supervisor who, in turn, introduces the worker to other members of the department. Induction and orientation procedures, if properly conducted, increase substantially the odds of the employee's remaining in the company.

Most new employees in the front office department are hired on a **probationary basis**, usually 90 days, to allow workers enough time to learn and perform their jobs well. After a successful probationary period, usually when employees reach no fault or no errors standards, they become regular workers and are given a raise as an incentive to continue to perform well and stay with the company. If, after the probationary period, reasonable standards of efficiency have not been met, employees should not be allowed to continue employment in that particular position.

INDUCTION AND THE PEER GROUP

The peer group is an important part of the new employee's orientation. New employees depend on their coworkers for approval and acceptance. For the newcomer, the pressure to conform is very strong. It is a good idea to involve the most representative members of the peer group in the orientation process. This practice will help the old employees and the new person get to know each other as soon as possible. In fact, the induction process should not be considered as completed until the full acceptance of the new employee by the peer group has been accomplished. To end the hiring process, the personnel department should open an individual record file for each employee in which personal information (such as address, telephone number or whom to call in case of emergency) and work data (such as starting wage and title of position) are recorded. The file is thereafter updated each time a change in status occurs, such as for changes in pay rate, disciplinary actions taken, written warnings, promotions, and special recognition.

TRAINING

The hospitality industry is notorious for attracting under-skilled workers, especially young workers coming right from high schools with a relatively low educational background. In addition, members of the hospitality work force tend to change jobs frequently, causing high turnover. On the other hand, most hospitality jobs are under the constant scrutiny of the public, hinging on face-to-face relationships where the incompetence of one employee may lose a guest forever. Because of this, a lodging property cannot afford to have an untrained or disinterested worker on the front office payroll. As a matter of fact, training should be a process of investing in employees to improve employment stabilization because if employee departure is decreased, employer profit increases.

An effective skills training program begins with the development of **job lists** and job **breakdowns.** A job list specifies the tasks that employees must perform in each position; for example, Figure 6.2 (Job description) above identifies 25 responsibilities of front desk clerks. A list can be compiled from these duties specifying the sequenced tasks to be performed in this position. Here is a possible job list of a front desk clerk's morning shift from beginning to end.

1. Punch in wearing uniform.
2. Peruse the incidence log book.
3. Count your cash bank.
4. Ascertain current room availability.
5. Check guests in and out.
6. Take reservations.

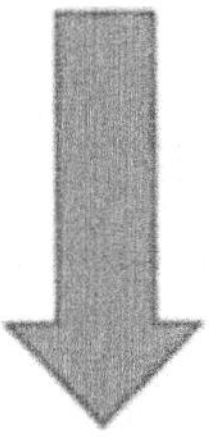

22. Count your cash bank.
23. Balance daily work.
24. Run shift reports.
25. Punch out.

A job breakdown usually specifies in detail how each task on the job should be performed. For instance, the task of checking in guests (number 5 above) can be broken into these steps:

1. Greet guest.
2. Verify the name of the reservation.
3. Punch in guest information in the computer.
4. Secure guest's credit information.
5. Assign room.

6. Ask guest if he/she needs assistance with luggage.
7. Wish guest a pleasant stay.

Training in the front office department should encompass four major areas: **technical skills, employee attitude, personal development,** and **knowledge of the property and the surrounding area.** Technical skills training include teaching workers how to perform the tasks described in their job description without error. In the case of a front office clerk, for example, it means teaching the person how to check guests in and out, take reservations over the phone, answer guests' questions, balance the cash after each shift, have security awareness, and so on. The employee will have reached regular performance standards when a minimum number of errors are found when the clerk takes over his/her shift. Technical training contributes to the success of both the organization and the individual.

Social skills are critical to providing service to guests and must be an essential qualification for front office work. Attitude training should create awareness of the relationships between the employee and guests, other employees, and the company. Workers must be trained to be courteous, friendly, and approachable, and to show keen attention to detail. Sensitivity toward fellow workers must also be taught, including toward people of other cultures, races, and religions which will help develop teamwork within a diversified group, almost always the case in lodging properties. Employees should have a positive attitude toward the company and its management by representing the property well and mirroring the philosophy of the establishment. As for social interaction, social skills can be developed primarily through practicing face-to-face conversations or by using role playing exercises. Some scenarios to be performed between a front desk employee and a trainer (or in the classroom) might follow these models:

SCENARIO 1

You are alone at the desk on a Saturday evening and a person approaches confidently saying,

"Hi, my name is Jenny Sampson and I have a reservation for tonight."

You greet Ms. Sampson warmly, check the list of arrivals and find no such name. The hotel has five twin rooms and three junior suites open for two nights but it will be at 100 percent occupancy on Monday. You ask Ms. Sampson:

"Do you happen to have a copy of your reservation, Ms. Sampson?"

And you hear,

"No, I'm sorry. I didn't bring it with me."

In order to accommodate this customer, you need to know what type of room she might have booked and the length of her stay. After asking her, she replies,

"My reservation is for a junior suite for three nights. Don't you have a record of it?"

Continue role playing the situation from here on.

SCENARIO 2

You are one of three front desk clerks checking out guests on a busy Monday morning. The next person on the line says,

"Hi. My name is Oliver, room 505. Can I have my bill, please?"

You answer: *"Certainly, Mr. Oliver."*

On looking at his folio, Mr. Oliver assures you that he has not made a telephone call appearing on the bill for $10.75.

At this point, you go into the back office to find the antecedents of the charge. The search shows a long distance telephone call made Saturday by the concierge to reserve tickets for Mr. Oliver for a 'Phantom of the Opera' production in a city nearby. The resort follows the policy of charging for any long distance phone call made on behalf of guests. Mr. Oliver refuses to accept the charge arguing,

"Well, I will not pay for a telephone call besides the surplus I had to shell out for the tickets. That would not be fair."

Continue role playing the situation from here knowing that the same case has happened in the past and that management insisted on collecting any long distance phone calls made on behalf of guests.

SCENARIO 3

It is Saturday and you are the morning-shift supervisor at a 5-star resort in Scottsdale, Arizona. There is a Cardinals' game in Phoenix and the property is ten rooms overbooked for that night. The front office manager has warned you that in no case are you to take any reservations and to make sure that all scheduled departures check out by 1 PM. At 11:00 AM you receive the following call from room 712:

"Hi, I am Morris, room 712. We are scheduled to leave this morning, but I'm afraid our flight has been delayed until tomorrow. We just got a call from the airline and they cannot put us on another plane until 7 AM Sunday. That is tomorrow. We would like to keep our room one more night."

You know that Mr. Morris is a regular guest at your resort but, after checking once again the latest room count, you find that there is no possible way of accommodating him this time. Several other guests wanting an extension of their stay have already been asked to leave.

"Sorry, Mr. Morris. There is no way possible that we can extend your stay. I wish we could help you this time but we are unable to do so."

Mr. Morris changes his tone of voice:

"Look here, young man, we have been customers of this resort for years. Talk to your manager or something. We need to stay another night."

Continue role playing the situation.

Training should also be provided to workers to improve their ability to make changes in their own lives. This type of training can range from personal grooming sessions to seminars and workshops that will aid in raising their perceptions of themselves as competent individuals. Finally, knowledge training should teach employees the layout of the property and the configuration of the surrounding area so that they can give directions to guests and inform them about hours of operation and main features of the different outlets, and driving directions and mileage to other cities in the region. For example, a bellperson, if asked, should be able to tell a guest how to get to the swimming pool, what type of menu the coffee shop offers, and how to get on I-25.

Lodging properties should have ongoing training programs in place. People in general tend to forget concepts or deviate from standing procedures as time goes by. Clear indications of the need to retrain personnel include an increase of oral and written complaints by guests. For instance, if management keeps getting negative comments about the time they spend checking out, employees at the front desk should be retrained in this procedure or the equipment evaluated to speed up operations. Another indication of a need for retraining may be a drop in productivity. For example, if in the past, bellpersons have been able to speedily deliver luggage to travelers arriving in buses but lately complaints have been received about the time it takes to bring the bags to the guestrooms, the method should be examined to ascertain whether standing luggage-handling procedures are adequately followed. These performance analyses should investigate the question "could the task be performed quicker, with the same level of quality?" If the answer is yes, the worker should be retrained to improve his or her performance. There is, however, a difference between **deficiency of knowledge**, in which the employee doesn't know how to do the job better and should be retrained, and **deficiency of execution**, in which the employee knows how to do the task correctly but decides not to for his or her own benefit. In this case, the employee should be reprimanded and asked to do the job according to established procedures.

The most efficient method of training in the front office department is **on-the-job training**, in which new employees are assigned to watch how the work should be performed, usually observing a supervisor or senior employee. Large lodging operations have designated trainers whose job is to train newcomers or retrain employees who are not performing up to standard. When employees need to be trained to operate new front office systems, vendors or representatives of the manufacturing company often conduct **demonstrations** at no cost to the employer; in this case the purchaser of the products. Training of supervisors and middle managers can be enhanced by sending them to conferences and workshops where new industry products are introduced and demonstrated. When employees already in the company are being prepared for advancement, companies should train them in the different operational aspects of the department by following a career ladder or schedule. Thus, committed employees who master each step of the cycle along the way may be promoted to management positions within the property or in other company establishments.

Training programs offer distinct advantages to employers and employees alike. The employer will benefit from having a more competent staff, and workers will become efficient sooner rather than having to learn on their own by trial and error. Workers achieve high levels of productivity when their training begins with learning only the best way to accomplish jobs. As training improves performance, employee self-esteem rises, and with it, the willingness to come to work and to increase earning power. Turnover and absenteeism are thus reduced.

The simplest and most efficient way to ascertain the effectiveness of training and retraining programs is by obtaining feedback from on-line questionnaires and guest comment cards. If many negative comments are received, training programs must be improved. Guest comments should be read at employee meetings. Negative comments should be discussed, without naming the employee who caused the problem, and the entire group should be challenged to find an appropriate solution, although the employee who received the adverse comments should be addressed privately.

There are nationwide companies, that offer training services to individual lodging properties and chains, which specialize in webinars, workshops, seminars, or customized on-line or on-site training aimed at achieving guest service excellence and front desk profit optimization. These companies can also be contracted for telephone mystery shopping services to identify operational deficiencies so that they can be corrected by re-training reservationists and other front office employees.

WORKER MOTIVATION

A basic goal of human resource policies should be to design procedures that motivate employees, inducing them to identify the firm's interests with their own. In other words, the objective is to make the goal of the employee coincide with those of the company. Adopting this approach, the company can cut back on costly supervision, presuming that competent employee performance will take place.

In most cases, employees are vital to the success of the lodging industry. A business that requires face-to-face interaction with people requires a work force that is motivated to deliver excellent service. But the work force usually available to the lodging industry has inherent fundamental problems, such as high turnover, a disinterested attitude, and low productivity. The problem is compounded by the fact that most lodging companies have limited financial resources to increase their employees' compensation beyond inflation rates. On the other hand, employees look to improve their own quality of life by achieving a satisfactory standard of living through job security and adequate compensation. However, adequate compensation, although necessary, is not enough to motivate the work force. People also look for a challenge, recognition, and the opportunity to be part of an organization that is successful. Therefore, to motivate employees the manager must understand what type of environment best utilizes workers' energy and directs them toward reaching a common goal. The first step is to establish a climate of mutual trust and respect, meaning that employees should never be looked down on from a position of superiority; instead, managers should be fair, caring, and approachable individuals. Good motivators must be capable of understanding people well and be sensitive to their individual needs and differences. Motivation is internal, complex, and individually patterned; what motivates one person might annoy someone else, and vice versa. Future front office managers should be aware of theories of motivation and understand how they can be applied to front office settings.

MASLOW'S THEORY OF MOTIVATION

Although first expressed in the 1950s, Abraham Maslow's thoughts on motivation are still relevant to employee motivation in lodging operations. It can be deduced from Maslow's work that employees will not be highly motivated if their basic needs have not been met. A worker's **physiological needs** must be satisfied first; that is, if front office employees are working in very poor conditions, such as in a steaming-hot, unventilated reservations area, all attempts to motivate them will fail. Likewise, if the workers' **security needs** for survival are not granted, motivation will be impossible. This would occur if a front office employee is allowed to work only 28 hours per week and therefore is unable to make enough money to pay for his or her rent. The fulfillment of **social needs** is also necessary to motivate people. A Hispanic employee, for instance, would be unhappy working in the front office in the midst of an Anglo workforce that refuses to accept him or her as part of the group. Conversely, an Anglo worker among non-accepting Hispanic workers will also be hard to motivate. **Self-esteem**, the fourth of Maslow's basic needs, is applicable to hourly employees who must also be satisfied before they can be motivated. For example, an outside porter in the front office department opening and closing car doors all day long, whose job is not appreciated by management and coworkers, is not likely to be motivated.

Front office managers must always realize that individuals have a scale of needs and that encouraging them to be courteous, polite, friendly, or productive does not work unless basic needs have been adequately satisfied. Motivation at the departmental level will be easier to achieve if all job descriptions and specifications consider both the needs of the organization and of the workers.

HERZBERG'S IDEAS ON MOTIVATION

Once employees' basic needs have been covered, front office managers must provide their employees with opportunities that are intrinsically satisfying or that embody responsibility. Frederick Herzberg proposes that workers can be motivated by recognition, feelings of achievement, job responsibility, and opportunities for advancement and growth. In other words, if employees feel wanted and are happy in their jobs, they will willingly contribute to the goals of the organization. A **career ladder program** to promote people from within can be implemented in the department to establish the possibility of advancement from lower entry-level jobs to supervisory and management positions.

There is a marked difference between motivation and manipulation of employees. Managers who attempt to influence workers to do what they want done seldom succeed. Niccolo Machiavelli, the cynical sixteenth-century writer, observed that because humans are selfish, greedy, ungrateful, and manipulative, they deserve not to be trusted and must be manipulated in turn, a theory hardly conducive to employee motivation. On the contrary, managers who know how to create a climate in which the individual can function to maximum capacity will be successful in motivating employees.

DAVID MCCLELLAND

McClelland, an American theorist in psychology, experimented with volunteers who were asked to throw rings over pegs without stipulating particular distance. Most people seemed to throw from arbitrary, random distances sometimes throwing close to pegs, sometimes farther away. However, a small group of volunteers, who McClelland identified as strongly achievement-motivated, took some care to measure and test distances to produce an ideal challenge—not too easy, and not too hard. McClelland deduced from this experiment that people need a balanced challenge to achieve motivation. This premise can be applied to front office employees: a worker who is given a very difficult task will be demotivated by his/her inability to complete it; on the other hand, an employee who finds his/her job too easy may be bored by it.

PRACTICAL MOTIVATIONAL TECHNIQUES

Besides understanding the theoretical approaches to motivation, front office managers can put in place practical programs and plans to motivate front office employees. Removing obstacles that often hinder performance may help workers to perform their tasks. Too much paper work, for instance, may be an obstacle to productivity; another could be a badly designed work area that does not take into consideration the human element. Lack of communication may create a feeling of uncertainty about what needs to be done, and people tend to perform well only when they understand what is expected of them. The simple act of listening often allows managers to hear useful comments from employees regarding work conditions, suggestions to improve work flow, and the existence of morale problems.

EMPLOYEE EVALUATION AND COMPENSATION

EVALUATION

One of the difficulties of defining the employer-employee relationship is the lack of performance homogeneity; that is, workers' productivities, skills, and attitudes vary from person to person. Some employees may be self-motivated problem solvers while others may elude responsibility in the workplace if not properly supervised. Given this, some mechanism in the workplace must be established to evaluate employee performance. The rationale behind employee appraisals is that if good reviews lead to rewards, employees will strive to receive favorable ratings. Similarly, they will attempt to avoid unfavorable reviews if these lead to penalties. Typically, performance appraisals increase employee productivity, since that is one of the behavioral responses that is rewarded.

The purpose of employee appraisals is twofold: to provide feedback to workers about how they are performing their jobs and to establish a basis for compensation on the quality level of their performance. The advantages of providing feedback to workers are substantial, as employees who do well need to be recognized for their efforts while those whose work needs improvement must be notified about their specific deficiencies in order for them to be corrected. Using ratings to determine wage payment and promotions helps motivate employees to work hard so they can reap the benefits awarded to those who do a good job. To be useful, evaluation methods must be fair, objective, based on pre-established standards of performance, and accepted by those being evaluated.

Because evaluations can be interpreted as subjective, employees may not always agree with the opinions of the evaluators. To overcome anxiety or hostility, workers should be involved in setting up the standards of performance against which they are to be appraised, provided that their goals are in line with those of the company. **Rating scales** are helpful tools for appraisal; they consist of a series of descriptors to which a numerical score is attached to determine the efficacy of workers in areas such as absenteeism, tardiness, grooming, following instructions and courtesy to guests. Figure 6.6 is a rating form with a scale of five points, where 1 indicates "superior" performance and 5 indicates "needs improvement." Most companies ask workers to fill out a rating form after a designated period of time, ranging from six months to a year, while the worker's supervisor or manager also fills out a form on the employee being evaluated. At a scheduled meeting, the perceptions of both the worker being appraised and the supervisor are compared and discussed. From that discussion, goals for the next evaluation period are agreed upon. The goals are again evaluated against actual performance after the next appraisal period has elapsed and new goals are set. Where performance is difficult to quantify, as in rating assistant managers or supervisors, the **critical incident method** may be used instead of the rating scale. In this case, the rater may periodically record observations of good or bad performance that are discussed at the time of the rating.

Any appraisal method used in the front office department should be a way of recognizing excellent performance and of identifying areas in which further training is needed, and should be done so that the person being evaluated sees the process as a means of self-improvement. That is, there should be a mutual discussion between superior and subordinate with regard to what conditions must be altered to change operational procedures or upgrade performance. These changes or efforts to upgrade become the objectives to be accomplished for the next evaluation period.

Employee being evaluated_______________________________________

Evaluator ____

Period of Evaluation: From__________________To:______________________

Date of Evaluation _________________________

Description	Rating Superior			Needs Improvement	
Absenteeism	1	2	3	4	5
Tardiness	1	2	3	4	5
Personal appearance	1	2	3	4	5
Following instructions	1	2	3	4	5
Courtesy to guests	1	2	3	4	5
Getting along with peers	1	2	3	4	5
Productivity level	1	2	3	4	5
Accepting responsibility	1	2	3	4	5

Goals/Objectives for next evaluation period

1. ____
2. ____
3. ____
4. ____
5. ____

Employee's signature ___________ Evaluator's signature___________

FIGURE 6.6 SAMPLE EMPLOYEE EVALUATION FORM

The first formal appraisal of employees should be conducted at the end of their probationary period. Afterward, evaluation should be done periodically, typically every six months to a year. It is common for lodging companies to have **pay scales** that start with a probationary rate and go up in accordance with time on the job. For example, an employee can be started at minimum wage for the first 90 days (probationary period) and then be raised a fair amount per year worked to a pre-established maximum hourly rate. Employees who exhibit extraordinary performance are awarded additional increases, regardless of time, based on their positive performance appraisals.

Because performance evaluations are emotionally charged events, reviews should be held in a private, neutral environment, such as in a small conference room. Evaluators should go into the review fully prepared and with an attitude that supports discussion, cooperation, and negotiation. It is better to sit beside the employee rather than across the table from her/him to minimize the boss/worker barrier. The meeting should be long enough to clearly delineate the workers' strengths and weaknesses, and show them how and to what degree they must improve their performance.

COMPENSATION

Compensation (pay increases) should be tied to performance. If an employee's productivity is high and the quality excellent, his or her compensation should be greater than that of an employee whose performance is well below standards. When compensation is tied to performance and the evaluation system is fair and unbiased, employees strive to do well at work in order to earn better wages and benefits. Most employees establish a relationship between the rewards they get from their job and the effort they put into it. The ideal **effort / compensation ratio** should be 1:1, meaning that the effort put into one's work should equal the reward received from it. If workers see that other employees in similar positions produce less but receive equal or higher wages than they do, they will soon be de-motivated. Managers should regard equity in compensation as a critical part of the motivational process.

CREATING WORKER SATISFACTION

One of the underlying purposes of motivating employees is to reduce turnover. Hovering at about 100 percent for line employees and often costing over $3,000 per hourly employee, turnover represents a substantial loss of income to lodging companies. Thus the challenge is to create worker satisfaction so that employees stay with the company for extended periods of time. Besides using motivational techniques and providing equitable compensation and fringe benefits, what else can the front office manager do to alleviate the problem of high turnover? Conducting **exit interviews** is the first step in attempting to solve high turnover; that is, finding out why employees leave in the first place. Exit interviews help management identify reasons for turnover, paving the way to corrective action. During the interview, departing employees should be asked to discuss the company's working conditions, pay rates, training, benefits and job security. If turnover is severe, current employees should be surveyed periodically regarding wages, benefits, and working conditions. Once the problem is identified, goals and objectives for a turnover-reduction plan should be set. Some of the most common reasons for high turnover are poor hiring techniques, inadequate orientation and training practices, no opportunity for advancement, poor supervision methods, bad department image, and lack of performance standards. Besides correcting these technical slips, front office managers should make employees feel like valuable members of the team, boosting their self-esteem by making sure that the department has a good reputation. The creation of a **career path program** within the department will make employees feel that there are opportunities for advancement. Encouraging employees to earn professional certification will help them develop the necessary expertise for advancement. The Educational Institute of the AH&LA offers certification in hospitality front office operations which grants recognition as front office professionals in the lodging industry. **Incentive programs** are intended to provide employees with such rewards as recognition and appreciation for the good work they perform. Commendation letters, gift certificates, bonuses, plaques, complimentary stays at the property, and designated parking spots in the garage are some of the incentives that may provide substantial employee satisfaction at no great cost.

Wellness programs, designed to prevent illness and enhance the well-being of employees, are helpful in reducing absenteeism. These programs include periodic medical examinations, sessions to improve dietary habits, weight control practices, exercise and fitness sessions, free or discounted meals, stress management workshops, and immunizations. **Employee assistance programs** can help retain employees who are substance abusers by helping workers overcome drug and alcohol addiction. Referring affected employees to counseling agencies and supporting them in their rehabilitation will help improve the company's retention of employees. **Transportation assistance** can also be a valuable incentive in keeping employees in the workplace. Because some front office employees may not own their own means of transportation, in cities where public transportation systems are reliable and can be used by employees to get to work, the company can provide financial assistance to purchase passes. In localities with poor or no public transportation, employers can provide vans for pickup and delivery of workers to a central location or organize a ride-sharing or carpooling program. With subsidies from state and federal government programs, lodging properties can offer **child** and **prenatal-care assistance** for workers, especially to young single parents. The practice of **participative management,** in which employees see themselves as part of the decision-making process, also increases employee satisfaction. As they contribute to operative decisions, workers become committed to the outcome of these decisions and get involved in the successful completion of common tasks.

When everything else has failed, the company may resort to creating **retention bonuses** by offering a percentage of a year's pay, spread over a period of several years, to those employees who stay with the company. In sum, any efforts aimed at maintaining high levels of morale, individual attention, and respect for hourly employees will increase service standards and guest satisfaction and reduce employee turnover.

EMPLOYEE DISCIPLINE

The implementation of a standard method of discipline is just as important as motivation for employers and employees alike. Corrective action for unacceptable or irresponsible behavior must be taken as soon as it occurs. Common misconduct cases that take place in the front office department are quarreling, insubordination, intoxication, excessive unexcused tardiness or absences, theft, and unauthorized or unlawful acts. Depending on the severity of the wrongdoing, discipline can range from a simple verbal warning to termination. The most effective method of disciplining employees is the **counseling session**. Counseling sessions should be conducted one-on-one to ensure confidentiality. In these sessions, the problem should be addressed in a straight-forward manner with the understanding that the only purpose of the meeting is to find a fast, permanent, and equitable solution to the matter in question. Listening to the employee (the other side of the story) is crucial as the worker, not the supervisor, often is in the right. It is important that at the end of the session a mutual agreement is reached and that there is a commitment on the part of the employee, if he/she is at fault, to correct the situation. Needless to say, if an employee persists in his or her wrong behavior, the company always reserves the right to apply punitive measures, as building positive discipline requires appropriate disciplinary action. If a violation occurs, disciplinary action follows this sequence: oral warning(s), written warning(s), suspension, and dismissal.

CULTURAL DIVERSITY AND THE FRONT OFFICE DEPARTMENT

The percentage of minority hourly employees working in the hospitality industry is very high; in some states, Spanish-speaking people employed in lodging establishments are the majority. In some cases, this diversity in the workplace can represent challenging management situations with communication, training, and operational performance. In the Southwest, for instance, the entire housekeeping department may be staffed with non-English speaking Hispanic workers. Cultural differences may also be serious obstacles to traditional management practices. While the North American culture has been built around a strong work ethic, with emphasis on efficiency and aiming at constantly improving mechanical and technological frontiers, minorities are often preoccupied with concepts like individualism, family, and leisure. However, language barriers and marked cultural differences do not imply incompetence. A job and its paycheck are very important to most minority employees. Whole families may depend on it so they are usually willing to work very hard to earn a living wage.

The vehicle that best promotes understanding is, without doubt, language. Managers and supervisors will be able to bridge the gap between cultures if they are able to communicate directly with the people they oversee day after day. An elementary knowledge of the language that can be used in daily operations is therefore invaluable, particularly in establishments in urban areas with large concentrations of minorities. Students in hospitality management programs should elect to study a modern language, particularly Spanish, prior to joining the industry after graduation.

On the other hand, dealing with multicultural issues can be a rewarding experience. Using effective communication skills and patience, managers and supervisors can successfully reach and train a diverse work force. Listening attentively and speaking slowly and clearly in elementary English are a must. The best method of training minorities with no command of the English language is to follow a "hands on," "learn-by-doing" approach.

Cultural awareness is another important aspect of managing a diverse work force. Some groups arrive in the United States with such respect for authority that they will never discuss or dispute a request that comes from the boss. Others will never volunteer an opinion if they are not specifically asked to do so. Some are shy and may wait until they are away from the group to ask an important question. Some lodging companies have **English for Vocational Purposes (EVP)** classes conducted at their facilities to teach foreign employees how to communicate with supervisors and peers on the job. This is a great benefit to them, helping insure their loyalty towards the property besides making them more competent in their work environment.

RACIAL DISCRIMINATION AND SEXUAL HARASSMENT

It is illegal to discriminate against any authorized-to-work individual in hiring or discharging practices. Racial problems in the workplace can lead to lack of productivity and costly lawsuits. Productivity can decline if some employees harbor resentments. They may decide to leave in search of businesses without racial tension. Lodging companies should have procedures in place to reduce friction between employees of different races and know how to respond when a racial incident occurs.

The property must have a written policy that prohibits discrimination based on race, national origin, sex, and physical impairment. It should also forbid discrimination in hiring, promoting, and terminating employees. Racial remarks or jokes should not be tolerated. The written policy must be communicated to all supervisors and employees, who should also be educated about the company's expectations regarding interracial behavior. When a racial incident does occur, action must be taken immediately to make sure that it does not escalate to a legal confrontation. A typical example of racial discrimination is that of minority employees being repeatedly passed over for pay raises or promotions on the basis of evaluation by majority superiors.

Sexual harassment is a subtle, hard-to-define form of discrimination. The vast majority of sexual harassment claims are filed by women against men. But there are exceptions as males may also be harassed by members of the opposite sex. However, it is not unusual to find that as much as 40 percent of women in the work force have suffered some sort of harassment in the workplace in the form of uninvited pressure for sexual favors, of which cornering, touching, leaning over, or sending provocative notes are the most common. The U.S. Equal Employment Opportunity Commission declared in 1980 that sexual harassment violates title VII of the 1964 Civil Rights Act. In a June 1998 decision by the U.S. Supreme Court, the guilt of all demonstrated acts of sexual harassment in the workplace extends not only to the perpetrator but also to the employer for which he or she works. For this reason, it is important for companies to have anti-harassment training in place to sensitize employees about sexual harassment. This can be done with workshops and speakers specialized in the field. In addition, the company's employee handbook must have clear descriptions of what may constitute sexual harassment, specifically acts such as staring, flirting, making suggestive gestures or remarks, and touching.

IMMIGRATION AND EQUAL EMPLOYMENT OPPORTUNITY (EEO)

Front office managers should be aware of two major federal programs aimed at regulating the workplace. These are the immigration control policy and the **equal employment opportunity (EEO)** policy. At the time of this writing additional legislation on immigration is making its way through Congress. It is incumbent upon lodging business owners to keep abreast of the changes likely to result.

The United States has historically been a high wage country compared to most of the world, so that its labor market has been an enticement to immigration. The proximity of the high wage labor market provides an opportunity for a significant illegal flow of immigrants from Latin America. To curtail this influx, the federal government imposed in 1986 norms which must be complied with by business nationwide. The US citizenship and immigration services require that employers document that each new employee is authorized to work in the United States. This is verified by having workers fill out the employment eligibility verification **form I-9**. Employers must record in section 2 of the form the following information:

1. Document of evidence of identity and employment authorization.
2. Authority issuing the document.
3. Number of the document.
4. Expiration date of the document, if any.
5. The date employment begins.

Employers found to be employing illegals are subject to an escalating set of fines and potential criminal penalties.

The U.S. Equal Employment Opportunity Commission is responsible for enforcing federal laws that make it illegal to discriminate against a job applicant or an employee because of the person's race, color, religion, sex (including pregnancy), age (40 or older), disability, genetic information or national origin (for example, persons with an accent). In an out-of-court settlement in California an employee was awarded damages after being discharged because his accent did not fit the company image. The EEOC determined that 'successful management of diversity in the workplace requires respect and understanding that people with different national or regional backgrounds speak with different accents.' It is also illegal to discriminate against a person because the person complained about discrimination, filed a charge of discrimination, or participated in an employment discrimination investigation or lawsuit. It is pertinent to note that women and minorities are not well represented in the ranks of management which has led to charges that there is a "glass ceiling" preventing advancement at the top. Another difficult area of application of the equal employment opportunity law has been employer attitude towards individuals who are HIV-positive or have AIDS. Fellow employees and guests may perceive a health risk from persons with this disease, despite medical evidence to the contrary.

KEY TERMS

Application form
Aptitude test
Career ladder program
Child assistant program
Contingency workers
Counseling session
Critical incident method
Deficiency of execution
Deficiency of knowledge
Demonstration (training by)
Effort/Compensation ratio
Employee assistance program

Employee attitude
Employee handbook
Employee qualifications
Employee requisition form
Employee security needs
Employment checklist
English for vocational purposes (EVP)
Equal employment opportunity (EEOC)
Exit interview
External recruiting
Form I-9
Fulltime employee
Halo effect
Human capital
Incentive program
Intelligence test
Interest test
Internal recruiting
Job description
Knowledge of the property
Knowledge of the surrounding area
On-call employee
On-the-job training
Orientation
Outsourcing
Participative management
Part-time employment
Pay scale
Personal development
Physiological needs
Pre-natal care assistance
Pre-screening interview
Probationary basis
Rating scales
Retention bonus
Self-esteem needs
Social needs
Technical skills
Temporary help

Transportation assistance
Wellness program

DISCUSSION AND REVIEW QUESTIONS

1. What is the difference between a part-time and a temporary worker?
2. What is the purpose of an employee requisition form?
3. Why could a company that develops exclusively from within be limiting itself regarding the composition of its work force?
4. Explain why an interviewer should not ask the question, "Do you own a car?"
5. What is the purpose of the prescreening interview?
6. **(a)** Why should front office managers and supervisors ask prospective employees questions regarding their technical skills?
   (b) List three questions that a supervisor should ask people looking for front office work to find out if they are technically qualified to perform the job.
7. What is the main reason for front office departments to hire employees on a probationary basis?
8. What three areas must be addressed when training workers in the front office department?
9. What is the difference between deficiency of knowledge and deficiency of execution?
10. What are the advantages of implementing a career ladder program in the front office department?

PRACTICAL SITUATIONS

Situation 6.1

Sexual harassment or Discrimination?

Review the following occurrences and be prepared to discuss them in an open forum.

1. One of your supervisors, John, often comments on Michelle's appearance, telling her how good she looks in her clothes.
2. Pat assigns time-consuming, complex projects to the men on his staff and short-term, simple assignments to the women. He believes he is doing the women a favor.
3. Co-workers Joan and Ann earned comparable appraisals and equal raises until Ann was promoted. Joan believes she was more deserving of the promotion because of extra effort and workload she has taken on. One day, Ann confided to her that she was dating her boss who pressured her into a relationship, saying that "it would pay off." Joan filed a grievance with the company.

ASSIGNMENT:

Was there sexual harassment or discrimination in these cases?

Situation 6.2

Do workers try to exploit the system?

Jennifer usually has some excuse for not showing up for work. The excuses during the past three months included four dental appointments, four car breakdowns, and three occasions for which she was unable to find a babysitter. You, as Jennifer's supervisor, find it difficult to schedule your department as a whole because of Jennifer's spur-of-the-moment absences. Mrs. Robinson, another supervisor in your department, has told you in confidence that Jennifer is an unmarried employee who collects government financial aid for her two dependent children. Because the financial aid is conditional upon Jennifer's earnings, Mrs. Robinson thinks that she is trying to keep her work hours low enough to continue qualifying for government aid.

LOBBY THE BARCLAY, NEW YORK
COURTESY OF INTERCONTINENTAL HOTELS GROUP

ASSIGNMENT:

What would be your approach to solving this situation?

Situation 6.3

Rooms Division turnaround?

The front office department of the Pacific Hotel in downtown Santa Barbara has been going downhill since the property changed ownership two years ago. Productivity in the rooms division is low, morale is down, and the annual turnover of employees is very high. Communication between the front desk and the housekeeping department is poor because most of the section housekeepers are from Central America and don't speak English. It is common to receive complaints by guests being sent to rooms that are not ready and of travelers waiting in the hotel lobby for long periods of time until they are roomed.

You have been sent to the Pacific Hotel on loan from a sister property for one year to help improve the current situation.

Concierge Desk
Courtesy InterContinental Hotels Group

ASSIGNMENT:

Present a written proposal to the general manager suggesting actions that should be taken to correct the current problems.

CASE STUDY 6.1

Analysis of operations and front office reorganization

After graduating from a hotel and restaurant management program, you have been hired by a nationwide lodging company and sent to work the first year in a resort property in the Northwest. Having completed the period of training successfully, the company has promoted you to front office manager of a downtown hotel in Seattle. The property is a four-star, 550-room hotel offering meeting facilities, two restaurants, bars, and a health center. The hotel also has the following problems:

Absenteeism. Prior to your arrival, the front office department has consistently reported an average of 30 hours of overtime daily for front desk and uniformed staff. The previous front office manager contended that this is primarily due to transportation and the necessity of relying on the city's transit system that is very unreliable for that particular route. According to one of the bellpersons, "if only there was a bus route nearby, my life would be a lot easier. Most of us live 25 minutes from work."

Turnover. The turnover rate of front desk and uniformed personnel is 90 percent annually. Estimates of replacing a front desk clerk range from $3,500 to $4,500. The exit interviews conducted by the human resources department have pinpointed some common reasons for the high turnover rate. Some employees claim that they can make more money at other establishments in town, which also guarantee a minimum of 35 hours of work per week. In this hotel, sometimes they have to work 50 hours while other weeks they work fewer than thirty. Most of the workers leaving stated that the morale in the department is low.

Guest complaints. The general manager gets a continuous flow of guest complaints about long lines at check-in and check-out times and having to wait over 20 minutes before their luggage is brought up to the rooms. There is also discontent that the concierge desk is not being manned consistently throughout the day. Several travelers from Japan disliked the fact that neither the concierge, front desk, nor the uniformed employees were able to speak a word of their language.

Productivity. It seems that the long lines at the front desk happen in spite of the fact that there are three or four clerks behind the counter at all times. The department also employed an assistant front office manager, shift supervisors and reservationists whose only job is taking and confirming reservations online and by phone.

ASSIGNMENT:

From the information given, establish a plan of action, including specific ways of applying Maslow's and Herzberg's theories.

CASE STUDY 6.2

Corporate reorganization of front office operations

A group of 8 independent properties in the Southwest have combined their organizational efforts under the name of Genro Inc. The owners of the properties hired a CEO to manage the group as a sole entity. One year after the formation of the company, the merger has proved to be a disappointment. The CEO has not been able to bring the properties together. It appears that the 12 units remain operationally autonomous to a large extent, and are not able to cooperate with each other. Some of the units are not up to the service quality levels portrayed in the company's advertising. While some establishments are luxury properties offering very good accommodations and services, other units are midsize in need of more efficient service. As a result, the public image of the group as a whole is poor.

Employee relations at the front offices of the medium-size units seem to be the major problem. The salaries and wages paid in these properties are lower than in the others. Workers know that there are differences in the weekly take-home checks, and those who are being paid less are showing signs of discontent. Some employees quit because they can get better wages and salaries elsewhere. As a result, the employee turnover rate is very high and complaints from guests are increasing by the day. Besides the wage issue, exit interviews have shown that employees leaving the midsize properties gripe about the front desk and reservations technology being obsolete and that the training of new workers is appalling for lack of skilled supervisors.

The new CEO has decided to tackle the problem and bring the working conditions of the front office operations of all the properties to optimum standards. To this effect, she has hired Jane Cruise as rooms division coordinator for the 12 units. Jane has been asked to work out a reorganization plan and present it in a formal meeting with the general managers of the 12 establishments.

ASSIGNMENT:

Based on the content of this chapter, imagine that you are Jane Cruise and present a detailed plan to the class explaining how you think the current situation at Genro Inc. could be improved.

PART 3

ROOMS RATES AND RESERVATIONS

CHAPTER 7

ROOM RATES AND REVENUE MANAGEMENT

CHAPTER OBJECTIVES

- Understand the principles of cost-based pricing.
- Learn how to work out average room rates using the Hubbart formula.
- Explain how to ascertain rough estimates of room costs for new properties.
- Discuss how to determine standard rates for different room types.
- Understand the relationship between rate discounts and higher occupancy.
- Define the principles of market-based pricing.
- Explain the concept of revenue management in lodging properties.
- Discuss the role of the front office manager as revenue management coordinator.
- Describe computerized revenue management systems.

OVERVIEW

This chapter describes strategies to determine the room rates that lodging properties should charge for overnight accommodations. Basically, the property's operating costs and the expected return on investment decide how much the average price of rooms should be where rates can range from a minimum to break even to the maximum allowed by supply and demand. The approach to determine rates for the different room types and the discounts commonly used by lodging properties are discussed.

Yield management is described as the process of understanding, anticipating and influencing consumer demand in order to maximize profitability from room reservations. It is a component of revenue management that involves the control of room inventories so they can be sold to the right customer at the right time for the right price. Revenue management is introduced as a further step for directing the capacity and sources of income by the application of consumer behavior analytics. The chapter ends describing the role of the front office manager as revenue management coordinator and discusses commercial computerized programs available on the market.

RATE CALCULATION

Graduates from hotel and restaurant management programs will most likely find that the rates at the lodging establishments where they are about to start work have already been established but, before they join the industry, they should acquire a thorough knowledge of how these rates are structured in order to generate enough revenue to achieve an adequate rooms division income. The rate structure of lodging properties can be arrived at by using complex cost and market research techniques or simply by adopting prices similar to those set by existing competitors in the area.

There are several variables involved in the determination of rates such as location of the property, economic conditions, season, and direct competition. Generally, pricing is based on **market-based rates**—the average rate of guest rooms set after analysis of the variables listed above, but occasionally, recent graduates will be involved in determining room rates if they form part of a lodging operation's **opening team**—the employees selected by a company to open a new establishment. In this case, the starting rate should be a **cost-based rate** and take into consideration the expected **return on investment (ROI)** which is defined as the ratio obtained by dividing profit by the owners' investment. The purpose of this calculation is to make sure that the minimum rate adopted allows for the project to be financially sound. Once the property's rates are decided on, some of the questions that need to be answered are these: When is there a good opportunity to raise prices? Will the raise cause the loss of customers and, therefore, revenue? Will the loss of some customers because of higher rates be compensated with the gain of fewer ones willing to pay more?

COST-BASED PRICING

Cost-based pricing is designed to cover operational costs given a certain level of service plus the expected return on investment. In this case the costs have to be calculated, keeping in mind what guests will expect by way of service. For example, the rates of a four-star property must be necessarily higher than those of a three-star establishment because customers of the former will be expecting better facilities and services. A logical train of thought would be not to charge, say, $150 per standard room per night at a mid-market hotel if the property next door is a luxury resort charging the same amount for similar accommodations.

THE HUBBART FORMULA

A method, classic by now, of ascertaining cost-based rates was developed in the 1940's by Roy Hubbart. The formula, based on the calculation of costs plus a fair return on investment, has been customarily used to work out average room rates for new or renovated properties. The average room rate is obtained by dividing the total operating costs plus the ROI minus the income from other revenue-generating departments (such as restaurants and bars) by the projected number of rooms sold. The formula for the average room rate follows:

$$\frac{\textbf{Operating costs + ROI – income from other revenue-generating departments}}{\textbf{Projected number of room nights sold}}$$

Where operating costs are those related to running the property, ROI is the targeted return on the investment after covering fixed expenses (insurance and depreciation) and taxes; income from other departments is that generated by sources other than rooms.

A simplified practical example for a 575-room property follows:

If annually:

1.	Total operating costs of the property of the new Royal Hotel	$13,100,000
2.	Desired return of investment (ROI)	10,000,000
3.	Income from other departments	6,250,000
4.	Projected number of room nights at 65% occupancy	136,510

The average room rate required is **$123.43** (13,100,000 + 10,000,000 – 6,250,000 / 136,510) or **16,849,429 annually** (136,510 x 123.43).

THE 1/1,000 RULE OF THUMB

A simple method to ascertain a rough estimate of the room cost for new properties is:

$$\frac{\textbf{Cost of land + cost of building + furniture, fixtures and equipment (FF\&E)}}{\textbf{Number of rooms of the property}}$$

The rule is simply based on the premise that operators should charge $1 per night for $1,000 of room cost to recover the value of the investment; that is, if the cost to build one room is $150,000, the rate to be charged per night should be around $150 to cover costs. This method doesn't allow for the income from other revenue-generating departments, such as restaurants and bars, for inflation or for the revaluation of the real estate, and it doesn't take into account the desired ROI. A simplified practical example follows:

If

1.	Cost of the land where the Royal Hotel was built	$20,000,000
2.	Cost of building the Royal Hotel	40,000,000
3.	Cost of the hotel's FF&E	15,000,000
4.	Number of rooms of the Royal Hotel	575

The cost of each room would be **$130,435** (20,000,000 + 40,000,000 + 15,000,000 / 575). The average room rate should be close to **$130** just to cover the investment (130,435 / 1,000).

COST-BASED RATES AND ROOM TYPES

Lodging properties offering a sole type of rooms, most Embassy Suites for instance, don't have any problem with the average price that they should charge per room when applying the Hubbart formula. However, when establishments consist of several types of guestrooms, as is the norm, the average rate method cannot be applied to the different rooms that are sold every night. This is the case because the structure of each category (twin, double, queen, king, junior suite, etc.) affect the demand for each type of room. For example, twin-bedded rooms are typically less desirable than double rooms which, in turn, are less desirable than queen and king types. If by working the average rate using the Hubbart formula we get, say, $150 per room night, it would be impractical to sell all room types at this rate. The question, therefore, is how to work out appropriate rates for the different room categories in the house. These standard or list price rates are also called **rack rates**, a term used because in the past the standard rates were posted by each room number on a grid at the front desk called the rack.

Table 7.1, shows a way to split up the average rate reflecting the different categories of rooms and is based on the Royal Hotel example given above. The hotel's 575 rooms consist of 100 twin, 75 double, 200 queen and 100 king-size rooms plus 100 junior suites. After applying the Hubbard formula we know that to reach the ROI desired, the average room rate required should be $123.43 per night. This was the first step in the process of room price determination. Now we need to break up this rate to decide those for the different room types.

Based on the projected 65 percent average occupancy, let us assume that the average occupancy for the different categories of rooms will be as follows:

Twin-size rooms	30%
Double-size rooms	40%
Queen-size room	80%
King-size rooms	94%
Junior suite	60%

The assumption is based on the fact that the demand would be highest for king-size rooms, lowest for twin rooms and in-between for double, queen and junior suites. We know that the original overall target revenue at 65% occupancy was $16,849,429 (575 x .65 x 365 = 136,510 rooms night and 136,510 x $123.43).

Type	# of rooms	% occupancy	Rooms sold	Rate	Revenue
Twin	100	30	30	$75	$2,250
Double	75	40	30	$90	$2,700
Queen	200	80	160	$110	$17,600
King	100	94	94	$125	$11,750
Jr. suite	100	60	60	$195	$11,700
Totals	**575**	**65**	**374**	**$46,000 average daily revenue**	

TABLE 7.1 STANDARD ROOM RATES DETERMINATION

This room price structure will generate $16,790,000 annually ($46,000 x 365), very close to the required revenue when the Hubbart formula was applied.

This standard rate approach, however, needs to be rethought for lodging properties which experience occupancy fluctuations because of seasonality. Charging lower rates during low season helps attract business, while setting higher rates during high season helps maximize revenues. Except if the property is located in areas with little occupancy fluctuations, such as in downtown New York or San Francisco, the most common approach for lodging establishments is to offer high and low season rates.

The same situation occurs when the average rates need to be split between weekdays (usually Monday through Thursday) and weekends (Friday through Sunday). Generally, weekend occupancy is lower than on week days as most businessmen travel during the work week. Likewise, lower rates on weekends are intended to attract families looking for packages and special vacation deals.

STANDARD RATE DISCOUNTS

Hoteliers managing properties with good weekday business should keep in mind that lodging properties must remain open over weekends as well when costs for overhead expenses, depreciation, insurance, taxes and energy still apply. By attracting business on weekends, these overhead costs can be reduced, although it is not always possible to draw weekend business unless a considerable reduction in price is offered. **Marginal pricing** attempts to market lower-than-normal room rates to cover the property's operational expenses while, possibly, generating some income to contribute towards fixed costs. But, how low should marginal rates be? Let's assume that operational costs represent about 26 percent of every revenue dollar.

Then:

Average room rate	$123
Less 26% operational expenses	-32
Contribution to overhead expenses	= 91

If we charge $32 per room we would be covering operational expenses. Any amount over $32 would contribute towards our overhead expenses.

However, it is often believed that demand will increase if prices are lowered but it is also a fact that the drop in revenue must be offset by a substantial augmentation of the property's occupancy. For example, if the Royal Hotel's current occupancy averages 60 percent and we decide to reduce room rates by 20 percent to attract more customers, we will need to reach a 75 percent occupancy to generate the same revenue. Table 7.2 shows the calculations.

Current		**20% rate deduction**
575 x .60 = 345 rooms sold	$123 x .20 = $25	123 – 25 = $98
345 x $123 = $42,435	$42,435 / 98 = 433 rooms or **75%** occupancy (433/575)	

TABLE 7.2 RELATIONSHIP BETWEEN RATE DEDUCTION AND OCCUPANCY

In addition, rate cutting may force other properties in the area to do likewise, initiating a price war which might not benefit anyone in the long run.

If management decides to charge a supplement for double occupancy, the double rate could be set as a percentage of the single rate, usually between ten and twenty percent. For instance, if the average rate for a queen-size room is $110 and the percentage to be added for double occupancy is fifteen, the rate for double occupancy in a queen-size room should be $126 ($110 x 1.15).

DISCOUNTED ROOM RATES

Listed **transient room rates** (rack) charged to full-paying guests are usually discounted when they are sold to specific types of guests. Lower room rates authorized by the sales department and/or management may include:

Group	for tour operators or for a guaranteed minimum of rooms booked.
AARP	for senior citizens.
AAA	for members of the American Automobile Association.
Government/State	for federal or state employees traveling on **per diem** (per day) stipends.
Corporate/Commercial	for companies that provide frequent business.
Family	for parents with children traveling together.
Convention	for guests attending a gathering involving many rooms.
Day use	for guests checking in and out the same day (usually, these rooms can be rented twice the same day).
Package	for a combination of room, meals and/or activities (such as use of spa and golf).
Complimentary	for meeting planners or special guests.

The property's daily revenue from selling rooms divided by the total of rooms sold daily at rack and discounted prices provides the **average daily rate (ADR),** or average of all the rates sold on any given day. It is the job of the front office manager to maximize the ADR in order to increase room revenue. Because of their lowering effect on the property's ADR, discounted rates should be closely monitored to ensure that reservationists and guest service agents are following the established discount policies. Complimentary rooms, in most companies, must be authorized by management.

Regardless of the method used to determine a property's rates, hoteliers should keep in mind that business customers in general are not sensitive to price because they can charge lodging expenses to the company's business account. On the other hand, leisure travelers, especially senior citizens, are usually motivated by lower prices, particularly in difficult economic times. Also, if location, accommodations and services are comparable, most travelers will select the lower priced establishments. It is obvious that when the demand for rooms equals or exceeds the property's room supply, the application of discounts should be minimized or even temporarily discontinued.

MARKET-BASED PRICING

Market-based pricing is a strategy based on the rates charged by the competition. In other words, some establishments determine their rates comparing them with those offered by other properties of similar characteristics in the area. The method may also take into consideration what customers are prepared to pay for the product and use this as a starting point. With higher demand, a property can offer the rooms at a higher rate. If demand falls, rates are lowered to keep customers interested. Once the rate is set, management tries to tailor costs in order to receive a reasonable rate of return. Nevertheless, it would be unwise to adopt room rates solely based on those of the competition because operators should always be guided by their own operational expenses and profit margins. In all cases, room rates adopted by any lodging establishment should be sufficient to cover costs, provide a fair return on invested capital, and be adequate to attract and retain the targeted clientele. In other words, room rates need to be low enough to maintain optimum occupancy while at the same time high enough to make a fair return on investment.

In markets where rivals compete mainly on price, low costs relative to those of competitors is the only competitive advantage that matters; however, a low-cost product must offer enough attributes to be attractive to prospective buyers. Low price, by itself is not always appealing to buyers. To be successful with a rate strategy, a lodging company has to study buyers' needs and behavior carefully to learn what they consider attractive, what they think has value, and what they are willing to pay for. **Competitive advantage** results when buyers are attracted to services or themes that are perceived as different, appealing, or superior to the competition, to the point that customers bond with the company and become its loyal followers.

ROOM RATES AND MEAL PLANS

Today, most lodging companies offer rates that include full or continental breakfast. In the US, most properties operating in faraway locations such as in isolated geographical or historical spots, often market rates that include lunch, dinner or both. The available room rates that include (or do not include) meal plans are:

European Plan (EP):	A rate that includes no meals.
Room and breakfast (R&B):	Usually offered at no extra cost.
American Plan (AP):	A price that includes all three meals each day, convenient to long-stay full-board residents or in locations where there are no restaurants nearby.
Modified American Plan (MAP):	Plan that includes breakfast and one other meal (usually dinner). This plan is convenient for guests who are likely to be visiting the area during the course of the day.

When meals are included in the room rate, the price is usually quoted 'per person.' For example, if a hotel charges $90 for a double-size room for one or two persons without meals and the prices for breakfast and **table d'hôte** dinner are $10 and $18 respectively, the price per person per night to be charged should be $73 ($45 + $10 + $18).

RATE AVERAGES

By calculating the averages of the prices charged for the different room categories, the front office manager can monitor the average revenue from rooms sold of each type on a daily basis. As it has already been discussed, the average daily rate is the cumulative rate paid by guests each night but it doesn't provide a breakdown of the prices charged by category. Other averages that provide similar information are:

Group average rate	calculated from the revenue of occupied rooms sold at discount prices to group business.
Rack average rate	provides the average price from occupied rooms sold at transient rates.
Gross average rate:	also known as **Rev-par,** results from dividing the rooms revenue by the total number of rooms occupied or not. It provides a measurement of performance per room available.

Market segment rate average determines the average price for government, corporate, AARP, etc. categories.

Double occupancy percentage gives the percentage of rooms sold to two or more guests compared to that of rooms sold to only one occupant. The ratio is obtained by dividing the number of guests minus the number of rooms sold by the number of rooms sold. The percentage for a hotel that sold 85 rooms to 118 guests would be **38.9** [(118 -85) / 85].

THE CONCEPT OF YIELD MANAGEMENT IN THE LODGING INDUSTRY

The **revenue potential** of a lodging property, its optimum yield, is reached if one hundred percent of its rooms are sold at rack rates (highest price possible); however in practice, this is never possible because of the different discounted rates applied on a daily basis. Thus, the yield is the percentage obtained by dividing the **actual revenue** realized for any given period of time by the **revenue potential** in the same period of time.

Let's compare the yield of the Royal boutique hotel, for the month of March, 2020 and its yield for the same month in 2021. The Royal is a 425-room property that sold 7,980 rooms in March, 2020 and 8,680 in the same month, 2021. The weighted average rack rate for both periods of time was $300. Management wants to ascertain if profitability had increased or decreased. The result is shown on Table 7.3:

Period	Revenue potential	Actual ADR	Actual revenue	Yield
March, 2020	$3,952,500 (425 x 31) x 300	$265	$2,114,700 (7,980 x 265)	53.50
March, 2021	$3,925,500 (425 x 31) x 300	$205	$1,779,400 (8,680 x 205)	45.33

Table 7.3 Yield comparison at the Royal Hotel

Although fewer number of rooms were sold in March, 2020 the profitability (yield) was better than in March, 2021 because the ADR in the first year was substantially higher. In this example, it is assumed that the rates at the Royal had not changed between March 2020 and March 2021.

REVENUE MANAGEMENT AT THE FRONT OFFICE

In the beginning was **yield management (YM)**, a revenue maximization technique that aims to increase net yields by allocating available room capacity at optimum price. In practice, YM has to do with the alignment of room price and guest demand; that is, rates are kept high when demand is high and low (to attract buyers) when demand is low. However, as has been stated before, high occupancy ratios at discounted prices are unsatisfactory if the property's profitability (yield) decreases. Revenue management differs from yield management in that while the latter is a method of managing yields, revenue management goes a step farther in directing the sources of income by applying observations of consumer behavior.

The revenue manager in large establishments ranks at the same level as other members of the executive committee. His/her role is to optimize the revenues of all revenue-generating departments. In smaller properties, the front office manager, in cooperation with the sales manager, is in charge of maximizing room revenues.

BACKGROUND

In the early 1980s, airlines began to look into the relationship between the percentage of seats sold, the **load factor,** and the revenue for each mile flown per passenger, the **yield**. The idea was to determine which fares to offer on which flights to maximize occupancy and, therefore, revenue. First, they believed that by lowering the fare, more passengers would be attracted and revenue maximized, but it was soon found that the total revenue could be less, not more. The conundrum was solved by assigning different fare levels to different flights on different days of the week and at different times of the day. For example, the fares of a flight departing at 5:00 AM were made lower than those of a flight taking off at 10:00 AM for the same destination. The discount enticed passengers to book the earlier flight helping the airline fill seats that would have been otherwise empty. Table 7.4 shows how fare reduction by airlines helped increase revenue.

Current revenue		**Revenue after lowering rates**	
100 seats x $300	= **$30,000**	70 seats x $300	= $21,000
		50 seats x 200	= $10,000
		50 seats x 150	= $ 7,500
		Total	**$ 38,500**

TABLE 7.4 RELATIONSHIP BETWEEN AIRLINE RATE REDUCTION AND LOAD FACTOR

In this simple example, the airline was running two flights with a total of 170 seats available at an average load factor of 100 and an average fare of $300 per passenger. It was then decided to lower rates to $150 for the first 50 seats sold; then, increase them to $200 for the next 50 seats, keeping the $300 for the remaining 70 seats. With this strategy, the airline managed to fill the planes and obtain a revenue of $38,500, an increase of 28.3%.

The same principle was adopted by the lodging industry. Companies began researching customer demand and behavior to determine whether the two could be forecasted so that rooms could be offered at different prices to maximize occupancy and obtain higher revenues. The practice is in full swing today; for example, a 310-room business hotel with an average occupancy of 80% on weekdays and an ADR of $210 could lower prices substantially for the first 62 rooms sold in order to reach 100% occupancy. Even if the ADR came down to, say, $175, the revenue would still be higher and the number of guests would be increased to boost sales in F & B outlets. The front office manager in this case could allow the sales department to book a group of up to 62 rooms at a substantially low price to increase occupancy. See Table 7.5:

CURRENT REVENUE		
Rooms sold at 80% occupancy	248	(310 x .80)
Revenue with $210 ADR	**$52,080**	(248 x 210)
New revenue		
Rooms sold at 100% occupancy	310	(310 x 1.0)
Revenue with $175 ADR	**$58,900**	(310 x 175)

Table 7.5 Relationship between rate reduction and occupancy in lodging properties

These should be the main goals of front office managers regarding revenue management:

- To maximize the **occupancy percentage,** calculated by dividing the total rooms occupied by the number of rooms available.
- To increase the **average daily rate** as much as possible. The ADR is calculated by dividing the room revenue by the number of rooms sold.
- To get the best **revenue per available room (RevPar).** The RevPar is calculated by dividing the room revenue by the number of rooms available.

This last measurement is more significant than the ADR because it provides an accurate picture of sales. So, if we sell 10 rooms of a 200-room property at $100 apiece, the ADR would be a substantial $100 but at the same time the product of a dismal occupancy. Using the RevPar measurement, the figure would be $5 ($1,000 / 200), revealing that the selling of rooms was poor at best. Table 7.6 is an example of how to calculate the three measurements. The property has 200 rooms, the number of rooms sold is 184, and total revenue is $19,320:

Occupancy percentage:	**92.0**	(184 / 200)
Average daily rate:	**$105**	($19,320 / 184)
Revenue per available room (RevPar):	**$97**	(19,320 / 200)

TABLE 7.6 MEASUREMENTS FROM DAILY ROOM SALES

REVENUE MANAGEMENT AND PRICE/VALUE PRICING

Most customers assign a value to the rooms and services (product) they buy. This perceived value is what, in their opinion, they get from the transaction minus the price they pay for it. As a result, the customer's perceived value should be a major determinant in the pricing strategies of lodging properties. For instance, upscale establishments may decide to price their accommodations quite high because their guests are willing to pay for the prestige of staying in luxury hotels or resorts. On the other hand, senior citizens on a fixed income will be looking for a competitive rate for a comfortable, clean room, efficient services and a tasty full breakfast; that is, a balanced relationship between price and value. If the same retired traveler feels that the price is higher than the value received, he/she will feel that there is an imbalance in the value/price relationship and will decide to stay somewhere else. Needless to say that if the perceived value is higher than the charged price, the traveler will be a customer for life, although in this case operators may have to determine if they are giving the house away and it is the right time to raise rates.

Because value/based pricing depends on the perceptions held by customers, hoteliers must consider elements that some travelers will see as important to them while others won't; for example, high tech connections, environmentally-friendly products, HBO, old movies or games that can be played on the TV screen may be seen by some, but not all, guests as value added to their room purchase. The strategy of some companies is to combine both reduced rates and added amenities for frequent customers encouraging them to develop **brand loyalty** because of the special value they receive from staying at their properties. Similar to the airlines' frequent-flyer programs, some lodging chains offer points that guests can exchange for extra services, such as being allowed to stay on concierge floors or getting a complimentary dinner in the restaurant after a certain number of stays.

In general, lodging customers will patronize establishments that charge a fair price for their product (room and services). It the rate per stay does not match their perception of value they may simply book with the competition. So, to fulfill the goals set in revenue management, hoteliers must keep one eye on profits and one eye on the customer. If the initial strategy doesn't work they must be prepared to make adjustments as required.

In all rate-setting practices, any secret business agreement with a competitor to fix prices—**business collusion**—undermines free market competition and is against the law. **Price gouging**, charging unreasonably high prices during high customer demand, is an illegal practice and subject to large fines. It is not atypical to drive along the main drag of small resort towns in the summer to find that the rates of every single motel are extremely high and not much different from each other. It is possible that these businesses are colluding in price gouging.

THE FRONT OFFICE MANAGER AS REVENUE MANAGEMENT COORDINATOR

Let's consider the role of the front office manager as revenue management coordinator. To implement revenue management programs, lodging properties should develop realistic goals to be achieved, particularly for occupancy and RevPar levels. After an analysis of the market's supply and demand, the property should map out the selling strategies needed to reach the goals initially set. An important component of revenue management is the control in advance of the room inventory available in the different **channels of distribution** as optimal revenues can be gained by effectively managing price, room availability, and purchasing conditions.

The basic strategy should be to assign prices to the different room categories that are posted in the distribution channels together with some restrictions aimed at maximizing revenue, such as duration of stay, or specific arrival and departure dates. For example, certain discounted prices can be gotten by customers only if the purchase is done in advance or if the traveler is a member of a company with whom there is a negotiated rate agreement. As some rooms are booked and others cancelled, different rates are made available and others turned off in both the distribution channels and in the establishment's reservation systems. The discounted room inventory is closed if a certain high level of occupancy is reached; at this time, only rack rates are made available.

Besides rate restrictions, front office managers can set **length of stay restrictions** in an attempt to balance the property's occupancy. It is possible that a particular day(s) of the week has a higher demand than have others; for instance, when a couple of nights are sold out and the previous or following nights are wide open. In these cases, stay restrictions may be implemented. This strategy applies mainly to smaller properties, casinos or resorts far from city centers that must maximize occupancy in high season, during special events, such as local fairs, or on holiday weekends.

When selling blocks of rooms to groups that also contract meeting space and meal functions, the total revenue should be considered, keeping in mind that, overall, profits derived from selling rooms are much higher than those realized from F & B functions. An effective approach is to move price-sensitive groups to low demand days.

Another task of the front office manager as revenue management coordinator is that of preparing short-term and long-term room sale forecasts so that adjustments to selling strategies in the different selling channels to meet RevPar objectives can be effected. If any of the channels, for example the company's national sales program on the Internet, is not generating satisfactory results the reasons should be investigated and adjustments to current strategies put in place.

A critical element in the revenue management process is the right selection of room-selling channels. Some of the options can be:

- The property's reservations website.
- The company's central reservations website.
- Global distribution systems; such as Travelocity or Expedia.
- Auction Internet sites, such as Priceline.com.
- Special-interest sites; for example, the Arizona Golf Association.
- Web and social media portals.
- The American Society of Travel Agents (ASTA).

A basic step in the development of a revenue management strategy is the establishment of the right rates following the price/value concept discussed above and of the room inventory to be allocated to the distribution channels.

The tasks of the front office manager related to revenue management include:

- Working with the sales department to maximize occupancy and RevPar.
- Assigning room inventories, rates and restrictions to channels in the computer reservation system.
- Determining rack rates daily based on occupancy.
- Closing specific discounted prices on all channels on dates when optimum occupancy is assured.

REVENUE MANAGEMENT PROGRAMS STRATEGIES

The application of revenue management techniques depends in all cases on the specific conditions of each individual property or company. Here is a list of possible marketing decisions that could be adopted to maximize RevPar:

- Develop a strategy to position all rates based upon demand.
- Monitor the market mix during weekdays and weekends separately to ensure that revenues are maximized.
- Analyze the competition's rates making sure that they are in line with those of the property. Benchmarking research companies like STR Global can provide reports on American, European, and Asian markets.
- Provide incentives in **global distribution systems (GDS)** to increase sales in periods of low occupancy.
- Attain an ideal **price-occupancy mix** to maximize profitability.
- Develop packages to attract price-sensitive families and groups in offseason periods.
- Lengthen guest stays by closing a specific day or days on the computer reservation system (GDS).
- Offer higher commission percentages for rooms on specific days.
- Advertise substantially discounted rates on dates of low demand to attract price-sensitive travelers.
- Require a two or three-day minimum stay on certain weekends when the demand for rooms is high.
- Maximize room rates when full occupancy is assured.
- Restrict the selling of discounted rates when occupancy is high. As occupancy climbs, consider closing out low room rates.
- Train front office staff in revenue management procedures.

In general, revenue management works best when demand is high and the front office manager can juggle blocks of rooms from one market segment to another. When demand falls substantially from normal levels price reductions should be automatically implemented.

COMPUTERIZED PRICE MANAGEMENT

There are several revenue management options on the market that offer programs to book the right guest at the right time at the right rate by simply using a few keystrokes. These systems do not tell front office managers what to do but provide the support needed to make the right decisions to maximize profitability. One company that offers revenue management programs is IdeaS which sells HTNG-certified software that is backed by SAS, known in the industry as the finest analytics firm in the world. The software package offers these features:

- A **best available rate (BAR)** module that allows for the selection of the optimal rate with the highest probability of selling based on arrival date and length of stay.
- A program for sending the property's best available rate to distribution channels without the need to manually enter the data.
- The possibility of optimizing demand and increasing revenue by accessing all properties instantly from anywhere in the world.
- A module for group management by which the groups' entire value can be determined, factoring in rooms, costs and commissions, conferencing and banqueting, as well as the value of any business being displaced before accepting the booking.
- A method to assess the property's performance on a daily, weekly, monthly, and annual basis against its financial goals, including charts and reports.
- A benchmarking option to compare rooms sold, revenue per available room (RevPar), and average daily rate with those of the competition.
- Integration of the software with other programs such as property management systems, central reservation and distribution systems, sales and catering systems, rate shopping engines, and rate distribution services.

The URL for IdeaS is http://www.ideas.com

Other features offered by revenue management software outputs include:

- Room statistics tracking no-shows, walk-ins and turn-aways that are useful to forecast occupancy accurately.
- Reports with sell prices for rooms, including special and discounted rates.
- Market segment reports.
- Future arrival dates status report.
- Booking graphs.

Keep in mind that revenue management programs ignore intangibles like the necessity to retain the property's corporate business and other regular customers. For instance, it is not a good idea to close availability when the demand for rooms from transient business is high and automatically deny reservations to regular guests who will be displaced to other competitor establishments with the possibility of losing them forever. Revenue management is designed to raise revenues in the short term but it doesn't have the capacity for long-term perspectives.

KEY TERMS

Actual revenue
American plan (AP)
Average daily rate (ADR)
Brand loyalty
Business collusion
Channel of distribution
Competitive advantage
Cost-based rate
Day-use rate
European plan (EP)
Global distribution system (GDS)
Hubbart formula
Length of stay restriction
Load factor
Marginal pricing
Market-based rate
Modified American plan (MAP)
Occupancy percentage
Opening team
Operating costs
Per diem
Price gouging
Price occupancy mix
Rack rates
Return on investment (ROI)
Revenue management
Revenue per available room (RevPar)
Revenue potential (rooms)
Table d'Hôte
Transient room rates
Yield management

DISCUSSION AND REVIEW QUESTIONS

1. What is the difference between market-based rate and cost-based rate?
2. When is the Hubbart Formula usually used? What is the formula?
3. In general, are rack rates higher or lower than AAA rates?

4. What is the average daily rate in a 510-room resort that sold 449 rooms while generating a revenue of $49,390 the night of March 2? What is the RevPar average?
5. A customer approaches the front desk of a hotel and tells the clerk that her per diem for room and dinner is $97.50. What does she mean by that?
6. What strategies should a front office manager follow to gain a competitive advantage over the hotel next door?
7. What is the formula to work out the RevPar in lodging properties?
8. The front office manager of the Royal resort calls a colleague in a hotel down the street and tells him: "*As you know, we are going to be packed next week. Let's go ahead and raise our room rates by twenty percent across the board.*" His pal answers: "*Yes, people won't have anywhere else to stay anyway. Everybody is booked up!*" Was this proposal lawful because of the law of supply and demand? Was it business collusion?
9. In your opinion, what are the advantages and disadvantages of selling rooms through global reservations systems?
10. List three strategies that a front office manager can adopt to maximize RevPar.

PRACTICAL SITUATIONS

Situation 7.1

Cost-based rate calculation

After several years as an industry professional, Jennifer Johnson has been assigned the job of coordinator of the opening team of a 310-room hotel soon to be inaugurated in Boise, Idaho. The corporate office has asked Jennifer to determine the minimal initial average room rate needed to cover the hotel's expenses and the company's projected annual ROI (15 percent of the initial $15,450,000 capital investment). Ms. Johnson was provided with the figures listed below:

ROI required	$2,317,500	(15,450,000 x .15)
Tax	927,000	
Annual property operating costs	3,181,000	
Interest to banks	1,100,000	
Income (profit) from other departments	1,236,000	
Estimated rooms division expenses	2,695,500	

Information received from the sales department indicates that the annual occupancy from the first year has been estimated at 62 percent.

ASSIGNMENT:

What is the minimum ADR that the property needs to set given the ROI and the amounts from operations listed above?

Situation 7.2

Measurements from daily business results

You are the front office manager of a ski lodge in Blue Sky, Montana. The lodge has 115 rooms, 95 of which were sold the night of February 15 generating a revenue of $11,564. The morning of February 16 you are supposed to work out last night's ADR, RevPar, and the occupancy percentage. All electronic systems are down and you are compelled to do the calculations by hand.

ASSIGNMENT:

What were the ADR, RevPar, and occupancy percentage for the night of February 15?

Situation 7.3

Discount rate dilemma

On a late Sunday evening, Jordan Ramirez is the only front office clerk working the desk at the Sunrise motel in Pensacola, Florida. On starting his shift at 4 PM that day, he was reminded by his colleague Anne that next Tuesday the motel is already booked at 90% capacity and not to accept any reservations at discounted rates. Ann told him that the front office manager was very specific about the need to increase the average daily rate and that no discounts are to be given on that Tuesday. Just before his shift is over, Jordan receives a call from Len Oswald, a guest who stays regularly at the Sunrise:

> *"Hello, this is Len Oswald. Can you please reserve a room for me this Tuesday? As usual, I would like a quiet corner room facing the pool on the fourth floor. Please don't forget to apply the $73.00 commercial rate I always get."*

Jordan's answer is:

> *"Sorry Mr. Oswald, we are almost full on Tuesday and we cannot grant you thecommercial rate this time. I could reserve you a room for $95.00."*
>
> *"Well, I don't think I want the room. My per diem is $70.00 and I cannot afford the rate you are offering me. I will book somewhere else. Good night."*

ASSIGNMENT:

Discuss this scenario with another student and be ready to give your opinion when asked by the instructor.

CASE STUDY 7.1

A practical yield management scenario (I)

Christopher Wang is the front office manager of a 229-room in Seattle, Washington. At yesterday's staff meeting, the property's general manager spoke of the need to increase occupancy to boost revenues in the food and beverage outlets, particularly in the restaurant and bar areas. The GM would like to increase the projected 65 percent occupancy for the next 3 months to 75 percent by offering discounts. However, she insists on achieving the same budgeted revenue from room sales. The budgeted ADR for the period had been set at $115.

ASSIGNMENT:

What decrease in dollars on the budgeted ADR can the hotel afford in order to increase occupancy from 65 to 75 percent without lowering the budgeted revenue from guestroom sales?

A practical yield management scenario (II)

At the end of the 90 days in which discounts to attract occupancy had been offered, the GM asked Christopher Wang if profitability had increased or decreased. Christopher decided to put into practice his knowledge of yield management to find out the profitability percentage using the yield management information learned in college. The results for the 3-month period had been as follows:

Occupancy	**78%**
ADR	**$89.40**

ASSIGNMENT:

Apply the yield formula and find out the difference between the expected yield and the yield actually achieved.

CHAPTER 8

SELLING ON THE JOB

CHAPTER OBJECTIVES

- Review how the analysis of a property and its surrounding areas is conducted.
- Identify the property's business market segments.
- Discuss how the target market segments can be reached.
- Emphasize the importance of selling at the front office.
- Explain the concept of front office salesmanship.
- Discuss group sales in lodging operations.
- Describe how to forecast advanced sales.
- Discuss E-sales in today's lodging operations.

OVERVIEW

The principal concern of front office employees in lodging operations is to sell guestrooms to prospective customers. When a person calls to inquire or at the time of registration, the value of renting a room can only be stressed by the front office employee on duty. Salesmanship includes the ability to describe rooms, amenities, and services to potential renters, such as the desirable location, appealing décor, a special view or a tempting selection of in-room guest supplies.

Selling a large number of rooms to groups requires knowledge on the part of the front office manager to evaluate and select those which will generate the most revenue for a specific period of time considering the group-transient mix potential. The ability the front office manager must have to forecast future sales based on bookings to date and on historical data is also emphasized in this chapter.

Because the Internet has woven its way into the fabric of everyday business, lodging companies are being forced to address how best to make electronic commerce a fundamental part of their business strategy.

SELLING IN LODGING OPERATIONS

Although the real task of identifying and bringing customers into lodging properties is the concern of the marketing department, these activities are related to the work of the front office manager as well. In fact, it is important for front office managers to acquire a thorough understanding of selling and marketing in lodging operations as in some cases, convention business can exceed fifty percent of the property's sales volume. The hospitality industry offers a large selection of products to the public, ranging from guestrooms, and food and beverage services to sophisticated convention packages that usually include concurrent meetings, exhibits, receptions, banquets, and recreational activities. Hospitality establishments, from the humble bed-and-breakfast operation to the megaresort, must develop a marketing program and a sales strategy that fulfill the needs of each property.

In practice, sales begins with the development of a marketing plan that basically includes the following components:

- Analyses of the property and of the surrounding area (what is to be sold).
- Identification of business segments or markets (who may be interested in the product the property offers).
- Ascertainment of ways to reach potential customers (how is the advertising and promotional effort going to be implemented).

The plan has to be based on the property's capabilities for it will be difficult for a hotel, for example, to sell conventions if the property has a large convention hall but no breakout rooms; or it will be hopeless to sell the concept of "golfing" if the nearest course is 50 miles away from the property or is accessible only by a circuitous, unpaved road.

Once the analyses are completed, the source of potential business must be identified. Can and should the establishment attempt to attract transient, group, convention, commercial, tour and travel, and/or banquet business from local, regional, national, and international markets? And how will these segments be attracted? In brief, marketing is all about finding out what potential guests want and providing that with the highest possible level of quality at reasonable cost in order to generate an acceptable profit.

IDENTIFICATION OF BUSINESS MARKET SEGMENTS

After the potential of the property and surrounding areas have been determined, sources of possible business must be identified. Prospective guests may have a wide range of reasons for wanting to stay at one establishment in particular; consideration must be given to the major urban centers in the area or to specific countries that have been, are or have the potential to be good business sources. For instance, the current largest number of European tourists to visit Arizona is from Germany. Other considerations to be weighed are natural attractions, sports stadiums, entertainment venues, cultural enclaves and major historical sites that are within range of the property. For example, an establishment that is near the Gettysburg battlefield will have excellent possibilities of attracting national and international history buffs.

Here are some possible sources of business:

- Corporate/Business guests
- Leisure travelers
- Transient guests
- Independent and group tourists
- Conventions, conferences, trade shows and business gatherings
- Catered functions and banquets
- Organized tours
- Social functions (such as weddings and fund raisers)
- Education/Religious/Fraternal organizations

Special market sub-segment trends present in specific environments should also be considered so as not to overlook any potential source of business. For instance, **special-interest travelers** to the area where the property is located may be looking for activities such as visiting archaeological sites, dancing, sports, art, film or musical events; **older travelers** usually prefer cultural and heritage attractions, **Road Scholar** educational trips or guided nature tours; **weekend travelers** may be attracted by value-for-dollar family packages or children-oriented activities; **nature tourists** prefer ecotourism trips, bird watching or photography.

REACHING THE TARGET MARKET SEGMENTS

Once the environmental analysis is complete, the plan addresses the opportunities, strategies, and tactics to reach the market segments identified as "potential customers." Generally, individual guests can be attracted by way of Internet, social media, signs and some media advertising. The role of travel agents as retailers to individual travelers has all but disappeared in the age of technology.

On the other hand, convention and group business may be found by Internet advertising, direct mail or contact with government agencies, civic organizations, company **meeting**

planners, and professional, religious and non-profit organizations. Tourists, tour groups, and international travelers may be reached through online advertising, tour operators, and information presented at tourism exhibitions and trade shows. Weekend and family business can usually be attracted by **packaging;** that is, combining rooms and complementary or discounted services into a single-price offering. Local and regional market segments can be reached by **personal selling**, either by telephone or face-to-face (**field sales**). **Inside sales** can be promoted by **suggestive selling** and by **merchandising** products. Sales can also be increased by **publicity**, a non-paid communication or information effort about the property by way of **news releases** and **press conferences.** For example, at the time I was front office manager at the hotel Meliá Aguadulce in southeastern Spain the actors in the movie Shalako (a western) were staying with us for several months. The cast included Brigitte Bardot and Sean Connery who were very famous at the time. We publicized the information and hundreds of movie fans booked in the hotel just to have a glance at our celebrities.

Lodging operations must have documented knowledge of their customers in order to develop a revenue management strategy. This knowledge will help companies and individual properties to market services to suit the needs of their clientele. Internal information from automated sales and records systems can be used to compile data. External sources can also be used, such as local convention and visitors' bureaus, tourism organizations or reports acquired from specialized data vendors.

SELLING ROOMS AT THE FRONT OFFICE

The main goal of the front office, in close cooperation with the reservations and sales department, is to sell as many guest rooms as possible at the highest feasible rate. In fact, most of the profit generated by lodging operations comes from selling guestrooms while the food and beverage division often may do little more than break even.

Basically, there are two ways to augment revenue; one is increasing occupancy, the second is charging more for rooms. For example, a resort with 250 rooms and an average daily rate (ADR) of $150 with an average annual occupancy of 82 percent will generate $11,223,750 revenue annually (250 x .82 x 150 x 365). If the occupancy were increased by just two percentage points, the annual revenue would be increased to $11,497,500 (250 x .84 x 150 x 365). If at the same time the ADR was raised from $150 to $160, the revenue would now be $12,264,000 (250 x .84 x 160 x 365). In most instances, the property's occupancy rises if rates are lowered and decreases if rates are increased. The challenge, however, for the front office staff is to maximize both occupancy and rates to benefit profits.

Front office employees must be thoroughly trained for the property to achieve optimum occupancy. If, for instance, a caller asks for a room with a queen-size bed and there are only rooms with twin-size beds left, the clerk should offer the twin-size room while allowing a reduction in price for the inconvenience. If the establishment is full on a specific day, the clerk should immediately offer the nearest date available adding that the caller would receive an upgraded type of room if he/she agrees to change the date; for example, she would be given a junior suite for the price of a standard double. If the caller cannot change the date, clerks should be trained to recommend an establishment of the same group that will likely return business to the property when it is full. Another way in which front office staff can increase occupancy is to boost repeat business. Because all guests staying in a property are potential future customers they should be approached for some forward selling using follow-up techniques such as e-mail marketing packages or special discounts.

The moment of departure is an excellent time to try some forward bookings when **face-to-face selling** can be put into practice by the front desk staff. It must always be remembered that a guest who is checking out is a potential future customer. A few selling questions to the departing guest by the front desk clerk can be:

Will you be coming back this way again, Mr. Butler?
Can we make a reservation for you for your next visit to town?
When do we hope to see you again, Ms. Hill?

FRONT OFFICE SALESMANSHIP

The employees in reservations and behind the front desk play an important sales role, a role that goes beyond checking customers in and out. Productive selling involves constantly offering conveniences; that is the seller, in this case the hospitality industry, provides a series of extras that consumers want. These may be excellent customer service, convenient location, desirable ambience, in-room amenities, or distinctive lodgings. In other words, the basic goal of a lodging establishment is to relate the values it offers to the values in demand by customers. The degree of success of a lodging operation should therefore be measured by this relationship of values.

Most travelers checking into a lodging property expect a great deal more than just a place to sleep. As stressed before, competent salesmanship consists in providing customers additional values through personal contact and service. Front office employees must think like professional salesmen by understanding guests and their wants and by taking a genuine interest in their comfort and welfare while they stay at the property.

Basically, there are three components to making a sale: a product, a customer, and a salesman. Consequently, front office employees should be knowledgeable of the product being sold and what its value is; they should understand potential customers and have a genuine desire to serve them. It is not enough for a reservationist, for example, to know only about the rooms to be sold; he/she should also know about the additional services that can be used as major selling points to influence travelers to book a room. Some additional services that can be part of a total package include these:

- Free continental or full breakfast
- Free local telephone calls
- Children under 12 registered free
- Babysitting services
- Small pets allowed
- Free extra amenities in guestrooms, like bathrobes and slipper
- Free Wi-Fi

It is the job of the front office to make potential guests aware of these benefits at the time of inquiring about rooms. A common mistake is for employees to take for granted that callers know about these special services.

Besides direct telephone information to callers, the property's webpage must prominently display all services that may appeal to people shopping for a room in the area. In this case, the computer should act as a convincing salesman by making the product enticing.

When dealing with direct sales, the front office employee should size up the customers. Do the potential guests know what they want? Do they seem to be price conscious? In the first case, if yes, the selling tactic should provide guests with exactly what they are looking for instead of confusing them by offering a variety of accommodations; in the second, if so, the clerk should offer a few room categories within the range of rates that he feels the traveler can afford to pay and list the various amenities and services that the price of the room entails.

Reservations agents should be trained to deal with savvy travelers who look for the lowest possible rate they can get. They may begin by checking the computer, coming up with a rate of, say, $190. Their next step is to call a toll-free number and ask for a corporate rate which may be $145. Pressing further they may ask "are there any other specials?" so the reservationist may find a weekend special rate of $105. This situation can often be avoided by the clerk politely taking control of the conversation and avoiding quoting the rock bottom rate, particularly if the property is close to being full.

A salesperson's pleasant personality is important so the customer likes him/her and the establishment. Politeness is a subtle form of respect that bolsters the customer's ego; after all, this is the hospitality business. A congenial clerk offers more than being a good listener by contributing to the conversation, like asking travelers about weather conditions on the road or expressing genuine pleasure in servicing them. Every guest is pleased to be given the red carpet treatment. The key to successful salesmanship is service, the willingness to help customers; a guest walking across the lobby who feels that the employees around him are unaware of his presence or a customer that stands in front of the registration desk while the clerk continues working on the computer screen will not feel that they are being served.

As our establishments are part of a service industry, their success is derived from satisfied, repeat guests. Taking a personal interest in each customer, understanding her needs, being sympathetic, making her feel important and creating an atmosphere of welcome will encourage guests to come back again and again. This is salesmanship.

GROUP SALES

Front office managers should be aware of the importance of group business while understanding that tour operators, meeting planners, convention and trade show organizers, and social institutions always attempt to book at the lowest possible rates. Although filling a property at rack rate prices is ideal, most large establishments must rely on group business to fill the house, particularly during low season. Two major disadvantages of group business are that the rooms are usually sold at discounted prices and that groups may drive out higher-yielding customers. An advantage is that it provides the property with assurance that a certain number of rooms will be occupied. The rationale is that it is better to have rooms occupied at discounted rates than to have them empty. Sometimes it is preferable to accept a convention, even if transient demand is high, in order not to lose that particular piece of business in the future.

Usually, tour operating companies want to reserve rooms during peak periods while establishments want to use group bookings to fill low season periods. This type of conflict of interests often results in the need for negotiations to reach a mutual agreement. It is clear that if the rooms would otherwise remain empty, the property's lowest bid would be to achieve the marginal cost of accepting the group. On the other hand, if the rooms might otherwise be occupied by customers who would have paid more, booking the group should be a second priority.

There are instances in which tour operators may require blocks of rooms. Such is the case for companies dealing with organized tours in the US or beachside resorts on the Mediterranean or Mexican coasts where large contingents of travelers are brought in charter flights most of the year. In this case, an agreement can be signed by which the property agrees to block a certain number of rooms in high season in return for a commitment by the tour operator to book rooms during periods of low business. Another option is to discount rates according to the number of bookings throughout the year. The purpose of discounting prices substantially is to encourage the tour operator to book off-peak season rooms. Generally, the rule of thumb is to level out the valleys in room occupancy by booking group business.

It is important when booking groups to impose cancellation deadlines. Rooms that failed to be occupied after the deadline should be paid in full by the booking party as it is not always possible to resell large numbers of rooms in a short period of time.

The following scenario is an example of the complexity of balancing rack rates and discounted group business occupancy: The rooms division director of a resort and spa has received a call from the sales department asking for advice on whether to accept a convention requesting to book the resort's 100 rooms from Monday, March 3 through Thursday, March 6 (4 nights) or a business group requesting 50 rooms arriving Tuesday the same week and departing Friday morning (3 nights). The historical records of the resort for Monday through Thursday of the same week for the last three years show the following average occupancy and rates:

Transient occupancy	40%
Corporate, government and other discount occupancy	20%
Rack rates	$210
Corporate, government and other discount rates	175

The rate quoted to the convention was $130 and to the business group $150. What should the rooms division director recommend? Table 8.1 shows the quantitative breakdown of the projected revenue for the dates in question (Monday through Thursday).

<u>**Convention**</u>		
Revenue from convention	100 x 4 = 400 rooms	
	400 x $130 =	$52,000
Revenue from rack rates		none
Revenue from discounted rates		none
Total from convention....		**$52,000**
<u>**Business Group**</u>		
Revenue from business group	50 x 3 = 150 rooms	
	150 x $150 =	$22,500
Revenue from rack rates	40 x 4 = 160 rooms	
	160 x $210 =	$33,600

Revenue from discounted rates	10 x 3 = 30 rooms	
	20 x 1 = 20 rooms	
	50 x $175	$ 8,750
	Total from group	**$64,850**

TABLE 8.1 BALANCING RACK RATE AND DISCOUNTED GROUP BUSINESS

It is clear that selling all the resort's rooms to the convention for 4 days would generate less revenue than selling 40% of the rooms to the business group for 3 days. In addition, some of the property's habitual guests would have to be displaced if all rooms are taken by the convention.

FORECASTING ADVANCED SALES

One of the basic functions of the front office manager is to determine future room availability. Room forecasting is based on the property's occupancy historical data; that is, being able to look back in time and see the number of rooms sold and average rates received during a certain month or even on a specific date in the past. Some of the factors considered in annual forecasting are:

- Historical occupancy percentages
- Local, regional and national economic factors
- Upcoming city special events
- Transient and convention reservations to date
- Changes in local competition
- Anticipated business trends

Figure 8.2 is an example of the annual forecast for a 300-room golf resort in Arizona's Valley of the Sun. The projections are based on the fact that national economic growth as a whole has remained flat from last year. Predictions indicate that the local economy will grow by 5 percent and that a new 500-room hotel has recently opened nearby. In this case, management decided to keep the overall monthly occupancy percentages from last year while increasing last year's rates 2.5 percent to compensate for inflation.

	Occupancy percentage	ADR	Remarks
January	85	255	High season
February	98	196	Boeing Corp. convention booked
March	82	214	
April	86	206	
May	78	206	
June	52	195	Remodeling of 80 guestrooms
July	50	194	Remodeling continues
August	78	180	End of remodeling
September	90	184	Technology convention booked
October	100	230	High season
November	100	230	High season
December	95	210	High season

FIGURE 8.2 ADVANCED SALES FORECAST

Long-term forecasting of guestrooms is necessary for several reasons. It is important for preparing the income statement for the annual budget, for scheduling labor and anticipating expenses in all departments, and for planning renovations or major repairs.

Once the advanced sales forecast is prepared, it is easy to project the revenue for every upcoming month and for the year as a whole. In the example provided in figure 8.1 the monthly occupancy percentages can be easily converted into rooms to be sold, and the totals multiplied by the projected monthly ADR to obtain the revenue for each month and for the year.

INCREASING SALES

There are occasions in which revenue-increasing efforts are necessary to generate more sales volume. Some common strategies are cutting prices, increasing product promotion, using a bigger sales force, and adding customer services. These attempts to improve sales are imperative in difficult times when there is no room in the operating budget to cut expenses to break even.

However, hoteliers should be aware that aggressive moves to capture a share of the market away from the competition often trigger retaliation in the way of price wars, bringing down everybody's revenues. When striving to widen the gap between an establishment and its competitor in quality or service, the attempt should be meaningful to effect substantial differences between products, as a small differentiation may not be appreciated by buyers; in other words, considerable investment should be made to create a robust competitive advantage. Most importantly, in these ever-changing market conditions, companies should be quick to adapt, meet customer needs, fulfill buyer wishes for something better, adopt new technological alternatives, and foresee new initiatives of competitors.

E-SALES

The use of the Internet has woven its way into the fabric of everyday business with lodging companies being forced to address how best to make electronic commerce a fundamental part of their business and their competitive strategies. Therefore, lodging operations need to define what strategic principles need to be observed in the new technological environment. A first step is to carefully analyze industry and competitive conditions and select strategies to match these conditions.

A winning strategy is one that stands apart from those of rivals and succeeds in drawing customers because of the value being delivered. It should not be just a matter of offering low rates but of giving more attention to on-line service, making on-line booking an experience that customers find appealing. Adopting cutting-edge Internet products and state-of-the-art software programs and following techniques that are efficient in reaching the target audience and in stimulating purchases brings success in today's environment.

It is also important to develop innovative websites offering features that capture viewer interest by being easy to read, with lots of visual appeal. Websites that are easy to navigate and are entertaining encourage potential customers to spend time on the site. The strategic issues can be narrowed down to:

1. How to make the Internet a fundamental part of the selling strategy.
2. How much emphasis to place on the Internet as a distribution channel for reaching customers.
3. Which Internet applications need to be implemented.

Basically, a website should provide customers with clear information about the property and how to book rooms directly with the property while at the same time being present on all major distribution channels. In fact, the Internet is a unique force for expanding the geographic area in which lodging companies have a market presence by opening booking opportunities to potential customers all over the world. Although English is commonly understood by businessmen everywhere, individual customers may be attracted by an option to browse in any of several languages as national boundaries mean little in an e-sales world.

KEY TERMS

Face-to-face selling
Field sales
Inside sales
Meeting planner
Merchandising
Nature tourism
News release
Older travelers
Packaging
Personal selling
Press conference
Publicity
Road Scholar tours
Special interest travelers
Suggestive selling
Weekend travelers

DISCUSSION AND REVIEW QUESTIONS

1. What are the four components of a lodging property's marketing plan?
2. List six possible sources of business in the lodging industry.
3. What is the difference between merchandising and publicity aimed at increasing room sales?
4. Which of the following decisions would generate more revenue in a resort annually:
   - Selling 90% of the rooms at an average daily rate of $182.54
   - Selling 92% of the rooms at an average daily rate of $178.00
5. What are the three components involved in making a sale?
6. What are the advantages and disadvantages in selling blocks of rooms to groups?
7. List three factors to be considered when forecasting annual room sales in lodging properties.
8. What two strategies could you adopt to increase room sales in your hotel?
9. Explain some ways of making E-sales appealing to potential customers.
10. Project the <u>annual</u> rooms revenue for a motel with a forecast of an average of 2,850 room nights sold monthly at an ADR of $89 from January through May, $105 from June through October, and $ 99 for November and December.

PRACTICAL SITUATIONS

Situation 8.1

Analysis of a property in the American Southwest
(The analysis can be conducted on any other property preferred by the instructor or students)

Kara Rice is a 3-year graduate from a hotel and restaurant management program. Her last two years in the industry have been as front office manager with a nationwide hotel chain with headquarters in the Northwest. Wishing to move up in the career ladder, Kara has accepted the position of rooms division director with the Enchantment Resort in Sedona, Arizona. Being new to the property and to the area, Miss Rice decides to conduct a thorough analysis of the resort and its surrounding area, including this specific information:

— What facilities and services can the resort offer to guests?
— What activities can the property advertise?
— What are the natural and historical attractions of the surrounding area?
— How can the climatic seasons of the Sedona area affect occupancy?
— What is the competition, and does the Enchantment have an advantageous edge over existing establishments in the area?
— What are the tourism counts and visitor profiles for the area?

Wedding gazebo
Courtesy Marriott International, Inc.

ASSIGMENT:

Prepare an analysis of the Enchantment Resort in Sedona, Arizona, from information gathered from the property's Internet page at www.enchantmentresort.com, the City of Sedona Webpage at www.visitsedona.com and the Arizona Office of Tourism: www.arizonaguide.com.

Situation 8.2

Identifying market segments

After thoroughly analyzing the facilities and services of the Enchantment resort (or any other property chosen) and the attractions of the surrounding areas, Kara Rice decides to identify the local, regional, national, and international segments and sub-segments that could be marketed by the resort.

ASSIGNMENT:

Based on the analyses conducted, identify the target segments and areas of origin of potential customers who might be attracted to the Enchantment Resort in Sedona, Arizona.

Situation 8.3

Ascertaining the package price

The Royal Hotel has received a request from the Nestle Purina Company to work out the price per person per night in single and double room occupancy for a tentative booking of a convention in downtown Los Angeles from August 15 (arrival) to August 18 (departure.) The hotel will charge a flat rate of $130 per room for single or double occupancy plus 11.5% city tax. Continental breakfast on August 16 and 17 will be priced at $8.50, lunch on August 17 at $16.50, and dinner on August 16 and 17 at $25.50 per person. There will be a surcharge of 15% for gratuities on all meals.

ASSIGNMENT:

Calculate the price per person per night for single and double occupancy that includes lodging and meal charges.

CASE STUDY 8.1

Balancing rack rate and discounted group business occupancy

Max Gonzalez has been promoted to front office manager of a resort and spa south of Pittsburgh. The date is January 10. Max has received three requests for group business for the second week of October:

- **The Friends of the Earth,** an ecological organization with headquarters in Philadelphia, wants to book the resort's 280 rooms from Monday, October 7 through Thursday, October 10 (4 days). They are willing to contract for a flat rate of $110 per room per night.
- **The Shriners** wish to reserve 40% of the hotel capacity. The group would arrive Monday, October 7 and depart Thursday, October 9 (3 days). They could pay a flat rate per room of $135 per night.
- **The Republican Women** wish to book 50% of the resort's room capacity at $125 flat rate per room. Their stay is from Tuesday, October 8 to Friday, October 11 (3 days).

Mr. Gonzalez has been asked by the sales manager of the resort to work out the optimum revenue from rooms that can be gained during the second week in October taking into consideration the number of rooms and rates that the groups require and the occupancy trends of the property for the week in question for the last five years. Max looks up the historical records of the resort and finds:

Daily minimum room occupancy percentages for the last five years during the second week in October, Monday through Thursday (4 days):

Transient and individual occupancy (rack rates)	50%
Corporate, government and other discounted occupancy	10%

Current ADR:

Rack rates	$150
Corporate, government and other discounted rates	$135

ASSIGNMENT:

Which group should the resort accept to maximize room revenue?
(Don't take into account the potential F & B business.)

CHAPTER 9

THE RESERVATION PROCESS

CHAPTER OBJECTIVES

- Review the sources of reservations used by the traveling public.
- Know the data required to make reservations online.
- Learn the difference between guaranteed and non-guaranteed reservations.
- Explain the underpinnings of the reservation process.
- Practice working out room availability by applying occupation historical factors.
- Discuss the dilemma of overbooking versus underselling a property.
- Describe online reservation programs.

OVERVIEW

The reservation process can be summarized as the booking of rooms according to the availability of space in the house. It could be compared to filling a glass to the brim without spilling any of the liquid. The process is particularly challenging as occupancy and availability are in a state of constant fluctuation; that is, guests are checking out or deciding to stay over longer while at the same time customers are making reservations, cancelling or postponing their arrival. In addition, rates must be brought down to increase occupancy when demand is low or raised to maximize revenue when demand is high. Although property management systems help determine the levels of occupancy and availability and suggest rates to be applied, front office managers need to develop an instinct for handling the different situations that arise in the process of maximizing both occupancy and rates while accommodating the needs of their customers.

Today, there are several web-based booking engines on the market that can be made compatible with the same database used by the property's management system. In addition, the reservations distribution landscape is changing with a new breed of third-party intermediaries, such as Google, Facebook, and Apple, which are becoming the preferred points of entry for customers to search for their travel shopping. The combination of high booking volumes controlled by these third-party intermediaries, the cost imposed for their services, and the pressure on rates are challenging hospitality companies to maintain profitability levels.

RESERVATIONS

The use of reservation software enables lodging properties to process bookings, keep timely room availability inventories, and generate reports which facilitate the reservation process. Most establishments are linked to central reservations systems that perform the functions of storing and monitoring the reservation data. Thus, it is the reservation central system, interfaced with the property's PMS, which communicates all information related to each particular booking and updates the reservation status at all times. Likewise, any booking entry posted at the property is registered at the central reservation location by electronic filing. A list of expected arrivals from the reservation data on file and preregistration materials can be printed at the property prior to the guests' arrival.

RESERVATION SOURCES

Front office managers must be aware of how prospective guests get information about their properties. The decision to maintain the different sources of possible business open should be taken by management after analyzing the number of bookings obtained from each one of them; that is, while it is critical to be present on the Internet, it might not pay off to have an expensive billboard in a doubtful location that doesn't generate enough reservations to warrant its cost. Prospective guests can obtain reservation information about lodging properties in numerous ways including:

- **Distribution channels**, such as Expedia, Travelocity, and Orbitz. It is vital to have a presence in these sources as many, if not most, travelers use them to book rooms.
- The company or franchise Internet page where customers can find hotels in the location they plan to visit, for example Marriott, Drury Hotels or Sheraton. These **affiliate reservation networks** constitute the chain's reservation system in which all participating operational units are represented.

- Central reservation networks for independent or non-chain properties: for instance, Pegasus Connect (former Utell) where customers can book rooms using the URL www.hotelbook.com.
- The property's own webpage, direct telephone number (usually toll-free) and, less commonly, fax.
- Social networking channels, such as Facebook and Twitter.
- Advertisements in magazines, such as airlines and tourism publications like *Conde Nast Traveler*, or in state, regional and local Chamber of Commerce periodicals.
- Ads in newspapers, particularly to inform the local and regional public about packages, such as ski-and-stay specials and weekend family packages.
- Google's search engine.
- Yellow pages.
- Billboards.
- Direct telephone-link panels for those properties near airports.
- Guest clerks in nearby lodging properties. A referral fee is usually offered to employees who recommend the property when theirs are full.
- Employees of auto rental companies and visitor information centers.

Special rates and/or packages are advertised by lodging companies through direct e-mail to customers or on their social media pages. Lodging properties which are members of a franchise, for example Days Inn, have access to a **central reservation system** provided by the franchisor that includes national marketing and advertising.

RESERVATION INFORMATION

Customers making reservations online are prompted by the program they are using to provide the information required to book directly. Those who call establishments by phone are asked by the property's answering agent to furnish the pertinent data. In all cases, the items solicited when making a reservation include:

- Date of arrival and departure.
- Number of adults and children in the party.
- Number of rooms and their type, such as twin, double or queen.
- Address and phone number.
- Special discounts applicable, such as AARP, government or frequent traveler.
- Smoking or nonsmoking room.
- Credit card information.
- Special requests to be specified by the traveler, such as a quiet location, a crib needed, access to handicapped chair, or short distance from the elevator.

GROUP RESERVATIONS

In most cases, group reservations in medium and large properties are handled by the sales department in cooperation with the front office. A block of rooms is reserved in the system from which individual group members can select accommodations. As the reservations start coming in, the status of the rooms in the block is changed from 'blocked' to 'booked.' After a pre-determined date, the **cut-off date,** unbooked rooms are released back to the property. The establishment should honor reservation requests received after the cut-off date if rooms are available although the rates may be raised from group to rack price. In some cases, the organizers of the event take the reservations directly and, prior to arrival, the property is given a **rooming list** with the information on the arriving attendees.

Group blocks should be reserved only after an agreement is drawn between the property and the group organizer specifying the dates of arrival and departure, the cut-off date, the number and types of rooms to be held, complimentary accommodations if any, and billing arrangements.

Sources of group business include these:

- **Organized tours** are a popular way of combining cultural and outdoor activities for travelers that have limited time and resources to pursue their interests in themes like sightseeing, ecotourism, adventure travel and religious pilgrimages. Travel agents and social organizations are the major sales outlets of such tours. They sell packages that include leasing bus or plane space, booking rooms and other services at lodging properties and often providing guides.
- **Conventions, conferences** and **trade shows** organized by companies, clubs or associations generate, besides room business, revenue from the renting of meeting and exhibition space and F&B functions. Typically, room reservations for conventions are made by individual attendees who contact the property directly.

It should be ascertained whether or not reserving blocks would result in taking away rooms from transient business. Given that group rates are usually discounted, it may be a bad idea to displace customers who pay full prices and generate higher revenues.

TYPES OF RESERVATIONS

With **non-guaranteed reservations** the property agrees to hold rooms for guests until a specific reservation cancellation hour on the day of arrival, usually 4 or 6:00 PM. This type of reservation does not guarantee that payment for a **no-show** will be received, but if the guest doesn't arrive by the agreed-upon hour, the establishment is free to sell the room to someone else. If the guest arrives after the predetermined time, he can be accommodated based on availability.

On the other hand, a **guaranteed reservation** assures the guest that the property will hold a room or rooms through the night. The guest or a distribution channel entity, in turn, agrees to pay for the accommodation whether he arrives or not, unless the reservation is cancelled according to the establishment's cancellation procedure, which usually is 24 hours before the arrival date. The commonest method of guaranteeing a room is the use of a credit or debit card. In some cases, reservations are guaranteed by corporations after an agreement has been signed in which the company accepts the responsibility for any no-show of its employees travelling on business. Occasionally, a reservation can be guaranteed by an **advance deposit** made in cash and, rarely, by a **voucher** issued by travel agencies.

RESERVATION CONFIRMATION

A reservation confirmation is a contractual agreement by the property to hold a room for a traveler who intends to occupy it. The confirmed reservation can be either guaranteed or non-guaranteed. If the reservation is guaranteed, the credit card information of the customer is filed. Computer systems automatically send an email message at the time the reservation is completed. The content generally includes:

- Name of the traveler.
- Date of arrival.
- Date of departure.
- Room type and rate.
- Number of rooms and persons.
- Special requests, such as a non-smoking room or a crib for a small child.
- Stipulations for cancellation.
- Confirmation number.

By entering the confirmation number in the computer, the record of the reservation can be retrieved and made available for any change or cancellation. If the reservation is cancelled, a cancellation number should be issued which can prove, in case of future misunderstanding, that both the property and the customer cancelled the booking. Most credit card companies will only reject no-show billings if the property has issued a cancellation number. There is no need to issue a cancellation number for a non-guaranteed reservation as the commitment elapses when the time deadline passes. In the case of advance deposits, the amount is returned if the reservation is properly cancelled.

RESERVATIONS REPORTS

Computerized systems generate a series of reports that help monitor current and future room availability. The **transaction report** provides information such as the number of daily reservations, cancellations, rooms blocked and no-shows. The tracking of reservations requests refused by the hotel because of lack of availability is provided by the **turnaway report.** If the demand for rooms is consistently larger than the number of available units, hoteliers may need this information when considering the expansion of the property.

The **arrival** and **departure reports** indicate the number of customers expected to arrive and that of guests who will depart on a specific day. The list of stayovers that day is also provided. The reports are printed at intervals during the day to facilitate guest check-outs and check-ins, and to provide information about the number of reservations to be taken at any given time.

RESERVATIONS AS A FIRST STEP IN GUESTS' STAY

The reservation process involves the important first contact between the potential guest and the lodging property; its final purpose is to provide customers with accommodations that best meet their needs and wants in type, location, and special features. It is up to the person taking the reservation to determine the kind of traveler they are talking to so that they can offer features that best fit that particular customer. For example, corporate travelers may want to hear about concierge floors or the availability of Ethernet service while a customer traveling with his family might be interested in knowing about recreational facilities of the establishment or babysitting availability.

In lodging operations, guestrooms are considered to be perishable goods as the revenue for a room not sold today is lost forever. In fact, a room not sold represents some income not earned for the hotel while daily operating expenses for running a potentially full house must be covered. If, for instance, a 100-room establishment achieves an average of 96 percent occupancy monthly this will represent four guestrooms empty every night or 120 rooms at the end of the month. If the ADR for the hotel is, say, $135, the loss of revenue would have been $16,200 (120 x 135). It is therefore vital that the front office department have a method in place to maximize room occupancy at all times.

The volume of reservation requests should determine the amount of employees and equipment required. Bookings in large lodging establishments are handled by a reservations manager supervising a reservations department within the front office; in smaller properties the task of reserving rooms is conducted by employees at the front desk. Reservations are the first part of a continuous process that leads to guests' registration, their stay, and their departure. In most lodging properties a computerized system is used to record reservations by way of a few keyboard entries or by directly receiving the bookings from an interfacing outside source. The basic purposes of the reservation process are:

- To provide availability of dates and room types.
- To create a record of the reservation from which a daily arrival list can be generated.
- To supply information on rates to be quoted based on updated occupancy.
- To establish a reference for guest identification, preferences, credit rating, and patronage.
- To provide a source for special promotional campaigns.

By looking at the computer screen, front office employees can confirm a reservation on the spot or offer room alternatives if the date and type of room that the customer requests are not available. The alternatives usually include suggesting a different date, offering a different type of room or recommending other company properties.

Inquiries about room bookings can also be made in person, commonly known as **walk-ins,** by telephone, by e-mail or by fax. When the reservation is made through a computer, a confirmation which can be printed by the customer is generated together with a confirmation number. In all other cases, the booking is recorded in the system and the customer is given a confirmation number and/or sent an e-mail acknowledgment of the reservation.

The process used to enter reservations in computerized systems varies from system to system but in general it follows this sequence:

- Entering the "advanced reservations" program.
- Calling up the availability for the date in question by room type.
- Filling out the customer information.
- Finalizing the booking.

After the process is completed, the room count is automatically adjusted to reduce the number of rooms available. If a specific room has been selected, the room number is flagged so that it cannot be assigned to someone else. The computer can generate a list in alphabetical order of expected arrivals for any date or search for a particular name in the files.

It is advisable for innkeepers to create computer-stored records of guests' preferences, also known as **guest history.** The data are linked to the reservations files and provide information to the front office staff of a caller's past record, such as the customers' preferred room type and location, address, and special service requirements. Nothing can please a guest more than being told by a front desk clerk at the time of registration: "Mrs. Foster, as usual, we have reserved for you a room overlooking the garden" or "Mr. Peterson, we have placed feather pillows in your room which we know you prefer."

UPSELLING

Reservationists and front desk agents should be trained in how to motivate a guest to reserve a room or rooms at prices higher than average, for example, increasing the clerk's ability to convince a guest to book a junior suite rather than a double-size room. To some customers the rate of the room is a concern, in which case upselling should not be attempted. If a customer asks for the lowest rate or for a $70 special as advertised at the airport it is obvious that he/she is not ready to rent a highly priced room. In this case high-pressure selling techniques should be avoided. On the other hand, business travelers who can charge costs to their expense accounts may be willing to pay for the extra cost of a larger-than-average or a room with a better view, so the clerk should offer a choice of rates and explain how price relates to value.

A good approach is to start with a high rate and see if the customer is willing to pay for it; if he isn't, the clerk should work down to the lower prices. In all cases, the clerk should know the location and layout of the rooms very well. Instead of asking, "What type of room are you looking for" the customer should be told, "We have a quiet room with a view on the river for $150. Is that suitable for you?" If the customer hesitates, the clerk could continue, "We still have a queen-size room on the park side for $125."

An effective room-selling method consists in offering guests a choice of rate categories leaving the selection to them. For example, a junior-suite for $160, a queen room for $140, or a room with a double bed for $120. Often, customers select the middle choice; in this case the queen room. Another approach is to start from the top down, quoting the highest-priced room first and hoping that the guest will feel that after rejecting the highest rate the next price is a good compromise.

Both reservationists and front desk clerks should be trained to view upselling as providing good service to guests by offering choices while increasing revenue for the establishment. Upselling should not be perceived by employees as a way to extract extra revenue out of unsuspecting or unwilling travelers.

ROOM AVAILABILITY

The starting point of room availability for the current day is the number of rooms occupied at the time of taking a count; for future dates it is the number of reservations on hand. The availability for the current day can be understood by using this simple method:

total rooms in the house
- **rooms occupied yesterday**
+ **predicted checkout for today**

- **today's arrivals**
= **rooms available for sale**

However, because of the fluctuations of incoming reservations, date changes, no-shows, and cancellations that take place constantly, the number of rooms that are really available can change by the hour. In practice, **historical records** are figured out from averaged-out data gathered over long periods of time. To magnify the challenge, these trends are in turn influenced by factors such as special local events, season, location of the property, and weather. Although experienced front office managers develop a feel for predicting (in most cases accurately) the ups and downs of room availability, occasionally the prediction is off, resulting in either overbooking or underselling guest rooms.

HISTORICAL FACTORS

Each lodging property should develop a chart of historical records for every week of the year with average percentages of the fluctuations of guests' departures and arrivals which can be applied when predicting room availability. The following are historical factors to be taken into consideration at the time of determining availability:

- Percentage of **overstays:** Guests who stay longer than planned.
- Percentage of **understays:** Guests who check out earlier than expected.
- Percentage of **cancellations:** Guests who cancel their arrival.
- Percentage of **4-PM** (or 6-PM) no-shows: guests with reservations based on arrival-time. The percentage of this type of no-show is usually high.
- Percentage of **guaranteed reservations:** Guests guarantee the payment of the room with a credit card. The percentage of this type of no-show is usually very low.

The following example shows a possible application of historical records to a room-availability scenario. Let's assume that it is the beginning of the morning shift on Monday, May 5, in a 346-room hotel in Nashville, Tennessee. The computer system shows:

Rooms occupied	302
Confirmed 4-PM reservations	15
Guaranteed reservations	273
Predicted check-outs today	230
Rooms out of order	1

The **house count** at the time of working it out is -15. (346 - 302 – 15 – 273 + 230 – 1). That is, according to the computer we are 15 rooms oversold or **in the hole.** However, the historical records of this hotel indicate that for weekdays in May, the average no-shows for 4-PM reservations has been 12 percent and for guaranteed reservations 2 percent; the average overstays for predicted checkouts have been 2 percent and the understays 6 percent. The predicted cancellations are 1 percent of the total daily reservations.

The room count now is +7 (-15 + 22) after allowing for historical records.

Allowance for 4-PM no shows	+ 2 rooms (15 x .12)
Allowance for guaranteed reservations	+ 5 rooms (273 x .02)
Allowance for overstays	- 6 rooms (302 x .02)
Allowance for understays	+ 18 rooms (302 x .06)
Allowance for cancellations	+ 3 rooms (288 x .01)
Total	**22 rooms**

In this situation, the front office manager could take the calculated risk of taking seven additional reservations early in the morning to reach one hundred percent occupancy. Needless to say that room counts have to be conducted throughout the day to adjust for any unexpected fluctuations.

In order to minimize the effect of no-shows on the property's occupancy, lodging operators must protect themselves by asking customers making reservations to provide a credit card payment guarantee. If this is not feasible, a limit on the time to hold the accommodation must be set; typically, the limit is either 4 or 6 PM of the date of arrival. After this time the establishment is not obliged to honor the reservation although, if rooms are available, they are usually kept on file for possible check-in later. The cancelled 6 PM reservations are added automatically to the computer's inventory of available rooms.

In the rare case that a traveler doesn't own a credit card, an advance deposit should be required, usually amounting to the cost of one night's stay. Digital payments can be received by lodging companies from practically any country and in any currency in the world using e-commerce companies. Allied Wallet, is a provider of digital payment solutions to online merchants worldwide capable of processing payments in 196 countries and in 164 currencies. The URL for Allied Wallet is www.alliedwallet.com.

The collection of charges from credit card companies for no shows is often problematic. Many customers attempt to avoid payment by providing elaborate explanations on the expectation that the property will withdraw the charge. The typical excuse given for trying to avoid payment is that the reservation was cancelled by phone.

OVERBOOKING

The front office manager must strive each day to achieve 100 percent occupancy by combining reservations booked in advance with the up-to-the-moment call-in and walk-in sales. As already emphasized, in order to sell out the property, front desk supervisors must take calculated risks, including the possibility of **walking a guest**—rejecting a guest who has a confirmed reservation. Although some lodging companies have standing policies against **overbooking,** the most common practice in the industry is to attempt to fill every room in the house every day. Obviously, the worst drawback in overselling is walking a guest. In this case, the establishment must honor its commitment by compensating the displaced person(s) to mitigate the inconvenience. Traditionally, the property may:

- Comp the room(s) at another facility of the same quality.
- Provide free transportation to the new location.
- Make the necessary telephone calls to notify others of the change of accommodation.
- Forward mail and messages.
- Offer a discount to be applied to a future reservation.
- Write a formal letter of apology.

Obviously, the clerk or manager on duty should profusely apologize, assure the guest that an alternative suitable accommodation has been made and that it will be complimentary for the inconvenience caused. On one occasion, the author was walked from a 4-star hotel in Stuttgart, Germany, and sent to a casual guest house nearby of inferior quality without receiving a simple apology. Needless to say, I never booked that hotel again.

Usually, the extent to which a property may oversell is up to the discretion of front office managers. On the other hand, some lodging companies have the policy of avoiding walking guests at all costs accepting, say, 98 percent occupancy as a perfect sell or **full house**.

If the policy for overbooking is 5 percent beyond the properties' total capacity, a simple method of determining the number of reservations to be accepted in a 330-room property can be illustrated as follows:

Rooms in the house	330
105 percent of 330	346
Minus stayovers	150
Minus today's reservations	140
Minus out-of-order rooms	1
OK to sell	**55 rooms**

From this calculation, the front office manager would tell the staff at the start of the day to accept 55 reservations, counting on an overbooking factor of 5 percent. Of course, the number of checkouts, stayovers, and cancellations should be monitored continuously as the day goes by.

Overbooking raises the issue of whether the practice is legal. The letter of the law indicates that a guest who fails to take up a confirmed accommodation is guilty of breach of contract, and a lodging property which fails to supply the accommodation is also guilty of breach of contract. On the other hand, hoteliers who suffer a certain number of no shows argue that overbooking is the most effective way to conduct business.

ON-LINE RESERVATIONS PROGRAMS

Technology is used in practically every reservations program of lodging operations. Hoteliers have the option of installing an in-house system using stand-alone PC's or contracting with companies that offer cloud-based online reservations capabilities.

Historically, travel industry reservations systems started in the 1960s with the Sabre Global Distribution System created for American Airlines. The lodging industry followed with Holidex, the Holiday Inn company world's first hotel computer reservation system (CRS). Today, there are several web-based booking engines on the market that can be made compatible with the same database used by the property's management system. The Easy Innkeeping Hotel Company, for instance, offers a web-based software product that includes a reservations program that integrates with GDS/ADS and credit card processing. The reservations module provides options to add and update bookings, generate reports, and so on. The program includes these features:

- A screen dashboard with icons for accessing the different components of the software.
- The reservations icon that displays daily, weekly, and monthly room availability charts.
- A chart that can be set up either by room type, guest name or room number.
- The room type chart shows a summary of available rooms. Each room can be expanded to see any reservation details and its housekeeping status.
- The quick reservations screen can be used to answer any incoming call that is being received or for walk-in customers at the counter. Here arrival and departure dates are entered.
- Guest information can be recalled from previous stays to update the state of the reservation or to select from the pool of available rooms, record the referral source, capture credit card details, and apply deposits if necessary.
- Once the reservation is completed, an e-mail can be sent automatically to confirm the booking.
- The "find reservation" icon can display any reservation already in the system.
- Guests can directly reserve rooms in the system, pay with a credit card, and receive automatic confirmations by e-mail.

The URL of Easy Innkeeping is www.easyinnkeeping.com and its webpage includes a step-by-step demo that explains in detail how to deal with any aspect of room reservations.

Computerized systems are formatted to keep a close inventory of reservations by controlling room availability and generating reservation-related reports. Table 9.1 shows a basic computer display for arrival, stayovers, and departures of a 310-room hotel.

Date	Stayover	Departures	Arrivals	Rooms sold	Rooms unsold
5/15	201	67	105	306	4
5/16	244	62	66	310	0
5/17	190	120	98	288	22

TABLE 9.1 RESERVATIONS REPORT FOR MAY 15, 20.., AT 08:05 AM

In addition, computerized systems can generate reports by room type, guest name and any other programmed characteristics. When a reservation, cancellation, no-show, walk-in or change is inputted, room availability is automatically updated.

THE FUTURE OF RESERVATIONS THROUGH DISTRIBUTION CHANNELS

The number of intermediaries in the digital travel market is wielding a substantial influence as controllers of the reservations traffic while imposing fees for directing customer bookings to lodging properties. The combination of high booking volume controlled by these third-party intermediaries, the cost imposed for their services, and the pressure on rates are challenging hospitality companies to maintain profit levels.

A report issued by AH&LA and STR emphasizes that the reservations distribution landscape is changing with a new breed of third-party intermediaries, such as Google, Facebook, and Apple, which are becoming the preferred points of entry for customers to do their travel shopping. This emerging new network of third-parties will charge substantial fees for referrals to lodging properties. Although they offer great opportunities, how the hotel brands manage them will be critical to the longer-term outcomes and hoteliers will have to remain vigilant to ensure that each new channel generates a reasonable return on investment. In addition, new technologies, like voice and map-activated apps, will become attractive substitutes to the traditional search engine browser. It is a fact that when these third parties send a hotel its business directly, they charge referral or media fees and these bookings still require an interfacing technology infrastructure to support the transactions, all adding to cost.

The report predicts that the prominence and transparency of rates on the Internet and emerging mobile applications, and the concern for keeping the same rates in all channels, may result in a single-rate pricing structure for many lodging properties. This will undermine the marketing function which is a discipline built on a foundation that calls for offering relevant products and services with corresponding prices by segment in order to best meet the needs of each customer group. In other words, rates will be diluted by the pressure to keep online rates as low as possible because of the propensity of lodging operations to think that the demand generated by lower prices will always compensate for the reduction in price. With the proliferation of distribution channels, it is imperative for lodging marketers to understand which promotional efforts are to be credited for their bookings.

KEY TERMS

Advance deposit
Affiliate reservation networks
Arrival report
Central reservation system
Cut-off date
Departure report
Distribution channels
Full house
Guaranteed reservation
Guest history
Historical records (reservations)
House count
In-the-hole
Non-guaranteed reservation
No-show
Organized tours
Overbooking
Overstay
Rooming list
Rooms in the hole
Transaction report (reservations)
Travel agency voucher
Turnaway report
Understay
Upselling
Voucher

Walk-in
Walking a guest

DISCUSSION AND REVIEW QUESTIONS

11. What do you understand by "affiliate reservation networks?"
12. On taking a reservation by phone, what **three** pieces of information would you ask a caller?
13. Describe the purpose of "rooming lists."
14. Why is it advisable for innkeepers to create computer-stored records of guests' preferences, also known as **guest history** records?
15. At the beginning of the morning shift, the computer system goes down. Work out the number of rooms available from the following information:

Total number of rooms of the property	310
Number of rooms occupied last night	305
Today's reservations	175
Today's departures	190

16. What is an acceptable protocol to have in place for "walked" guests?
17. Discuss the pros and cons of overbooking in lodging establishments.
18. What guest information is necessary for a front desk clerk to guarantee a reservation?
19. What is the purpose of a reservation cancellation number?
20. What management reports can be generated from reservation data?

PRACTICAL SITUATIONS

Situation 9.1

Managing Occupancy

Frank Weiss is the front office manager of the 350-room Juan de Fuca Hotel in Juneau, Alaska. It is 8 o'clock in the morning and the computer is down. Last night, the occupancy percentage was 90. The hotel's predicted number of stay-overs is six rooms and that of under-stays three. One hundred and twenty rooms are scheduled to depart by 1 PM, check-out time. The number of reservations is 82. Based on historical records, 2 percent of these reservations will not show up. No rooms are out of order.

Frank receives a call from the marine division of Alaska Travel Inc. wanting to reserve 55 rooms for the passengers of the cruise ship Polar Star which is making an unscheduled docking at Juneau's harbor because of engine malfunction.

ASSIGNMENT:

1. What is the hotel's room count?
2. Should Frank accept the reservation of the 55 rooms?

Situation 9.2

Analysis of a Room Reservation

You are planning a trip to Orlando, Florida, with your spouse and two small children. Because it is the first out-of-the-state family vacation that you have taken, you want to book a room in a hotel or resort that is part of a national chain to ensure that you have a flawless experience. Your reservation is from June 18th (arrival) until June 25 (departure). Go online and find out the cost of a room per night using the following sources:

- Travelocity: www.travelocity.com
- lmt: www.lastminutetravel.com
- The central reservation URL of the chain to which the hotel/resort belongs.
- The Webpage of the hotel/resort.

In addition, call the hotel/resort directly for price information.

ASSIGNMENT:

Compile a report after making the contacts listed above, including all prices quoted to you, a critique of the webpages visited, and a review of the conversation with the reservation clerk on duty when you made the call.

Situation 9.3

Daily Room Count

Natalia Kraska has been working as a reservation supervisor at a 500-room resort in Marina Del Rey, California. The resort computers are down, and she has to gather and organize the filed written backup records for the day's arrivals. After tallying the reservations by category she completes the following account:

Rooms occupied yesterday	452
Reservations guaranteed for late-arrival	170
Predicted checkouts for today	130
Rooms out of order none	
Confirmed 4 PM reservations	22

Historical records applicable to the date considered:

Average no-shows for 4PM reservations	15%
Average no-shows for late-arrival	2%
Average overstays for predicted checkouts	4%
Average under-stays	5%
Average cancellations for total reservations	2%

ASSIGNMENT:

What is the room count for the day at the beginning of the morning shift?

CASE STUDY 9.1

Overbooking

Andrew Palmer is supervising the evening shift at a 235-room hotel located near the Anaheim Convention Center. At 11:45 PM, he receives a call from the visitor's center at the Long Beach Municipal airport requesting two rooms for the night for a VIP and his family who have just missed their outbound flight. Andrew asks the caller to stay on the line while he finds out whether he can accept the reservation. Looking at the status report on the computer screen, he reads the following:

Rooms occupied	230
Rooms out of order	0
Guaranteed arrivals	6
Rooms available	- 1

Mr. Palmer knows that according to the historical records of the hotel, 5 percent of daily reservations are no-shows. The total reservations for the day are 146 rooms.

Andrew has always been nervous about having to make overbooking decisions. This situation reminds him of the ethics discussions he had in college on whether or not to take advantage of guests in order to improve the bottom line. At the same time, he is also aware of the standing policy of the front desk to sell out every night if at all possible.

Andrew pulls out the backup paperwork for the remaining reservations. They show the following:

1 room—Letter signed by the front office manager 3 months ago confirming the reservation of a business executive from Peru. No credit card guarantee.

1 room—Reservation form filled out by the hotel's sales manager for a meeting planner arriving to inspect the property for a future convention.

4 rooms—Mastercard-guaranteed for late arrival.

Andrew knows that he is already one room in the hole. Nevertheless, recognizing that it is almost midnight he decides to make sure that the hotel is sold out that night. He goes back to the telephone and accepts the two rooms for the VIP waiting at the airport.

ASSIGNMENT:

Consider the situation and argue in favor or against Andrew's decision. What would you have done?

PART 4

FRONT OFFICE OPERATIONS

CHAPTER 10

REGISTRATION AND GUEST ACCOUNTING

CHAPTER OBJECTIVES

- Describe the procedures involved during the registration phase at the front desk.
- Explain the advantages of preregistering guests.
- Learn about custody of guest property.
- Explain the need for establishing credit at the time of registration.
- Discuss the check-in process.
- Learn about legal registration requirements pertaining to travelers and innkeepers.
- Describe the methods used for recordkeeping of charges and credits during guests' stay.

OVERVIEW

The basic process of rooming guests involves the task of assigning a number of rooms to a given number of incoming customers until the house is full. Registration of guests should be conducted as quickly as possible to avoid long lines and delays but, at the same time, check-in should be accurate for it is during this time that lasting impressions are made. Sequentially, the major steps in registering guests include processing the reservation, if any, assigning the room, and getting a method of payment.

The registration process is also the time for the front desk to gather information on how guests plan to settle their accounts when they check out. This chapter also describes procedures to ensure that all charges and credits are posted accurately to the right accounts during guests' stay.

GUEST ARRIVAL

Guests may arrive at lodging properties by car, bus, van or simply by walking from a railroad or bus station nearby. In large hotels, an outside porter (doorperson) opens the door of vehicles, welcomes arriving travelers, and signals to a uniformed attendant (bellperson) to carry luggage if customers ask for this service. A parking valet is summoned to the curb if guests' vehicles are to be driven to a designated parking lot. In smaller properties, the bell staff is usually positioned by the bell stand from where they are ready to assist customers with their bags if they so desire or to direct them to the location of the front desk.

Preparations for guests' registration usually begin with the night clerk printing an **arrival report** with the names of the day's incoming travelers. The morning shift agent then assigns rooms to the expected check-ins, blocking these in the computer. Attention is given to special requests specified on reservations, such as rooms with ocean view, non-smoking and near or away from the elevator. The arrival report may also indicate whether the rooms are reserved for early arrival or to be held for late registration, if the customers are attending a convention at the property, who is a **VIP,** if fruit or flowers are to be sent as a courtesy of management, or whether there is mail or messages waiting for the incoming guests. Unexpected early or walk-in arrivals may require juggling around blocked rooms as the property begins to fill.

Front office employees must be aware of the different characteristics of the property's room inventory when assigning accommodations to the day's arrivals. Some common definitions of room types are:

- **Single:** A room booked for one person.
- **Double:** A room booked for two people or a room with one double-size bed.
- **Triple:** A room booked for three people.
- **Quad:** A room booked for four people.
- **Twin:** A room with two twin-size beds.
- **Queen:** A room with one queen-size bed.
- **King:** A room with one king-size bed.
- **Double/double; queen/queen;** or **king/king:** Rooms with two beds of the same size.
- **Parlor:** A room with a convertible or Murphy bed.
- **Suite:** A combination living room and bedroom.
- **Adjacent rooms:** Rooms next to each other.
- **Connecting rooms:** Rooms with a connecting door between them.
- **ADA-accessible:** A room designed for disabled travelers.

The arrival function includes the guests' registration and rooming. Generally, the allocation of rooms for incoming travelers should be prioritized as follows:

1. Guests with special requirements because of disability.
2. VIPs to be assigned the best located rooms in the house.
3. Members of the chain or property loyalty program.
4. Regular guests asking for specific rooms, such as adjacent to each other or connecting.
5. Other travelers.

Once the guest is at the desk, the clerk verifies his/her name, the type of room desired, the rate, the number of people in the party, the billing and e-mail addresses, and the expected departure date. This information constitutes the registration record of the guest. Most lodging establishments request identification at check-in, such as driver's license, military card or passport, to comply with statutes issued by local authorities.

In receiving arrivals, the uniformed personnel first and the front desk agent later are in charge of welcoming the newcomer and of introducing the establishment's characteristics to guests. An efficient staff indicates an efficient property. Because this is the moment when the traveler experiences the first impression of the establishment there are polite words and phrases that should be repeated again and again by all employees who come in contact with customers, especially "please" and "thank you."

THE GUESTS' NAME

Nothing pleases guests more than hearing their names repeated throughout their stay in a hospitality establishment. Although in parts of the US first names are often used, this may be considered insulting by older and foreign guests. It is preferable to use the last name with the designation Mr., Ms. or Mrs. The first to recognize guests should be the bell staff if they happen to see their names on the nametags on their luggage; the registration agent is second, getting the name from the reservation information in the computer. If the guest has asked for assistance with luggage, the bellperson should be attentive enough to get the name from the person at the front office or from the bags' nametags and repeat it as he/she ushers the guest towards the elevator: "This way please, Mrs. Lowenthal." Having heard her name three times, Mrs. Lowenthal probably can't help feeling more relaxed and appreciative.

Section housekeepers should be provided with guests' names on the list of rooms to be cleaned from which they can read the name of the person registered before knocking at the guestroom door. When they are about to service the room, they can look up the name and, if the guest answers, be ready to say, "Mrs. Lowenthal, this is the housekeeper. Can I make up your room?" Room service should do the same by writing the name of the guest on the order. In this case, when tapping on the door, the server can say, "Mrs. Lowenthal, this is the waiter with your breakfast." Mrs. Lowenthal will hear yet again her name at the time of checking out when the clerk will say: "Thank you very much, Mrs. Lowenthal. Come back to see us again."

PREREGISTRATION OF GUESTS

During the reservation process, guests are asked to provide most of the information needed to complete their registration at the time they arrive at the property. Preregistering guests who have reserved rooms helps speed up check-in. All that is needed is for the guest to verify the information printed by the computer on a registration form, sign it, and receive the room door-opening card from the clerk. This service is greatly appreciated by travelers who don't have to provide the same data about themselves twice. A few alternatives to guest registration at the front desk are to complete the check-in process at a concierge desk (for VIPs) or to do so in the courtesy van for hotels near airports.

Preregistration is also a common practice for groups and conventions to speed up the check-in process. Groups may arrive at the property within a short time of each other and a long wait in line does not make for good guest relations. As with regular guests, rooms are assigned before arrival and registration involves just signing individual registration cards, saving time otherwise used for making the room assignment. On the day of arrival, the preregistered rooms are blocked off in the computer, the room numbers are assigned and the card keys are placed in individual envelopes to be handed to guests.

HANDLING GUEST MAIL

Messages, letters, and packages for guests staying in the house are handled by the head porter in large hotels. Classic properties in the United States and most European hotels still have pigeon holes for every room where guest mail is kept. New technologies, however, have considerably reduced the need to handle mail, especially with devices such as voice mail, e-mail, and ePads.

In smaller properties, the front desk handles mail and messages for guests. In this case, it is advisable to use a container with alphabetical dividers in which the pieces are kept. If the mail or messages are for incoming customers, the reservation entry in the computer should be flagged with the phrase "has mail."

CUSTODY OF GUEST PROPERTY

According to Adjusters International, a disaster recovery consultant company, traditionally under common law an innkeeper was liable for loss or damage to guests' property for the full value, unless the loss was caused by an act of nature, such as tornadoes or earthquakes, civil unrest, or the fault of the guest. Today this general rule still exists although states have modified the law by enacting statutes that limit the hotel's liability, provided that it complies with the statutory requirements.

Although amounts vary from state to state, liability ordinarily is limited to a specific figure. Lodging properties typically post conspicuous notices indicating that valuables worth more than a certain amount, for example $500, must be deposited in the property's safe in order to be covered for any loss. A Rhode Island statute, for instance, states that if an establishment provides a safe for depositing money, jewelry, and the like, informs guests by posting a notice to that effect, and guests fail to deposit their valuables in the safe, the property is not liable for any loss of the valuables. It also states that the property is not obligated to accept valuables for safekeeping that exceed $500 in value. If a guest deposits property with a value exceeding $500 in the safe, the hotel is not responsible for loss of the property for more than $500, unless there is a special agreement for a greater amount.

Another example is a New Mexico statute which states that the establishment is liable to its guests for loss of their property that is caused by the theft of its staff, up to a limit of $1,000. However, if the property provides a suitable safe for keeping valuables and informs guests by posting a printed notice in guestrooms and guests fail to deposit their valuables in the safe, the establishment is not liable.

Since statues vary by state, it is important that front office employees are familiar with the law in the state where they operate. The website www.adjustersinternational.com offers descriptions of the various state statutes.

Most lodging properties offer in-room safes but, if this is not the case, lodging properties have a duty to accept guests' articles for safe keeping. In practice, most hotels install a safe deposit box in the front office area and make this part of the front office's responsibility. Typically, guests are asked to place valuables for deposit in an envelope made from strong paper which should be sealed in the presence of a front office clerk. The envelope is marked with the guest's name and room number and a receipt is issued that may include the approximate value to avoid possible disagreement later on. The guest must produce the receipt when reclaiming the envelope or show proof of his/her identity if the receipt has been lost. If it is, the guest should sign a waiver discharging the property of any further liability.

An alternative to a large safe deposit box is to provide individual smaller deposit boxes in the front office area. These safes require the use of two keys, one held by the front office, the second issued to the guest against a signature. The guest is asked to sign a log book every time he or she wishes to open the box, allowing the guest service agent to compare signatures.

ESTABLISHING CREDIT

During the registration process information on how guests plan to settle their accounts is gathered. A phrase like "How do you intend to settle your account, Mrs. Lowenthal?" should be used. The most common method of establishing credit for guests is for them to provide a credit or debit card number and its expiration date at the time of making the reservation or when registering as transient at the property. Often, the name on the credit card is asked for when reserving by phone or online and proof of identification, such as a driver's license, when registering in person.

The on-line credit card validator or authorization terminal provides instantaneous approval or denial of the card tendered and issues an **authorization code** (or **denial code)** for the guests' anticipated transactions. For instance, for a guest registering for two nights in a $100-per-night room, a $300 authorization might be asked from the credit card company to allow for room taxes and other chargeable services. In some cases, credit card companies assign a **floor limit** or maximum amount allowed to be charged on behalf of the guest. When the amount exceeds the floor limit, the front office should contact the credit card company to request additional credit to cover the transaction. Ideally, lodging establishments should install a PMS that includes interfaced credit card processing capabilities.

When guests stay for an extended period of time, a property may decide to reserve credit in the credit card account for the amount anticipated to be necessary to cover charges. When a guest decides to check out earlier than planned, the establishment should notify the credit card company to release the unused portion of the reserved credit.

CREDIT FOR GROUPS

Tour or other groups staying in the property may ask to establish a **master account** where the charges incurred by the group as a whole are posted. Typically these charges include room and tax and functions, all other charges being the responsibility of the individuals in the group.

Often, lodging properties agree to bill the guest's company for the total or partial charges in the folio. **Direct billing** arrangements must be established between the property and the company in writing which involves the completion of a credit application. At check-out, the group leader is asked to sign the bill after approving its total, and a statement is sent to the company for payment. Charges to be invoiced may include these:

- All charges
- All charges except for incidentals
- Room only
- Room and breakfast
- Room, breakfast and one meal
- Room and meals

If the agreement doesn't cover all charges, a second folio to be settled directly by guests is opened to cover the amounts not included in the direct billing agreement. In this case, credit information must be obtained from each member of the group.

A very small number of travelers do not possess a credit card. In this case an advance deposit is required at the time the reservation is made or cash is collected at the time of check-in. In general, cash is understood as bank notes, bank checks, traveler's checks or money orders. If a guest pays cash for one night only, it is the responsibility of the front desk to collect the cost of the room(s) plus tax for the next day(s). If the price of the room is not collected ahead of time, the "guest" may decide to leave without checking out at the front desk. These "guests," called **skippers,** can be recognized by trained housekeepers as they tend to travel light or with no luggage at all.

Usually, the following rules are adopted by hotels to reduce losses:

1. Checks issued by a second or third party are not acceptable.
2. No checks drawn on a foreign bank are accepted.
3. Post-dated checks are not accepted.
4. The use of electronic check conversion machines by lodging establishments is a must. These check processing systems verify check payments, credit cards, and gift cards using a magnetic card reader. Checkreadi, for instance, offer dial up or Internet check-reader services for check verification that protect against bad, bounced, and insufficient-funds check loss. The equipment provides an integrated modem for direct access to electronic check processing. Checkreadi's URL is www.checkreadi.com.
5. No checks should be cashed for minors.
6. No cash should be refunded if an initial payment was made by personal check.
7. Any personal check should be made payable to the property, not to "cash," unless the check is intended specifically to obtain cash.
8. Guests paying cash at registration are not allowed to charge expenses to their room account. A **no-post status** is entered in the computer to inform all outlets that these guests cannot charge any service to their folios.

Guests who pay cash at the time of registration are not extended in-house credit; that is the computer system is set to not allow the employees of revenue outlets to post charges to guest accounts that are not authorized for in-house credit.

Some lodging properties allow guests to cash personal checks with credit cards that provide a check-cashing guarantee; in this case, the front office agent should write the card information on the back of the check. If credit is denied by a credit card company, the registration clerk should ask for a different card or for another means of payment. If the guest can provide no other type of credit, the clerk must refer the issue to his/her supervisor who should discuss the matter in private with the guest.

TRAVELER'S CHECKS

Prior to credit cards, the use of traveler's checks was one of the major methods of establishing credit at hotels, the others being bank checks and currency; today they are used by customers who don't want to use credit or debit cards or carry a lot of cash. Traveler's checks are issued by major banks and financial institutions in different currencies. Customers buy them in their own countries and then make payments or change them into the currency of the countries they are visiting.

Customers have to sign traveler's checks at the time of purchase and they don't become valid until they are countersigned in the presence of a merchant. Traveler's checks bear a commission fee, paid by the buyer, which is applied to defray the cost of administration and to cover insurance against accidental loss or theft. To avoid forgery of the bearer's signature, a clerk cashing traveler's checks should ask for documentary evidence of identity, such as a passport.

Front office employees receiving traveler's checks in payment for services should ask that checks be signed in their presence and verify that the two signatures are similar. The exchange value is then worked out and the property's commission (if any) deducted from the total. Table 10.1 is an example of a traveler's check transaction at a hotel in the United States. A guest wants to settle his $398.50 account at check-out with ten American Express 50-pound sterling traveler's check denominations issued in Edinburgh, Scotland.

Currency Exchange:	1 GBP =	1.61605 USD
Total bill	$398.50	
Hotel commission	0.02 %	
Traveler's check currency value in US$	$808.02	(500 x 1.61605)
Hotel commission	- 16.16	(808.02 x 0.02)
Hotel bill	- 398.50	

Change back to guest = $393.36

Table 10.1 Settling a bill in the US with British-pound traveler's checks

GUEST CHECK-IN

An effective front office operation should show the state of readiness of all rooms at any given time. Situations where travelers are impatiently waiting in the lobby to register and be assigned accommodations should always be avoided. Fortunately, room management software programs show up-to-the-moment information on guestroom status as well as on room availability. By entering any room number on the keyboard upon a guest's arrival, the guest service agent on duty can learn whether a room is ready for occupancy or is still on-change. Changes in room status are communicated instantly by the housekeeping department using an interfaced module. The clerk on duty can also find the characteristics of any room type, for example, which king-size room is available at a specific moment. Some of the registration-related reports that can be generated by a PMS are these:

- Alphabetical listing of guests with reservations.
- Alphabetical listing of registered guests.
- List of groups by date of arrival.
- Report of vacant rooms by number or type.
- Report of status of guest rooms at any given time.

Most lodging properties set a specific time, usually 2 PM, as the earliest time travelers can check in. However, often customers arrive before that hour which makes it challenging to have their rooms ready particularly if the house was full the previous night. Because guests feel inconvenienced when they have to wait in the lobby, the front desk staff should urge the housekeeping department to provide them with ready rooms as early as possible.

Arriving guests are checked against the arrivals report where their names are listed in alphabetical order. If travelers have not been preregistered, they are usually asked to sign a computer-generated registration form and to initial the type of room that has been assigned, its price, and the departure date. The purpose of registration is fourfold:

1. To satisfy the legal requirements of keeping a record of guests' stays.
2. To provide an internal record of guests checked in.
3. To confirm the acceptance by the guest of the terms and conditions of the accommodation.
4. To record the credit card number to pay for the total of the stay or for incidental charges if the room has been prepaid.

The guest information gathered during the reservation process may be transferred at the time of registration. The front desk agent usually gets the guest's record on the computer screen and proceeds to check in the traveler by filling the fields and adding the allocated room number, the guest's address, phone number, and e-mail information if they are not already in the system. For walk-in travelers the information is entered manually into the computer. When the property is full and walk-in customers cannot be accommodated, the guest service agent should express regret and offer assistance in locating lodging in a nearby establishment.

In most states, guests are required to sign a printout of the arrival record. This information becomes the source for creating a **guest history record** which can be used as a marketing tool by the sales department and in registering the guest on future visits to the property.

The computer system can tell the current status of every room in the house at all times. If a room is occupied, the screen will tell who is occupying it, for how long, and for how much. If the room is vacant, the system will show if it is ready for occupancy, blocked or out of order. As the registration process continues, the computer will remove allocated rooms from the list of available rooms. In the same way, the electronic memory of the system combines current room availability with the advance reservations program so that front office employees can see at a glance whether a particular room is flagged for future occupancy.

The status of guestrooms changes constantly during the day. The most common terms generally used in the lodging industry by both the front office and the housekeeping departments to indicate the state of guestrooms at any given time are:

- **Vacant and ready** the room has been inspected, and is ready for occupancy.
- **Vacant (on-change)** the room is not yet ready for re-sale.
- **Check-out** the guest has departed or is scheduled for departure today.
- **Late check-out** the guest is scheduled to depart later than the property's check-out time.
- **Do not disturb (DND)** the guest has placed the DND sign on the door.
- **Occupied** the room is occupied.
- **Sleep-out** a guest is registered but the room has not been used.
- **Out-of-order** the room cannot be sold.

Housekeeping departments using computerized programs also have access to room status information. For instance, when a guest is checked out at the front desk, housekeeping is alerted that the room needs cleaning; in turn, when the room is serviced and inspected, housekeeping enters the vacant-and-ready status that informs the front office that the room is available. The interface between housekeeping and front desk can also be made by entering a designated code in the telephone network.

SPECIAL REQUESTS

Registration is the time to determine guests' needs in order to avoid telephone calls from their rooms or that they reappear at the front desk asking for something they had requested at the time of making the reservation. In most cases, failure to follow up on requests made at check-in will cause a great deal of inconvenience at the time of checking out. For example, if a tour guide requested that all room charges be billed to a master folio and that all other services be posted to each tour member as incidentals, it would be very difficult at check-out time to separate total room charges from the incidentals of each guest. It is at the time of registration when billing and special requests should be identified. Some special requests to be determined by the check-in clerk include master and split folios, wake-up calls, and arrangements for transportation to the airport.

Once the registration form is signed and the credit details settled, the guest is provided with a key card and any information pertaining to the property, called a **rooming slip,** which usually contains a descriptive map for the location of restaurants, pool, workout room, and any other information about the property. Some establishments provide guests with a copy of the registration form and a passport-type handout with information about all facilities, like hours of operation of the outlets and telephone numbers they can use if service is required.

GROUP REGISTRATION

The arrival of groups can present a challenge to the front desk staff as it may involve registering many guests at the same time. One way of avoiding long lines at the desk is by using a separate table in the lobby to accommodate the group's arrival. For large groups, the tables should be equipped with interfaced computer terminals capable of providing a complete check-in process. The ideal scenario is when an organization allows each member to sign all charges to the master account; that is, when the company pays for everything. In this case, the group attendees do not have to show any method of payment at check-in. On the other hand, if each member of the group is responsible for all charges or for incidentals, individual credit card information is needed at the time of registration.

The distribution of luggage to the rooms by the bellstand can also present a challenge. The best approach is to schedule a sufficient number of uniformed personnel to deliver the bags within a reasonable period of time. Tour companies should have easily distinguishable luggage tags with guests' names attached to each bag for the bell staff to match with the room numbers listed on the master rooming sheet.

ESCORTING THE GUEST TO THE ROOM

After the registration process is completed, uniformed services provide escort assistance to guests on request. The bell staff should be knowledgeable of the area where the property is located and of the facilities offered by the establishment. After welcoming the guest, the bellperson should indicate the way to the room while explaining the location of outlets and services. This is the sequence usually followed to show the room to guests:

- Turning the light on.
- Checking that the room appearance is satisfactory.

- Placing bags on the luggage rack.
- Explaining how all fixtures in the room work.
- Mentioning equipment and supplies provided and services offered.
- Describing the establishment facilities and giving hours of operation.
- Mentioning the location of the nearest ice and vending machines.
- Wishing the guest a pleasant stay.

AUTOMATED CHECK-IN

Lobby check-in kiosks and computer terminals are being used nowadays as viable alternatives to desk registration, although they are not considered replacements for traditional front-office registration. The purpose is to provide the option of self-check-in as an alternative for those travelers who prefer this method rather than waiting in line at front desks. Although the directions on the screens are simple, often, the mechanical check-in is facilitated by an agent next to the kiosk who adds a personal touch to the experience while helping guests who need a quick walk-through of the technology. Automated check-in terminals are particularly useful when travelers walk into the registration areas of hotels only to find a long line of people trying to register. With check-in terminals, a transaction that could last several minutes can be completed in no more than thirty seconds on average.

Most kiosks are activated by credit card which is recognized by the machine. The screen displays the details of the reservation made previously that guests must confirm before they are issued a card key for access to their rooms. If the machine doesn't recognize the credit card, it senses that the owner is a transient guest and displays a menu showing the room types available and their prices. The traveler chooses a suitable accommodation and the machine prompts him/her to continue registering.

An advantage for hoteliers is that self-check-in machines can lower expenses by speeding up the registration process, especially for guests anxious to register and go upstairs. On the other hand, because check-ins are performed without any interaction between staff and guests, the major disadvantage is the loss of personal contact between the customer and the service agent so characteristic of hospitality operations. Most travelers prefer to be greeted by a pleasant, welcoming agent who can answer questions related to their stay at the property.

MOBILE CHECK-IN

As travelers are more mobile and global than ever before, lodging companies are adopting their check-in procedures to accommodate them. It is estimated that a large percentage of business travelers aged 21-39 use mobile devices for a faster, easier and convenient check-in.

Marriott Hotels, for instance, initially launched the mobile check-in at properties in the US and Canada and at 20 Marriott Hotels in 19 other countries. The company expects to complete the full global roll-out of mobile check-in and check-out services at all of its 500 properties by 2014.

Guests who use their Marriott app at Marriott properties can enjoy the following features:

- Mobile check-in up to two hours before their arrival.
- Automatic notification when the room is ready.
- Immediate handing of the guestroom key at the designated Mobile Check-in desk.

WAKE-UP CALLS

Although most rooms are equipped with electronic alarm clock/radio units and travelers use their smartphones for automated wake up, some guests ask the front office to be called by the property's automated wake-up systems. Needless to say this service is of paramount importance for travelers as, if it fails, a guest can miss a flight or a critical business meeting.

The DuVoice Corporation, offers the InnDesk Web Console that can be integrated in lodging PMS systems. The program can deliver customized announcements, from the simple "This is your wake-up call" message to "Thank you for staying at the Royal Hotel. Be sure to join us for our breakfast buffet..." or "The weather forecast today is for sun and 74 degrees Fahrenheit." The messages can be updated on a daily basis. The number of wakeup call retries and the intervals between retry attempts before determining that the guest has failed to answer can also be programmed. The calls can be set and delivered in several languages. The language from the guest portfolio in the PMS is automatically received on check-in or can be selected manually in the console.

DuVoice's InnDesk Web Console wake-up-call system allows guests to control by themselves the time they want to be woken up using the room telephone which provides an easy-to-use menu to be followed. If the guest fails to answer the call and the retries that follow, the system will register it as a failed wakeup call. The front office staff is then alerted by a printed message showing the guest name and room number of the failed call. Any time that there is a question about whether a wakeup call was correctly delivered, the front office staff can refer to the report issued by InnDesk. The report states the time each wakeup call was set, who set it (if guest or front office employee), and when the call and each retry was attempted. The DuVoice URL is www.duvoice.com.

MISHAPS THAT CAN TAKE PLACE AT CHECK-IN TIME

Some common errors that can take place during registration include:

- *A guest who arrives with a confirmed reservation which cannot be found because misspelling of the name or otherwise.* If rooms are available, the front desk clerk should check in the guest first and look for the reservation later.
- *A guest who arrives with a confirmed reservation and no rooms are available.* The guest is walked following the guidelines stated in the property's standard operating procedures (SOPs). Walking VIPs, celebrities, meeting planners, and returning customers should be avoided if at all possible. The front office manager or manager on duty should in person look after the guest to be walked.
- *A guest is given the cardkey of a room that is not ready or properly cleaned.* The traveler should be checked in an upgraded room, if available, to compensate for the inconvenience.
- *A guest stating that the rate quoted by a reservationist is lower than the price announced to him at check-in.* If the quote is in writing, the price should be honored.

Upgrading the room reserved while charging the original price quoted is a common way of compensating guests for any inconvenience caused by the staff. For example, if a traveler has to wait a long time for a room with a double-size bed being made ready by housekeeping, the front office manager may decide to assign a room with, say, a king-size bed to compensate for the delay. Assigning a room with a nice view rather than one which overlooks an inside patio may also be appropriate to make up for the trouble.

PMS CHECK-IN

Registration functions offered by automated systems are prompted for front desk agents to follow. Although the software modules differ from company to company, all of them are easy to operate and practically error-proof. The comprehensive PMS on the cloud sold by Hotelogix, for instance, offers the following features:

- Automatic allocation of rooms to guests on check-in for maximum yield and optimal usage of room inventory.
- Printing of check-in card with an option to do so in advance of registration.
- Optional self-service check-in and out in kiosks.
- Multiple guest names and sharers per room.
- Cancellation of check-ins before the start of night audit.
- Group check-ins.
- Direct interface with online credit card payments and secure web-based credit card payments.

- Automatic allocation of meals and other add-on services for inclusive rates.

The URL for Hotelogix is www.hotelogix.com .

LEGAL REGISTRATION REQUIREMENTS

Generally, an innkeeper is obliged to receive all persons who present themselves as guests. The relationship between innkeeper and guest is a mutual contractual one by which the traveler requests an accommodation and the innkeeper provides one that the customer can afford. In the US, a traveler may stay at a hotel without registering as it is not legally mandatory for a guest to sign a register as evidence of the contract. It is a mere matter of oral consent, and is legal without further formality. However, a guest of the registered occupant of a room who shares such room with him/her without the knowledge or consent of the innkeeper will not be treated as a guest of the hotel. Likewise, if a registered guest, without permission from anyone representing the property, transferred a room to another person, that person is not considered to be a guest and doesn't have the legal right to enter or remain on the premises against the will of the innkeeper.

In the absence of a specific constitutional state or local law requiring guests to show ID, a lodging property in the US that turns away a prospective guest solely for refusal to show ID would almost certainly be in violation of their state's innkeeper's law. This is not the case in other countries. In the European Union (EU) for instance, the collection of hotel guest data for use by security services is mandatory. In fact, within the EU, Article 45 of the Schengen Implementing Convention makes hotel guest registration data a requirement of member states and specifies the information to be collected. In British Columbia, Canada, innkeepers must provide and keep a suitable method for the registration of all persons provided with sleeping, camping or other accommodation. The registration records must be open at all times for inspection by the police.

THE RIGHTS OF TRAVELERS

Hospitality establishments are places that travelers need to use for lodging and eating, and it is therefore the business of hospitality operators to provide services to all customers. This common law practice of old was reasserted by the Civil Rights Act of 1964, which determined that the Constitution grants all individuals the right of freedom of contract and that it protects travelers against discrimination in favor or against any person because of race, religion, gender, or age. Subsequently, the Civil Rights Act was extended to cover disabled guests. In 1991, the **Americans with Disabilities Act (ADA)** mandated the elimination of discrimination against individuals with disabilities. It is therefore, illegal to refuse service on the basis of disability; for example, to a person in a wheelchair. Because a goal of the act is to ensure that goods and services are provided to disabled persons, hospitality establishments must adjust their facilities to accommodate guests with disabilities such as by providing accessible bathrooms.

The law also protects the privacy of guests. For example, the management of a hospitality establishment cannot consent to a search by the police of a guest's room without a warrant nor does it have a legal right to disclose phone calls made by a guest without due legal process.

Owners of hospitality properties, however, can reserve the right to refuse service in cases of disorderly conduct, inappropriate attire, breaking a nonsmoking regulation, or being underage. Hotel operators can request police assistance to remove individuals who have been asked to leave the premises on sufficient grounds. Private clubs that are not places of public entertainment can limit attendance to members and their guests.

THE RIGHTS OF INNKEEPERS

Some legal reasons for refusing to receive a guest include lack of room availability, drunk or disorderly behavior or the person's inability to pay for hotel services. However, because of the legalities involved in refusing certain customers, management should be consulted in any questionable case.

Although guests have a right to privacy, an innkeeper has the prerogative of being in control of the establishment's rooms. Management has the right to move a guest to a new room for reasonable cause or the right to enter a room in case of an emergency. The innkeeper also has the right to evict guests for nonpayment of rooms or services, for misconduct, and for overstaying an agreed-upon time limit. Management cannot use force to eject guests but can resort to **lock out**—the act of preventing access to a room while the occupier is away—until a settlement is reached.

ACCOUNTING RECORDS OF CHARGES AND CREDITS DURING THE GUEST'S STAY

As soon as the guest is checked into the system, an electronic folio is created and the accounting process begins. During the guests' stay, a series of transactions take place that need to be processed and posted in each account. The PMS guest-account management program facilitates control of all guests' outstanding balances. Large lodging establishments offer a number of revenue-generating outlets which guests can use while staying at the property, such as restaurants, bars, valet service, spa, telephone, gift shop, in-room movies and minibars. Most of these outlets are interfaced with the property management system allowing for any purchase to be charged to the electronic guest's accounts automatically.

The **guest's folio** (account) is debited with the charges guests incurred from the restaurant, bar, spa, cash advances, telephone, and so on. Thus, the guest folio shows with the stroke of a key, besides the rate charged for the room, a detailed record of all business transactions that have taken place between individual guests and the establishment's interfaced outlets. The basic purpose of accounting systems in lodging operations is twofold:

- To keep accurate records of guest charges and credits.
- To generate analytical reports of all transactions.

Likewise, the folio is credited with payments, rebates, discounts, advanced deposits, allowances, and adjustments. When the total of debits minus the credits on a folio is zero (typically after the guest has checked out), all charges have been taken care of and the transaction phase of the guest's stay at the property is completed.

Guests can take care of their accounts' debit balances by paying with a credit or debit card, cash, traveler's and bank checks or by charging the amount to the **city ledger,** the account comprising those folios whose totals will be billed to a company or organization that maintains a line of credit with the establishment. The city ledger balance is credited when payment is received later on from the holders of each account.

Obviously, all charges incurred at points-of-sale should be posted in the system as soon as they take place as guests may decide to check out at any given moment. The aggregate of outstanding balances of the folios of all guests in the property is called the **transient guest ledger.** The purpose of this ledger is to record in detail all the charges and credit transactions pertaining to guest accounts during the period between registration and departure. Each individual folio must be carefully monitored to ensure that the amount charged by the guest is within the credit established at check-in. The guest accounting module can be programmed to set guest credit limits and flag those folios which are close to or have exceeded the credit ceiling. In most first-class lodging properties, guests can review their individual folios on their in-room television sets that interface with the property's accounting program and can check out at their convenience without having to line up at the front desk.

KEY TERMS

Americans with Disabilities Act (ADA)

Arrival report
Authorization code
City ledger
Credit denial
Credit floor limit
Direct billing
Floor limit
Group master account
Guest discrimination
Guest folio
Guest history record
Lock-out room
Master account
No-post status
Ready room
Rooming slip
Room on-change
Skipper
Transient guest ledger
VIP

DISCUSSION AND REVIEW QUESTIONS

1. What is the purpose of the arrival report?
2. When allocating rooms for the day's arrivals, which type of reservations should be given priority?
3. Describe the process of preregistering guests in lodging operations. Why is preregistration particularly important for group arrivals?
4. How would you provide custody of your guests' property if the hotel you manage did not have in-room safes?
5. What do you understand by a guest having a credit floor limit of $2,000?
6. What is the difference between a master account folio and a folio where incidentals are posted?
7. List three recommended rules for check-cashing in lodging operations.
8. What are two requirements a front desk clerk should insist on when cashing traveler's checks?
9. Which are the two main purposes of keeping guest-history records at the front office?

10. Give three legal reasons for refusing lodging to a person who wishes to check in at your motel.

PRACTICAL SITUATIONS

Situation 10.1

Currency exchange at the front desk

John Bond was on duty at the front desk of a downtown Washington D.C. hotel on a Sunday evening. John had just graduated from a hotel and restaurant management community college program where he was taught how to deal with traveler's check transactions although this was the first time he had to exchange any foreign currency on the job. He was going to be put to the task that evening.

Ms. Cameron, a guest in room 1004 approached the desk and told John that she had a flight at 5 AM the following morning and that she wished to settle her account that evening in cash rather than with the credit card she had showed at the time of registration. She added that she had six 50-Euro traveler's checks and that she would pay the rest in US dollars. John asked the guest to come back to the desk in about 20 minutes to pay the bill.

The clerk brought up Ms. Cameron's folio in the computer. The balance was $505.25 to which she added room and taxes for that night, bringing the total to $781.00.

In-room digital safe
Courtesy of Safeplace Safes

ASSIGNMENT:

Put yourself in John bond's position and find out how much was needed in US dollars to settle the bill. Search www.google.xe.com/ucc (Currency Converter Widget) to find out today's currency exchange and apply it to the six 50-Euro denominations. The hotel's exchange commission is 0.03 % to be deducted from the total currency value.

How many US dollars will Ms. Cameron have to come up with to settle the bill?

Situation 10.2

The guide dog.

Bill Bane had just been promoted to office manager at the Broadmoor Hotel and Spa, Colorado Springs. On a Wednesday afternoon, Bill was working on the front office annual budget in the backroom when he was approached by Jane Gomez, the clerk on duty, asking what to do about the registration of a VIP party from California with a reservation for two rooms for three nights.

According to the agent, the customers were traveling with a large German-shepherd dog clad in a yellow cloth. The canine was behaving badly, barking and pulling at its harness in an attempt to smell the legs of people lined up for check-in. Jane told Mr. Bane that it appeared that the Californians were trying to have the dog admitted to the resort by pretending that the canine was an assistance dog. "Guide dogs don't behave like that," said Ms. Gomez. "The cloth is obviously a ruse intended for us to permit the dog to stay."

Bill was aware of the strict rules of the house not to allow any pets in guestrooms, let alone a large, barking, unruly dog. Mr. Bane opened the door to the front desk to address the issue.

ASSIGNMENT:

Pretend that you are Bill Bane. Your instructor will impersonate the guest who is determined to check the dog into the hotel. How would you deal with the situation?

Situation 10.3

Guest accounting

You have applied for a position of front desk clerk at a four-star hotel in Duluth, Minnesota. One of the requisites before obtaining the job is to take a test, together with other candidates, on front office operation topics. The first exercise is to tabulate a series of guest transactions as they would appear on a folio at the end the day's business. Below are the transactions listed in no particular order for room 705:

Long distance call	$3.75
Valet charge	18.50
Restaurant overcharge	10.00
Room	155.00
Tax	12.25
Advanced payment	100.00
Breakfast buffet	12.00
Senior discount on room	26.00
Transfer charge (lounge)	28.00 to room 507
Paid-out to taxi driver	19.00
Room	155.00
Tax	12.25
Previous balance pickup	390.25
Restaurant	85.40

ASSIGNMENT:

On a piece of notepaper, open a column for **charges**, one for **credits** and a third one for **balance**. Use the formula that follows to arrive at the account's **net outstanding balance:**

Previous balance + Debits – Credits = net outstanding balance

CASE STUDY 10.1

Exclusion of a guest from premises

A guest checked into a hotel, paying in advance for her lodging for a week at a time. After 1 month, the front office manager of the establishment told the general manager that several female guests were upset by the presence of the woman because she had been a prostitute before she registered in the hotel.

The manager told the front office to remove her belongings in a proper manner and to notify her that she no longer had a room at the hotel. The guest asked why she was forced to leave and she was told that no explanation was due as to why. Alleging humiliation by the conduct of management, the plaintiff filed a civil suit against the property to recover damages.

In court, the manager gave the reason that the plaintiff had been a prostitute before she came to the hotel, stating that some guests were upset by her presence, threatening to leave if she stayed. The plaintiff answered that, in spite of any right the inn may have had to remove her, she had been insulted and had suffered indignity because of the manner in which she was removed. The innkeeper insisted that the presence of the expelled guest would have injured his business.

Lobby Casa Magna Marriott Puerto Vallarta
Courtesy of Marriott International, Inc.

ASSIGNMENT:

Discuss this case and decide whether or not management infringed on the legal rights of the plaintiff. How would you have handled this case?

CHAPTER 11

THE NIGHT AUDIT

CHAPTER OBJECTIVES

- Explain the duties and responsibilities of the night auditor in lodging operations.
- Describe the accounting principles on which the night audit is based.
- List the components of the night audit process.
- Discuss the accounting cycle of debits and credits.
- Explain the objectives of the night audit process.
- List the steps followed to complete the night audit cycle.
- Describe the components of a night audit report.

OVERVIEW

Although most, if not all, lodging properties today use computerized accounting systems, technology is only as accurate as the data provided. It is therefore important that graduates from hotel and restaurant programs understand the process of account record keeping. A sudden failure of the property's computerized system should not be an obstacle to **balancing up accounts**—the final calculation of the day's transactions done by the night auditor.

The main purpose of the night audit is to verify the accuracy of all accounts at the end of the day's business cycle. Thus, the night audit is the process which provides management accurate information of revenues generated and account receivables owed to the operation. This chapter provides a sample of a night audit report for a 310-room property with several revenue-generating outlets from which students can gain insight on night auditing procedures in lodging properties.

THE NIGHT AUDITOR

The night auditor shift provides an excellent opportunity for hospitality students to understand the accounting procedures that take place daily in lodging operations. No employee should be promoted to front office manager without a complete grasp of how business transactions are processed, how all records are reconciled and balanced to the penny before guests begin to check out the following morning, and how the various financial reports are compiled.

In small and medium-size lodging hotels the night audit team is responsible not only for closing out the day's financial transactions, but also for providing services which are the responsibility of day-time front desk employees such as registering and checking out guests. Working the **(graveyard) night shift** may be tiring at first but it can provide a sense of accomplishment because it is during this time that the day's results are obtained and all accounts are balanced. On the other hand, it can be a frustrating experience when errors are made and a lot of time is spent squaring off the numbers. On occasion, the totals of debits and credits appear to be equal but one error may have offset another mistake or the wrong account may have been debited or credited, causing the auditing process to be a painfully laborious experience.

Basically, the night auditor is responsible for reconciling and closing out daily business activities. The financial procedures undertaken cover the reconciliation of the day's cash transactions, printing various reports, and balancing all accounts. Table 11.1 is a summarized night auditor's job description.

Job Title: Night auditor

Job responsibility: In charge of the overall operation of the front office during the night shift. Specific duties include closing and balancing the accounts kept at the front office.

Responsible to: Front office manager (In some establishments, the night auditor reports directly to the property's controller.)

DUTIES AND RESPONSIBILITIES:

1. Registering customers following the property's SOPs.
2. Checking out guests.
3. Receiving and recording guests' payments.
4. Posting charges.
5. Completing the night audit, including all financial and statistical reports.
6. Preparing the status report listing occupied, vacant, and out-of-order rooms.
7. Processing wake-up-call requests.

8. Keeping a log book where important information and unusual incidents are recorded.
9. Operating the telephone, taking reservations, writing down messages and answering inquiries.
10. Keeping and balancing a cash bank for the night shift's transactions.
11. Performing any other required assignments and duties.

TABLE 11.1 ABBREVIATED SAMPLE OF A NIGHT AUDITOR'S JOB DESCRIPTION

Prior to the age of technology, the night audit was a specialized position where an employee with a thorough knowledge of bookkeeping was necessary. Today, it is a matter of following the key-pushing instructions given by the company that installs the accounting software.

THE NIGHT AUDIT

The night audit generally takes place during the third shift of the day (11:00 PM to 7 AM). The audit in hospitality operations is based on the double-entry bookkeeping system in which accounts are debited and credited using the simple equation **balance = debits – credits.** This method serves as an error-detection tool for if at any given time the sum of debits and credits for all accounts is not equal in value to each other, an error has occurred. An example of a double-entry bookkeeping method would be that of a guest charging to his room a $35.00 meal in one of the hotel's restaurants. The transaction is recorded by debiting the guest's folio and crediting the restaurant outlet in the amount of $35.00. At the end of the day, the outlet will show a credit and the guest's account a debit for $35.00.

Basically, the night audit is a detailed account of daily charges and credits added and subtracted to an **opening balance**—the accounts receivable amount brought forward from yesterday's business cycle—to obtain a **closing balance** at the end of today's business cycle.

The two outstanding totals to be balanced by the night auditor are the **transient guest ledger's** (unpaid account receivables or guest folios of guests staying at the property) and the **city ledger's** (unpaid accounts receivable by nonregistered customers, credit card companies, and direct bill accounts).

When balancing the guest ledger, the total outstanding debit sum of all registered guest accounts obtained must equal the sum of the unsettled balances of all guest folios. Likewise, when balancing the city ledger, the total outstanding debit sum obtained must equal the sum of all pending nonregistered accounts. When balancing the **bank deposit**, the amount obtained must match the actual amounts collected in cash, checks, and credit card payments. The basic daily night auditing process can be summarized like this:

Opening balance (yesterday's outstanding balance) + **Charges** – **Credits** (today's) = **Outstanding** (closing) **Balance**

Table 11.2 provides an example of summarized transactions from the night audit in a lodging establishment.

Yesterday's outstanding balance:		**$62,848.99**
Today's total revenue: (all charges from business transactions)	+	**24,854.44**
Today's write-offs (discounts and paid outs)	-	**763.03**
Today's cash payments (cash, checks, transfers)	-	**18,393.75**
Today's credit card payments	-	**17,041.61**

From this information, the night auditor will work out the closing (ending) balance as follows:

Today's ending balance = **$51,505.04** (62,848.99 + 24,854.44 – 763.03 – 18,393.75 – 17,041.61)

Table 11.2 Example of summarized audit transactions

The accounting cycle of charges and credits can then be summarized:

The charge or credit is created

↓

Charge or credit is posted to guest or city ledger account

↓

Night auditor verifies and summarizes all postings

Besides its normal accounting functions, the night-auditing process is designed to safeguard the property from dishonest employees and from the omission or inaccuracy of data input. In other words, the accounting system should be capable of detecting the theft of cash by the staff or of a charge being posted to the wrong account. In addition, the night audit generates reports necessary to keep business statistics and transcripts of the day's debits and credits.

ACCOUNTS RECEIVABLE

The **accounts receivable** kept at the front office that are the responsibility of the night auditor are the transient guest ledger (for guests currently staying at the property) and the city ledger (for customers not staying in the house). An example of a guest ledger account is that of a Mr. Smith staying in room 1005; an example of a city leger account is that of a local lawyer charging a business luncheon to his office open account. City ledger accounts include:

- Businesses that use the property's services charged to a direct bill account.
- Guests who have checked out and have charged the bill to their company.
- Guests who have left the property for a short time and plan to return to complete their stay.
- Reservation deposits.
- Guests who have skipped payment.

NIGHT AUDIT PROCEDURES

To initiate the audit, the night clerk enters the PMS designated keys to generate the end-of-day revenue summary and detailed reports, occupancy data, and other business statistics. The objectives of the night audit process can be summarized as:

- To verify the accuracy of all postings to transient and city ledger accounts.
- To balance guest folios.
- To total the day's financial transactions.
- To gather statistical data.
- To compile the end-of-day reports.
- To ensure that outstanding financial data is backed up.

The **trial balance** is a test performed before the night audit report is finalized. It indicates whether or not all the day's debit and credit transactions are accounted for. If any of the totals is not in balance, the night auditor must find out where the errors or omissions have taken place in order to correct them. After the night audit is completed, the change of date is established. Ideally, this **date roll** should take place before the earliest departures of the following day to ensure that all charges of the previous day are accounted for and posted in the corresponding ledgers.

In large operations, the cashiers of the different revenue-generating outlets deposit their banks with the total of cash and credit card sales by the end of the day in a designated drop. The night auditor prints out the total cash and credit card sales reports that include:

- The day's total cash and credit card sales from the front desk and all outlets.
- The payments received from credit cards companies, direct bill, and other accounts credited to the city ledger.
- Cash and check advance deposits.

The following morning, the property's general cashier or controller reconciles the money found from all drops with the reading in the night audit report. The balanced bank deposit should read:

Total cash sales and advance deposits
+ **Total credit card sales**
+ **Payments received from city ledger accounts** (including credit card companies)
+ **Paid outs**
= **Total bank deposit**

In smaller properties, each front desk shift operates with a small bank, say $500, while a change safe is accessible 24 hours. When the clerks do their shift drops, they deposit the amount collected plus the money taken from the change safe (if any), keeping the $500 constant in the bank. Any discrepancies between the amount of funds on hand and the PMS readings are listed as **over/under.**

PMS NIGHT AUDIT

The interface with points of sale, call accounting telephone systems, and other revenue generating sources permits the automatic posting of charges to the guests' folios. All transactional details of all accounts are kept in the memory of the computer system rather than in individual paper folios. The software used will guide the night auditor through a series of prompts and commands to input or retrieve data directly at the front desk.

One of the first night auditing tasks to be performed is to post room and tax charges to all folios using the PMS "room" and "tax" options. Before posting room-and-tax charges, the auditor verifies that the proper rates have been charged to the guests' folios. For example, if a rack rate has been charged to an AARP traveler or vice-versa the auditor will correct the mistake. After all room charges have been posted, a printed **room-rate report** listing all room prices charged the previous night is generated for management review.

The next step is to print the reports for the day's transactions. The number of reports varies from house to house but the list generally includes a detail of the day's revenue, a list of guests in the house, the day's check-ins and check-outs, and the city and guest ledger transactions. Typically, the night audit cycle follows these basic steps:

1. Verify that all outlet charges have been posted. Complete outstanding postings (if any). The totals of the outlets summary should match the totals of individual postings. Balance all departments.
2. Reconcile the front desk and housekeeping room status. If a room is shown as vacant in the housekeeping report and there is a balance in the corresponding folio, the guest may have not come to the desk to check out in which case the folio should be balanced to zero by crediting the amount to the guest's credit card. If the guest is a skipper, the balance is also brought to zero by transferring the amount to the city ledger for further investigation.
3. Verify pending no-show reservations to ensure that a guest has not been checked in as a walk-in. Because customers who have guaranteed reservations but did not arrive may be billed as no-shows, attention should be given to the possibility that the reservation had been cancelled or changed to another date.
4. Post room and tax and generate the room-rate report after verifying discrepancies (if any).
5. Generate the day's **revenue report** and operational statistics by outlet.
6. Reconcile accounts receivable.
7. Run trial balance
8. Print the **high balance report** identifying the guests who are nearing their credit floor limit.
9. Prepare a summary of front desk cash, and credit card transactions.
10. Compare the postings of cash payments and paid outs with the actual cash on hand. Make a cash drop for the shift.
11. Print out these reports to be used in case of computer malfunction:
    - Alphabetical list of guests.
    - **Room status report** to be handed to housekeeping when this department opens early in the morning.
    - Guest ledger report with balances of all guest accounts.
    - Report of scheduled arrivals and departures.
    - End-of-day report.
    - Comparison of the transaction totals by outlet with the end-of-day report totals.
    - Saving the output on a backup devise, such as a computer disc.

In some properties, folios of guests who are departing the next morning are printed out and placed under the guestroom door to speed up check-outs.

Table 11.2 is an abbreviated night audit report of a 310-room hotel with two restaurants, a lounge, banquet service and athletic center. For expedience, the CURRENT MONTH-TO-DATE and LAST YEAR MONTH-TO-DATE columns have been omitted.

CONCEPT	DOLLAR AMOUNT
REVENUE	
Guest Room Revenue	44,392
TOTAL ROOM REVENUE	44,392
Room Tax (7%)	3,107
Occupancy Tax (0.20%)	89
TOTAL TAX	3,196
Atrium restaurant	
Food revenue	8,082
Beverage revenue	891
Antares restaurant	
Food revenue	5,105
Beverage revenue	774
Applause lounge	
Beverage revenue	2,035
Room service	
Food revenue	840
Beverage revenue	125
Banquets	
Food revenue	6,615
Beverage revenue	1,050
TOTAL FOOD SALES	20,642
TOTAL BEVERAGE SALES	4,875
TOTAL F&B SALES TAX (6.5%)	1,659
TOTAL F&B OUTLET TIPS	5,150
ROOM RENTAL	525
Long Distance Revenue	301
Other Miscellaneous Revenue Postings	45
TOTAL PHONE & MISCELLANEOUS REVENUE	453
ATHLETIC CLUB REVENUE	3,033
TOTAL REVENUE	**83,925**
SETTLEMENTS	
Advance Deposit Cash	0

Advance Deposit Check	790
Electronic Funds Deposit (EFT)	0
TOTAL ADVANCE PAID	790
Received on Account (ROA) Cash & Check	1,200
Guest Cash and checks	902
Paid-outs	95
TOTAL PAIDS	2,197
Refunds and adjustments	20
Bad debt	0
Write-offs	45
TOTAL NON-COLLECT SALES	65
GIFT CERTIFICATES	205
CREDIT CARDS	35,776
TOTAL SETTLED	**39,033**

BASIC BALANCE

Yesterday Outstanding	193,492
+ Today Total Revenue	83,925
- Today Total Settled	39,033
= TODAY OUTSTANDING	**238,384**

BANK DEPOSIT

Cash 2,987 (790 + 2,197)

Credit card 35,776

Total Bank Deposit 38,763

STATISTICS

Total Room Revenue	44,392
Available rooms	309
Singles	83
Multiples	193
Guaranteed no-show	1
TOTAL OCCUPIED	276
- Sleeper Adjustments	0
- Guaranteed no-show adjustments	1
= ADJUSTED TOTAL OCCUPIED	277
Percent occupancy	89.4

ADR	$161
RevPAR	$144
Comp Rooms	0
Vacant rooms	34
OOO Rooms	1
Total Guests	662
Source:	
Walk-in	22
Property Reservations	48
Call Center	99
GDS/Internet	41
National Sales Office (NSO)	10
Gold Key Rooms	54

COMP ROOMS REDEEMED

No comp certificates redeemed

ADJUSTMENTS POSTINGS

Folio 88392 Room 225 Amount $20.00 Reason: Room rate adjustment

PHONE ADJUSTMENTS

There are no manual phone adjustments

IN-HOUSE "CASH" PAYING GUESTS

Room 301 Folio 88105 Name: P. Lawson Nights: 5 CODE: Gov Rate: $120

LIST OF GUARANTEED NO-SHOW ACCOUNTS

Folio 88093 Name: Ramirez, Luis Status: Billed

LIST OF IN-HOUSE GUESTS WITH A BALANCE OVER $1,000

Folio 87993 Name: Perry, Bryon Balance: $1,788 Departure: January 12 Room 605

Manager Signature______________________

Date______________________________

Table 11.2 Abbreviated night audit report

From the information provided on Table 11.2, it is clear that:

- If settlements are deducted from the total revenue, the day's actual **accounts receivable** is obtained (83,925 – 39,033 = **44,892**).
- If yesterday's accounts receivable balance is added to today's accounts receivable amount, the **outstanding accounts receivable** to be brought forward to the next day is (193,492 + 44,892 = **238,384**).

KEY TERMS

Accounts receivable
Balancing up accounts
Bank deposit
City ledger
Closing balance
Date roll
Graveyard shift
High-balance report
Night shift
Opening balance
Outstanding balance
Over/under (cash)
Revenue report
Room-rate report
Room status report
Total cash and credit card sales
Transient guest ledger
Trial balance

DISCUSSION AND REVIEW QUESTIONS

1. What does the outstanding accounts receivable balance comprise?
2. If you were interviewing for a hospitality job, how would you answer the question "what is the main purpose of the night audit report?"
3. After the night audit is finalized, the auditor finds that the folio for room 776 shows a **credit** balance of $209. How could this be the case?
4. Mr. Trotter hands you a check for $394.65 to settle the account of his daughter who checked out from the hotel a week ago. He had arranged to pay the bill after

her departure. What ledger should be credited to bring the balance of the account to zero?

5. A customer checks into a hotel on a Tuesday. She had come by the property the previous Friday to leave a cash-advance deposit of $100 towards the total of her stay. If you were the guest agent registering the guest, how would you handle the $100 deposit? What account would you debit and which would you credit?
6. What is the date roll? When should the date roll be conducted?
7. Tim Moakes is the night auditor at the Royal Court Hotel, London. At the end of his shift, he finds that the no-show guaranteed reservation list has two names, Mr. John Lee and Mrs. K. Cartwright. What should Tim verify before billing the credit card companies used to make the reservation?
8. What steps are involved in preparing the night audit?
9. What are the pros and cons of working as a night auditor in a lodging establishment?
10. Work out the outstanding balance from this information:

Today total revenue	85,000.50
Yesterday outstanding	99,100.85
Today total settled	31,111.90

PRACTICAL SITUATIONS

Situation 11.1

Balancing the night shift's cash bank

Calculate the over or short of your cash bank before making the drop deposit for your shift as a night auditor. The beginning bank was $150.00.

Bills and checks	$500.25
Coins	55.05
Credit card transactions	191.60
Paid-out voucher	22.50
Total PMS cash and credit card reading	621.40

Situation 11.2

Night audit bank deposit

Niccolo Monti is the night auditor of a hotel in San Francisco. The PMS readings closing the day's work were:

Dante's restaurant cash sales	$893.50
Toscana restaurant cash sales	1,059.90
Room service cash sales	145.00
Today's sales charged to credit cards	3,001.00
City ledger payment received	2,020.10
Credit cards payment received	5,334.20

The following morning, the general cashier finds out that the cash from all deposits is $12,353.70.

Was the total from cash transactions balanced out with the PMS reading? By how much was it over (short)?

Situation 11.3

Balancing Accounts Receivable

As night auditor of a resort in Southern Arizona you experience a malfunction of the PMS just after printing out the day's trial balance. The readings at the time the PMS went down were:

Today's total revenue	18,994.50
Today's cash sales	500.00
Today's credit card sales	2,244.90
Yesterday's outstanding accounts receivable	53,033.10
Today's city ledger payments received	9,844.00

GUESTROOM BOSTON MARRIOTT CAMBRIDGE
COURTESY OF MARRIOTT INTERNATIONAL, INC.

ASSIGNMENT:

Work out the accounts receivable balance.

CASE STUDY 11.1

Working out the Outstanding Balance

CONCEPT	DOLLAR AMOUNT
REVENUE	
Guest Room Revenue	38,005
TOTAL ROOM REVENUE	38,005
Room Tax (7%)	
Occupancy Tax (0.20%)	
TOTAL TAX	
Atrium restaurant	
Food revenue	7,477
Beverage revenue	505
Antares restaurant	
Food revenue	4,329
Beverage revenue	615
Applause lounge	
Beverage revenue	2,722
Room service	
Food revenue	590
Beverage revenue	301
Banquets	
Food revenue	5,493
Beverage revenue	1,114
TOTAL FOOD SALES	
TOTAL BEVERAGE SALES	
TOTAL F&B SALES TAX (6.5%)	
TOTAL F&B OUTLET TIPS	3,090
ROOM RENTAL	772
Long Distance Revenue	409
Other Miscellaneous Re venue Postings	84
TOTAL PHONE & MISCELLANEOUS REVENUE	
ATHLETIC CLUB REVENUE	2,216
TOTAL REVENUE	
SETTLEMENTS	
Advance Deposit Cash	0

Advance Deposit Check	100
TOTAL ADVANCE PAID	
ROA Cash & Check	0
Guest Cash and checks	1,005
Paid-outs	75
TOTAL PAIDS	
Refunds and adjustments	99
Bad debt	0
Write-offs	53
TOTAL NON-COLLECT SALES	
GIFT CERTIFICATES	210
CREDIT CARDS	29,881
TOTAL SETTLED	

BASIC BALANCE

Yesterday Outstanding
+ Today Total Revenue
- Today Total Settled
= **TODAY OUTSTANDING**

Drury Inn & Suites Arnold, MO
Courtesy Drury Hotels

ASSIGNMENT:

Fill in all gaps on the template and work out the Today Outstanding Balance from the information given.

CHAPTER 12

GUEST CHECK-OUT

CHAPTER OBJECTIVES

- Explain what the front desk should do if guests do not vacate their rooms on their scheduled departure date.
- Describe procedures to check out guests.
- List the options guests have for checking out.
- Discuss the methods of payment guests have to settle their accounts.
- Learn about what to do if a guest decides to check out after the scheduled departure time.
- Discuss the importance of gathering guest history records.
- Understand the role of technology in the check-out process.

OVERVIEW

Because check-out is the last opportunity front office employees have to interact with guests, these employees must show excellent interpersonal skills to ensure that the last impression travelers take with them is a positive one. This lasting impression is likely to influence his/her decision to return to the establishment again. In addition, clerks must be capable of explaining billing details and handling any discontent brought up by the departing traveler.

Check-out is the final stage of the guest stay. The activities involved in the departure process include settling the balance on guests' folios, changing the status of the room from occupied to vacant, and gathering guests' thoughts on their stay. This chapter describes the check-out process in lodging properties.

DEPARTURE

As guests sometimes decide to extend their stay without giving advanced notice, the front desk must ascertain whether or not the scheduled departures for the day take place. The verification should be made as early as possible because the guest may leave the room early only to return later on in the day. If, after accounting for the day's check-outs and incoming travelers from the reservations on file, the house is full, guests must be notified that they are to vacate their rooms by the posted departure time. If guests cannot be reached and the rooms are needed, the housekeeping department is asked to pack up their belongings and have the luggage brought down to the bell stand storage room until the guest shows up. In this case the rooms must also be checked out of the system so that the door card is made inoperative and the room is accessible only to the new incoming guest. If the house is not full that day, the guest is allowed to stay on without causing any unnecessary ado, although he/she should be contacted as soon as possible to determine the length of the stay.

Guests should be asked to review their folios to ensure accuracy and to find out if they wish to use the method of payment chosen at check-in, as they may have established credit by presenting a debit or credit card and decide afterwards to settle their accounts by cash. Once the bill has been settled, the clerk should ask if luggage assistance is needed. If this is the case, a bellperson is summoned to the desk to help the departing customers with their belongings. The check-out process ends with the clerk asking if a reservation to a new destination down the road is needed or if they would like to reserve a future date at the property. When a room has been checked out, its status is automatically changed from occupied to vacant. The housekeeping department then cleans the room and changes its status once again from vacant to vacant-and-ready after the final inspection has been completed.

The front desk clerk checking out guests should inquire about their stay and address any complaints that may exist. Letting guests depart without clearing up an unresolved problem will probably result in their not coming back.

CHECK-OUT OPTIONS

Scheduled departures should be communicated to all departments, especially to housekeeping that needs the information for giving priority to departing rooms to prepare them for incoming guests. Guests may choose one of the following departing options:

- Check out at the front desk
- Check out using the in-room TV screen
- Check out by telephone
- Check out using a lobby kiosk or computer terminal
- Check out from a mobile device.
- Not checking out at all

In busy times, checking out at the front desk presents the problem of guests having to wait in line. There are travelers who don't mind waiting to make sure that everything is in order before they leave; others stop at the desk to get an updated bill with a zero balance to show their companies that all charges have been taken care of.

The use of the in-room interfaced TV screen to check out is convenient because guests can review their charges at leisure although they are not able to get a paper statement unless the room is equipped with a printer. It is obvious that the check-out option via TV is only available to guests with a valid credit card and not to those on a **cash-only basis**. When checking out by telephone, guests usually ask the front desk to check them out and send the bill to their e-mail addresses.

If the property provides bills placed under the guestroom door early in the morning, travelers generally don't bother checking out for they already have their printed statements. If they incur additional charges after the bill has been delivered to the room, the amount will have to be settled at the front desk; if they depart without settling late charges these are billed to their credit cards on file.

Self-check-out terminals in the lobby also allow for guests to access their folio and review its content. The machine asks users to punch numbers using a keypad or swipe the credit or debit card through a slot to complete the check-out process. The terminal is interfaced with the PMS and updates the room status from occupied to vacant automatically.

The front office must be in close contact with the housekeeping department to find out if guests have vacated their rooms. After the check-out is completed, the stay record is added to each guest's individual history data on file, including the dates of stay, rooms used, bill totals, and any special likes or dislikes each departing guest may have. The data can be used for sales and marketing purposes or to help a reservationist access the records when the guest books accommodations in the future. Table 12.1 is an abbreviated example of the folio of a departing guest:

Guest Name:	*Bill Christy*	Room number:	652
Arrival date:	1/15/20.	Departure date:	1/16/20..

Date	Room #	Concept	Debit	Credit	Balance
1/15	652	Room	118.00		
1/15	652	Tax	14.16		
1/15	652	Atrium Rest	59.50		
1/15	652	Applause lounge	18.25		
1/15	652	In-room Movie	9.75		
1/16	652	Long distance	10.50		
1/16	652	Subtotal	230.16		
1/16	652	Amexco		230.16	0

TABLE 12.1 EXAMPLE OF A FOLIO AFTER THE GUEST'S CHECK-OUT

CHECK-OUT PROCEDURES

The check-out process ends the guest's stay at the property. As written before, the procedure generally includes determining the level of satisfaction experienced by the guest during his/her stay, settling the outstanding balance, and updating the guest's records. Most departures occur in lodging properties between 7:00 and 9:00 AM.

The step-by-step procedure may begin with greeting the guest and asking if he/she is checking out. If so, the room number is verified and the folio printed. It is a good idea to ask departing customers if they have charged any services at any of the property's outlets recently (in case the amount was not yet posted at the point of sale) or if they have used the in-room minibar (if it is not PMS interfaced). The clerk should also verify if the guest's account is flagged on the screen for pending messages or for any other reason.

Once all charges are approved by the guest and the method of payment is chosen, the credit is posted, the account balance brought to zero, and a copy of the folio is given to the departing person. If the account is to be direct billed, the guest should be asked to sign the folio as an acceptance for all charges and the total transferred from the transient to the city ledger.

METHODS OF PAYMENT

The use of a debit or credit card is the method that guests use most often to settle their accounts. By pressing the credit card-payment option key, the debit balance in the folio is brought to zero while the system transfers the amount from the transient ledger to the credit card company account in the city ledger. The credit card company billed settles its debit balance periodically by transferring money to the establishment's bank account.

Guests can also settle their accounts using cash, bank or traveler's checks. If the currency used is foreign, the cashier will have to convert it at the current exchange rate. It is customary for hotels to keep a small percentage from the total to cover a commission for the transaction.

Folio totals can also be transferred to direct billing accounts in the city ledger. In this case, the accounting department is responsible for billing and collecting outstanding amounts. As already discussed, direct billing as a method of payment is only accepted if the credit has been arranged beforehand between the entity and the lodging establishment.

It is not uncommon to have to use more than one method of payment to bring the folio to a zero balance. For instance, a guest may decide to pay for the incidental charges on his account, and have the room and taxes, meals, and phone charges billed to his company. Table 12.2 is an example of a combined method of payment.

Guest Name:	***Bill Christy***	Room number:	**652**
Arrival date:	1/15/20.	Departure date:	1/16/20..

Company: Purina Corporation, Flagstaff, AZ

Date	Room #	Concept	Debit	Credit	Balance
1/15	652	Room	118.00		
1/15	652	Tax	14.16		
1/15	652	Atrium Rest	59.50		
1/15	652	Applause lounge	18.25		
1/15	652	In-room Movie	9.75		
1/16	652	Long distance	10.50		
1/16	652	Subtotal	230.16		
1/16	652	Cash		38.50	
1/16	652	Direct bill		191.66	0

TABLE 12.2 EXAMPLE OF A COMBINED METHOD OF SETTLING A FOLIO ACCOUNT

A summary of the steps involved in the check-out process include:

1. The guest is asked about additional recent charges.
2. The outstanding amounts (if any) are posted to the account.
3. The folio is printed.
4. The guest is asked to verify all posting on the folio.
5. Adjustments to the folio are applied if necessary.
6. The method of payment is determined (cash, check, credit/debit card, direct bill).
7. The payment or transfer to another account is posted to the folio, bringing its balance to zero.
8. The room status in the system is automatically updated.
9. The stay is automatically recorded in the guest history PMS program.
10. The guest service agent asks the departing guest if the accommodation was satisfactory.
11. The clerk offers help for future reservations.

Departing customers should be asked if the establishment can do anything to improve its service, thanked for their stay at the property, and invited to return in the near future. If a guest complains about the service received or about the in-room supplies or equipment, he/she should be thanked for bringing it to attention and told that the issue will be reported to management for correction. The problem, comment or suggestion should be entered in the **log book** or a manager on duty summoned to the desk if the situation requires immediate attention.

A common method of eliciting feedback from departing guests is to have them fill out comment cards at check-out and have the comments deposited in a box at the counter. Some companies send e-mails a few days after the guests' departures to elicit information about their stay. Front desk employees should offer help to reserve accommodations for departing guests somewhere down the road or for a return trip to the property in the future. Often, a reminder to make a reservation to guests in transit leads to additional business with a sister property in a different location.

LATE CHECK-OUTS

It is common for some guests not to depart by the stated check-out time. When guests ask permission for a late check-out, they should be notified about any additional room fee the property charges for the extra time involved.

The extra charge for late check-outs may upset customers, particularly if they are frequent guests. The front office should have guidelines in place for the staff to deal with situations which could annoy customers to the point of deciding never to return to the establishment. For example, a guest who has stayed for three days in a hotel having generated an $800 bill, will probably be upset if the hotel decides to charge a $25 additional fee for staying two hours over the established departure time. On the other hand, if a guest decides to keep the room for, say, five extra hours, the extra fee would be a reasonable way for the hotel to cover the cost of housekeeping having to clean the room because of extra labor time.

PENDING ACCOUNT BALANCES

There is always the possibility that a charge shows up as unpaid after the guest has checked out and his folio has been brought to a zero balance. Examples of **late charges** are those related to services provided to guests just before they leave, such as breakfast or minibar consumptions. If the late charge is minimal and the additional cost involved in billing the guest is larger than the unpaid amount, it is a good idea to credit the amount to a "lost revenue" account. On the other hand, if recovering the total of the unpaid amount is worthwhile the front desk can either charge the guest's credit or debit card or send a bill directly to the guest's mailing address with a note explaining the nature of the late charge.

Guest balances not settled at check-out are credited to the corresponding outlet and debited to a city ledger account pending for collection. If the collection of the billed charges is successful, the pending account on the city ledger will be brought to zero; if the collection proves to be unsuccessful, the outstanding balance is credited and charged to an **"uncollectables" account**.

GUEST HISTORY RECORDS

After guests have checked out, their stay is registered in the PMS guest-history program which records information like the geographical distribution of customers, zip codes, and e-mail addresses. This data help direct the advertising efforts to areas where potential customer pools are located. Knowing the origin of the reservations made by customers is also important, as it represents the background of the property's clientele. For example, if a Best Western property receives very few bookings from the BW central reservation system, an investigation of why this is happening should be conducted. Perhaps advertised rates are too high compared with those of a BW establishment of the same category in the same location. Lowering the price to compete with neighbors may be the right thing to do. Likewise, if the records show that the property is not receiving bookings from corporate accounts, an aggressive sales and marketing campaign to attract this market segment might be appropriate.

The program can also be used to give credit points to guests who are frequent travelers. Often, the points assigned after a stay, can be used by guests with other entities participating in the program, such as airlines or car rental companies.

PMS CHECK-OUT

As with reservations and check-in programs, hoteliers have the option of installing an in-house system using stand-alone PC's or contracting with companies that offer cloud-based online check-out capabilities. In both cases, the check-out module used will guide the front desk staff on how to complete the procedure. The software program used by Hotelogix, for instance, offers the following options:

- Folio printing
- Late check-out with choice to post an extra charge for the room
- Moving charges between the check-out account and direct billing
- Voiding or transferring of transactions
- Group check-outs
- Method of payment, including check, debit or credit card, and direct bill

- Direct interface with credit card payments
- Credit card processing
- Payment in multiple currencies
- Automatic posting of room charges
- Automatic invoicing to corporate accounts

The URL of Hotelogix is www.hotelogix.com and its webpage includes a step-by-step demo that explains in detail how to operate the check-out modules.

After applying all credits to the folio, its balance should be zero. If the method of payment is cash, the amount tendered will increase the "cash" balance in the system. If the folio total is paid with a credit/debit card or is transferred to "direct bill," these amounts will increase the balances in the city ledger. After the night audit is completed, a "method of payment" report will show the totals received from cash, credit card, and direct bill transactions.

Once guests are checked out, their names, room numbers, and accounts are expunged from the PMS database while the program changes the status of the empty room. The room status report module will show the condition of every room in the house on the front desk and housekeeping department computer screens.

KEY TERMS

Cash-only basis
Late charge
Log book
Self-check-out terminal
Uncollectable account

DISCUSSION AND REVIEW QUESTIONS

1. List the payment options available to lodging properties guests.
2. From a hotel perspective, what is the difference between a debit and a credit card?
3. What is the name of the report that provides the physical situation a guestroom is in?
4. A front desk clerk finds out that a guest has departed without settling a $45.35 long distance call. What should the clerk do?
5. A front desk clerk finds out that a guest has departed without paying for a $.50 local call. What should the clerk do?
6. Why is it important to keep records about guests' history in lodging properties?

7. Go to www.xe.com and convert 50 euros into US dollars using the day's currency exchange.
8. Go to www.xe.com and convert $50 into Euros using the day's currency exchange.
9. How many US dollars should a front desk clerk hand to a traveler from the United Kingdom who asks to exchange 50 pounds? No commission is charged by this property.
10. The required check-out time at the Intercontinental Hotel in Perth, Australia is set at 11:00 AM. A guest requests permission to check out at noon that day. If you were the clerk answering the request, how would you answer?

PRACTICAL SITUATIONS

Situation 12.1

Guest complaint during check-out

Two years after graduating from a hotel and restaurant management program you have been hired as front office manager at a ski resort in Vermont. It is Monday morning and you start your work by checking the logbook kept at the front desk for unusual incidents. Bill Murray, who was on duty during the morning shift on Sunday, wrote the following entry to your attention:

> *Hi, Laura. Sorry to have to report that our regular guest Jay Jensen complained very bitterly about the way he was treated when he checked in Friday evening. According to Mr. Jensen, he was given the cardkey to a room that was not ready. After having to come down to the desk to be assigned to a different room he was given the card to 707 which, as you know, faces the indoor patio and is quite noisy because of the vending machine nearby. He came down to the front desk again asking for a different room and felt that the clerk on duty at the time sort of threw a new cardkey on the counter without offering any apology for the whole episode. My feeling is that the new clerk we have just hired may not know how important Mr. Jensen is to us. As you know, he regularly sends a lot of business our way.*

ASSIGNMENT:

Compose a formal letter to be sent to Jay Jensen in response to his bad experience. The main purpose of the letter should be to ensure that Mr. Jensen will continue to be a guest at the resort.

Situation 12.2

Guest folio at check-out

Carmen Rubio is the morning shift supervisor at the King's Inn in Yuma, Arizona. There is a sudden electricity blackout and the PMS system goes down although, fortunately, the access to the Internet at the front office is still on. Mr. Oliver, a guest from Bolivia, asks to be checked out and insists on receiving a copy of his account showing a zero balance. Mr. Oliver gives Carmen the folio that was put under his guestroom door earlier that morning.

Carmen asks Mr. Oliver if he had any extra charges pending, to which the guest answered that he had just had a bloody Mary at the bar. He also mentioned that he wanted to pay cash for the minibar charge and for the morning drink, leaving the rest on his Visa credit card account. The copy of the folio that was put under the guest's door read:

Room	$225.00
Tax	22.50
Long distance	35.75
Dinner	64.25
Bar	12.50
Minibar	5.00

FRONT DESK
COURTESY INTERCONTINENTAL HOTELS GROUP

ASSIGNMENT:

From the information provided, type a folio-style statement using the Microsoft Word program, showing a zero balance on the account.

Situation 12.3

Check-out outline for front desk clerks

You have been hired as front office manager of a hotel in La Jolla, California. The 250-room property uses a PMS which includes a computerized check-out module. Upon taking over your new position, you find out that there are no standing operating procedures for the check-out process at the front desk. You quickly realize that the procedure outline is necessary, particularly to be handed out to new clerk hires. Be sure to cover all phases of guest check-out.

ASSIGNMENT:

Having the content of this chapter as guidance, write an outline of the major topics that should be included in the check-out procedure list for front desk guest service agents.

CASE STUDY 12.1

Reconstructing a guest folio prior to check-out

David Martin has had a successful career so far in the lodging industry. He graduated with honors from a community college in Mississippi with a degree in accounting. Immediately after graduation he was hired by a local hotel as front office clerk and, after two years, promoted to night auditor, shift supervisor, and assistant front office manager.

Four years later, David decides to apply for a position as rooms division director with a hospitality company based in Dallas, Texas. He passes the first interview and is now going through the second interview process at the company's headquarter. David is presented with the following case to be resolved with paper and pencil.

Two employees of the Paragon company, Joanna Sterling and Rita Chu, checked into a twin-size room of the Royal Hotel (room 2205), on May 15, 20.. Only one folio was opened for room 2005 at check-in. Three days later, at check-out, their folio showed the following transactions:

Date	Room #	Concept	Debit	Credit
5/15				250.00 AD
5/15	2205	Room	245.00	
5/15	2205	Tax	24.50	
5/15	2205	Restaurant	193.00	
5/15	2205	Lounge	73.25	
5/16	2205	Adjust. lounge		10.00
5/16	2205	Room	245.00	
5/16	2205	Tax	24.50	
5/16	2205	Rest	59.20	
5/16	2205	In-room movie	9.00	
5/16	2205	Lounge	44.90	
5/16	2205	Local calls	2.50	
5/16	2205	Long distance	12.80	
5/17	2205	Room	245.00	
5/17	2205	Tax	24.50	
5/17	2205	Spa	60.00	
5/17	2205	Pool bar	98.30	
5/17	2205	Long distance	17.50	
5/18	2205	Local calls	1.50	
5/18	2205	Business office	54.60	

On checking out, Ms. Sterling and Chu had the following requests at the front desk:

1. *Ms. Sterling requested that her share of room and tax and all long distance charges be billed to the Paragon Company. She wished to pay cash for the 5/16 local calls, the pool bar and the spa charges.*
2. *Ms. Chu also requested that her share of room and tax, the business office, and the 5/18 local call charges be billed to the company. She wants to pay with her Visa credit card for the in-room movie, restaurant, and lounge charges.*

Lobby Drury San Antonio Airport Hotel
Courtesy of Drury Hotels

ASSIGNMENT:

1. Apply the corresponding credits and transfers to the original folio, leaving a balance to be direct billed to the Paragon Company that includes room and tax, long distance, the 5/18 local calls and business office charges minus the advance deposit. Bring the folio balance to zero.
2. Open a new folio for Ms. Sterling that includes the 5/16 local calls, the pool bar and spa charges. Bring the folio balance to zero.
3. Open a new folio for Ms. Chu that includes the in-room movie, restaurant, and lounge charges. Bring the folio balance to zero.
4. Explain how this cumbersome situation could have been prevented at the time these guests checked into the hotel.

PART 5

FRONT OFFICE FINANCIAL CONTROLS, SECURITY AND JOB-SEEKING STRATEGIES

CHAPTER 13

OPERATIONAL CONTROLS

CHAPTER OBJECTIVES

- Understand the purpose of operating budgets in the front office department.
- Learn the process of compiling operating budgets.
- Explain the structure and purpose of the profit and loss statement and variance analyses.
- Discuss control of productivity in the front office department.
- Describe how to monitor labor costs through payroll control.
- Learn how to interpret operational data using financial ratios.
- Explain how to establish cash controls at the front office.

OVERVIEW

The control of resources in hospitality is by way of budgets, inventories, and accounting procedures. **Operating budgets** are used to forecast sales, expenses, and profits and to limit operational costs to predetermined percentages of projected revenues. Operational controls take effect when financial statements providing data on how the rooms department is performing are analyzed and interpreted. Two important operational statements generated during the course of the fiscal year are the **profit and loss statement (P&L)** and the **variance analysis.**

Two of the most critical challenges front office managers-in-training face as they start their careers are the calculation and interpretation of financial ratios. The ratios that supervisors and managers use most are calculated from operational data gathered in income statements. The important operational ratios that can be worked out from income statements are discussed in this chapter.

Because cash is so tempting, effective internal controls to ensure the accuracy of accounting records are necessary. All front desk employees handling cash should follow established control guidelines when transacting receipts and disbursements.

ACCOUNTING CONTROLS

Front office managers must regularly assess the operational performance of their department against pre-established forecasts and standards usually set by upper management. The purpose of this assessment is to find out how well (or how badly) the department has done operationally and to redirect efforts to optimize future results.

The control function begins with the compilation of an annual operating budget for the rooms division of the property, of which the front office department is a part. The front office manager must project labor and operating expenses for the upcoming year which, once approved by upper management, become the operational expense parameters.

Because most department expenses are a function of revenue, their totals must be justified. For example, if the labor cost percentage for a projected revenue of $10,000 is 9.0, this percentage is still expected if the revenue drops to $9,000. As the year progresses, the front office department receives monthly profit and loss statements showing the revenue achieved by the rooms division and the totals of expenses by category. The front office manager uses this information to monitor costs and readjust expense amounts if they are larger than expected. Statistical information can also be used to control productivity in the department by comparing the results obtained with budget indicators. For instance, if the total front office payroll per occupied room was budgeted at $14.00 and the actual amount is $25.00, the productivity of front office employees was lower than expected. On the other hand, if the payroll to the rooms-occupied ratio was lower than $14.00, the productivity was better than planned.

FRONT OFFICE OPERATING BUDGET

An operating budget is essentially a financial plan that allocates funds for expenditures by department for a determined period of time, generally one year. It is also a means of control that provides a measure of performance. Budgeting in large lodging operations requires a full cooperative effort of all department heads and the property's controller, who is usually in charge of preparing the final document before it is presented to the general manager for approval. Budgets are generally compiled for one-year time spans and are divided into 12 months, although some companies divide the year into thirteen 28-day segments to avoid distortion in the comparison of working periods (not all months have the same number of working days). Preparation of the operating budget in large lodging properties requires several months of planning and is usually finalized just before the budgeting cycle begins. The budget can start on January 1 (calendar year), or at the beginning of the company's fiscal year. Once top management has established its guidelines and amounts for each department, the respective departmental budgets are distributed down through each level. One of these levels is the front office department.

The front office department budget is part of the rooms division budget, which also includes the housekeeping department. The front office manager's participation in determining the amounts allocated to the front office department is essential if she/he is to be held accountable for the departmental control of expenses.

The basic structure of budgets for revenue-generating divisions is this:

Revenue (Sales) – **Costs** (Expenses) = **Departmental Income** (Departmental Profit).

The revenue of the rooms division consists mostly of the dollars (or any other currency) to be generated by the sale of rooms at a certain unit price (*number of rooms sold* **x** *average daily rate [ADR]*). For example, if the projection for selling rooms is 100,000 in one year and the ADR projected is $190 for each room sold, the anticipated annual revenue will be $19,000,000 (100,000 x 190).

The costs of the rooms division consist of the expenses incurred by the front office and housekeeping departments. Typically they include **salaries and wages** and **other expenses.** The percent of expenses is obtained by dividing the projected cost of each expense category by the projected revenue. For example, if we project spending $100,000 in the "customer goodwill" category and the projected revenue is $19,000,000, the ratio will be 0.0053, or .53 percent (100,000 : 19,000,000). Conversely, if we know the percentage and want to find out the cost of expenses as a percent of the revenue, we would multiply the percentage by the revenue divided by 100; in this case .53 x 19,000,000 = 10,070,000 and 10,070,000 : 100 = 100,700.

CONSOLIDATED ROOMS SALES SUMMARY

The first step in the budget process is the compilation of the **consolidated rooms sales summary** in which the rooms division director, director of sales, and front office manager are directly involved. The summary is a projection of revenues for the 12 months of the upcoming year based on the forecasted percentage of occupancy and average daily rate. The projections are calculated from factors such as the room bookings at hand, historical data of rooms sold in previous years, upcoming local events, state of the local economy, and changes in the competition (for example, if a major lodging establishment competitor nearby has closed down or if a new one has been recently opened). Table 13.1 is a consolidated room sales summary for a 450-room hotel that includes the predicted percent occupancy by month, number of rooms projected to be sold, average daily rate, and total revenue. In this example, the average occupancy for the year is 81 percent, the number of rooms to be sold 132,897, the average daily rate $105, and the projected revenue $14,131,142. Last year's budget figures for January through October are real; those for November and December are tentative, as these months have not yet elapsed at the time the budget is finalized.

	UPCOMING YEAR BUDGET				LAST YEAR'S BUDGET			
Month	**Occup. %**	**Rooms**	**ADR**	**Rev. $**	**Occup. %**	**Rooms**	**ADR**	**Revenue $**
January	63	8,788	95	834,860	65	9,067	71	643,757
February	78	9,828	106	1,041,768	80	10,080	75	756,000
March	78	10,881	110	1,196,910	78	10,881	77	837,837
April	80	10,800	106	1,144,800	80	10,800	80	864,000
May	81	11,300	94	1,062,200	88	12,276	85	1,043,460
June	85	11,475	126	1,445,850	89	12,015	86	1,033,290
July	95	13,252	131	1,736,012	95	13,252	88	1,166,176
August	90	12,555	135	1,694,925	93	12,973	87	1,128,651
September	88	11,880	95	1,128,600	90	12,150	85	1,032,750
October	87	12,136	90	1,092,240	87	12,136	85	1,031,560
November	81	10,935	89	973,215	81*	10,935	78	852,930
December	65	9,067	86	779,762	70*	9,765	75	732,375
Total	**81%**	**132,897**	**$105**	**14,131,142**	**83%**	**136,330**	**$81**	**11,122,786**

* Estimated

TABLE 13.1 SAMPLE CONSOLIDATED ROOM SALES SUMMARY

Once the rooms division revenue is forecast, the front office manager and executive housekeeper ascertain the expenses predicted for the year. Typical basic expense categories of the rooms division are *front office salaries,* housekeeping salaries, *payroll taxes* and *employee benefits, reservation commissions,* cleaning supplies, linen replacements, guest supplies, *digital communication, PMS-related costs* (front office share), *postage, printing and stationery supplies, uniforms,* laundry supplies, *customer goodwill,* and *auto expenses* (usually airport vans and limousines). Of these categories, the front office expenses have been printed in italics; the expenses not in italics belong in the housekeeping department. The categories of payroll taxes, employee benefits, printing and stationery supplies, and uniforms are shared by the two departments. The amounts to be allocated to each expense category are ascertained taking into consideration the percentages from previous years and factors such as predicted increases in salaries and wages, adding extra employees to the department and purchasing new uniforms for the front desk or bell personnel. The challenge for department heads when requesting expense allocations is to keep the cost percentages as low as possible while maintaining an optimum level of service and quality.

After the budget has been finalized and approved by management, it becomes the plan of operation for the upcoming year. The front office manager must henceforth operate the department within the budget's limitations so that the percentages of amounts spent in each expense category do not exceed the percentages budgeted. It is important to understand that the cost percentages are a function of the actual revenue achieved. For example, if the projected cost of auto expense has been set at 1.2 percent of $500,000 revenue for the month of March, the dollar allocation for March will be $6,000 (500,000 x .012). However, if the revenue is less or more than projected, the dollar allocation has to be adjusted accordingly. For instance, if the revenue drops to $450,000, the allocation for auto expense becomes $5,400 (450,000 x .012). If the revenue reaches $600,000, the allocation changes to $7,200 (600,000 x .012). In other words, as revenue fluctuates, budgeted percentages should stay the same.

Whenever any substantial deviation from the budget occurs, the front office manager will be asked to explain the variance. If the variance is found to be correctable, a plan of action is usually agreed upon with upper management. Figure 13.2 is a sample budget for the rooms division of the King's Hotel. The revenue for the upcoming year has been projected higher than the current year's to reflect an increase in room rates. Occupancy percentages have been kept the same as in the current year, assuming that a slowdown in the local economy does not allow a larger occupancy.

	UPCOMING YEAR		LAST YEAR	
	Dollars ($)	**Percentage (%)**	**Dollars ($)**	**Percentage (%)**
REVENUE	**14,131,142**	**100.0**	**11,122,786**	**100.0**
Salaries & Wages				
Front Office	748,951	5.3	556,139	5.0
Housekeeping	1,342,458	9.5	1,001,051	9.0
Total	2,091,409	14.8	1,557,190	14.0
Taxes and Benefits	593,508	4.2	444,911	4.0
TOTAL PAYROLL2	2,684,917	19.0	2,002,101	18.0
Other Expenses				
Reservation Commissions	282,623	2.0	222,456	2.0
PMS-related expenses	494,590	3.5	344,806	3.1
Cleaning Supplies	155,443	1.1	122,351	1.1
Linen Replacements	141,311	1.0	111,227	1.0
Guest Supplies	310,885	2.2	222,456	2.0
Digital Communication	28,262	.2	22,246	.2
Postage	800 –	800	–	
Printing & Stationery	14,131	.1	11,123	.1
Uniforms	70,656	.5	55,614	.5
Laundry Supplies	56,525	.4	44,491	.4
Customer Goodwill	84,787	.6	66,737	.6
Auto Expense	113,049	.8	88.982	.8
TOT. OTHER EXP	1,753,062	12.4	1,313,286	11.8
TOTAL EXPENSES	437,979	31.4	3,315,387	29.8
DEPART. PROFIT	**9,693,163**	**68.8**	**7,807,399**	**70.2**

Table 13.2 Sample Rooms Division Budget (Summary)

Salaries and wages have been increased by 0.3 percent from last year's in the front office anticipating a rise in pay. Payroll taxes and employee benefits will be up 0.2 percent overall as predicted by the hotel's controller. The cost percentages for all front office-related categories of "other expenses" have been kept as in the previous year except for "PMS expenses" after changing to a new provider anticipating better service. The departmental profit (income) projected is obtained by subtracting all expenses from the forecasted revenue. In this example, the income has been projected to be 68.8 percent of the revenue, down from 70.2 percent from the previous year. A departmental profit of 68.8 cents for every dollar of room sales is a fair target for rooms divisions in the lodging industry.

To justify the expenses in the category of salaries and wages, both front office manager and executive housekeeper must submit a statement showing the amounts needed to pay employees in both departments. The allocation to cover salaries is easy to work out as it consists of adding up the yearly pay of salaried employees. To figure out the wages of hourly workers, calculations must be made depending on the levels of occupancy of the property; for example, if the establishment's room occupancy is low on weekends, fewer clerks will be needed to cover weekend shifts, while a full crew will be necessary on weekdays. The calculation of the "taxes and benefits" category is generally done by the property's controller and is based on the cost of employee meals, payroll taxes, insurance, vacation pay, and other benefits. In practice, the controller will apply a percentage to the "total salaries and wages" category based on previous years' costs plus any increment to expenses foreseen for the upcoming year.

THE PROFIT AND LOSS STATEMENT

Once the year is underway, every hotel division and department receives a monthly status report generated by the accounting department called the profit and loss statement (P&L). This statement shows the property's revenue and expenses for the month and includes a variance analysis column that indicates the changes in revenue and expenses from budget by category. The purpose of the analysis of variance is to alert department heads of percentage changes from those projected in the budget. If the cost percentages are higher than planned, the causes for the difference must be identified and explained to management and a plan to correct them in the future implemented. Table 13.3 is a sample profit and loss statement for the rooms division for the month of May, showing a column with the actual results, a column with the budgeted amounts, and the percentage variance between the two, which can be positive or negative. A positive variance in revenue and income indicates that sales have been larger than forecasted and that the departmental profit percentage has been better than predicted. On the contrary, a positive variance in costs indicates that the expense percentages have been larger than planned; negative variances indicate the opposite.

Variance Report for the Period May 1 to May 31

	Actual $	Actual %	Budgeted $	Budgeted %	Variance %
REVENUE	1,115,300	100.0	1,062,200	100.0	+ 5.0
Salaries & Wages					
Front Office	57,996	5.2	56,286	5.3	- .1
Housekeeping	104,838	9.4	100,890	9.5	- .1
Total	162,834	14.6	157,176	14.8	- .2
Taxes and Benefits	43,497	3.9	44,604	4.2	- .3
TOTAL PAYROLL	206,331	18.5	201,780	19.0	- .5
Other Expenses					
Reservation Commissions	22,306	2.0	21,240	2.0	—
PMS-related expenses	41,266	3.7	37.170	3.5	+ .2
Cleaning Supplies	15,614	1.4	11,682	1.1	+ .3
Linen Replacements	8,922	.8	10,620	1.0	- .2
Guest Supplies	22,306	2.0	23,364	2.2	- .2
Digital Communication	2,231	.2	2,124	.2	—
Postage	114	—	65	—	—
Printing & Stationery	2,231	.2	1,062	.1	+ .1
Uniforms	3,346	.3	5,310	.5	- .2
Laundry Supplies	4,461	.4	4,248	.4	—
Customer Goodwill	4,461	.4	6,372	.6	- .2
Auto Expense	10,038	.9	8,496	.8	+ .1
TOT. OTHER EXPENSES	137,296	12.3	131,753	12.4	- .1
TOTAL EXPENSES	343,627	30.8	333,533	31.4	- .6
DEPART. PROFIT	**771,673**	**69.2**	**728,467**	**68.6**	**+ .6**

Table 13.3 Sample Rooms Division P&L and Variance Report

In Table 13.3, the results in all categories, as indicted by the respective percentages, are as planned or better, except for "PMS-related expenses," "cleaning supplies," "printing and stationery" and "auto expense," where the percentages obtained are positive and therefore over budget. The executive housekeeper will need to investigate the causes for the increases in cost percentages for "cleaning expenses" while the front office manager will have to do the same for "PMS-related," "auto expense," and "printing & stationery." The departmental profit line at the bottom of Table 13.3 indicates that the overall performance of the rooms division for the month of May was better than predicted by six tenths of one percent (69.2 – 68.6 = + .6).

PRODUCTIVITY CONTROL

Productivity is a measure of output compared to input. An example of output is the number of customers checked in or out in a certain period of time. Inputs are the investments made by a business to provide products or services, the materials used to have the job done, and the work of the company's employees. In the hospitality industry, the overall result of productivity is measured by the profit, that is, *revenue – labor expenses.* The average departmental profit for the rooms division in lodging establishments ranges around 70 percent; that is, for every dollar made from selling rooms to guests, 30 cents should be cost and the remaining 70 cents departmental profit.

Indispensable factors to reach high levels of productivity, apart from the influence of department heads, are appropriate investments in the design, technology and equipment of the facilities. The effects of internal factors, particularly those of labor, on productivity can be controlled by front office managers. Effective labor management practices contribute to increased profits; an employee who has been adequately trained and is motivated to perform well can increase work output by using a minimum amount of time to perform a certain task. Front desk personnel competently servicing an optimum number of customers and guests during their shifts will provide better productivity to the company and, therefore, an increase in the company's profit.

Productivity, however, must go hand in hand with quality. It is to no advantage to achieve high productivity if the product is defective. To reach quality control, the front office department must adhere to specifications and controls. A useful formula to control productivity in the lodging industry is

revenue : hours of work required = dollars per labor hour.

PAYROLL CONTROL

Front office managers must develop a formal system of accurate reporting of payroll to accounting. The report is a record of hours worked daily by all employees in the department. The system must include a means of controlling overtime work. An effective way to control overtime work is to request that all supervisors get authorization for any overtime before it occurs.

The hours worked by hourly employees are in most cases recorded on digital clocks. Workers are asked to slide an identification card or punch a digital time clock or software-driven device at the beginning and end of their shift. During orientation, these procedures must be explained to employees in detail, such as not clocking in until they are in uniform and ready to start work, and clocking out at the time they stop working and not after. Most companies allow a half hour for lunch on company time. Managers and shift supervisors should not ask employees to perform any duties off the clock, as that is against labor laws. Sliding a time card in or out for another employee is cause for disciplinary action.

FINANCIAL RATIOS

There are several important operational ratios that can be worked out from income statements. The following front-office-related financial ratios will help students pursuing a career in the lodging industry interpret operational data:

- **Average daily rate:** *Room revenue : paid room nights sold*

This dollar figure is key to generating income. If costs related to labor are kept under control, a higher rate will increase the property's bottom line. The average daily rate of a hotel that generates $1,092,240 from selling 12,136 rooms in one month will be $90 (1,092,240 : 12,136).

- **Cost of labor percentage:** *Payroll + related expenses : total revenue*

This ratio is useful to monitor labor costs and can be interpreted as an indicator of productivity. A "normal" rooms division ratio would be between 18 and 22 percent of sales. If the total monthly payroll expense is $206,331 and the revenue for the same period is $1,115,300, the labor cost percentage is 18.50 (206,331 : 1,115,300).

- **Occupancy percentage:** *Rooms sold : Rooms available*

This ratio explains the property's ability to sell rooms. The rate for lodging establishments' average room occupancy in the US has been between 60 and 70 percent. A

450-room hotel that sells 12,136 in the month of October will have achieved an occupancy percentage of 87 (450 x 31 = 13,950 and then 12,136 : 13,950 = 87).

- **Profit margin:** *Income (Profit) : Revenue (Sales)*

Being a measure of profitability, this ratio indicates the bottom line of the rooms division. It measures the ability to generate revenue and to control expenses. Profit margins for the rooms division of well-managed lodging properties range around 70 percent. The profit margin percentage of a resort that has generated a monthly revenue of $1,115,300 and an income of $771,673 is 69.2 (771,673 : 1,115,300). This means that for every dollar in room sales, 69.2 cents are departmental profit.

- **RevPar rate:** *Room revenue : number of available rooms for sale*

The difference between RevPar and ADR is that RevPar measures how well a lodging establishment has been able to fill its guestrooms. While ADR is obtained by dividing the revenue by the number of occupied rooms, RevPar is calculated dividing the same revenue by the number of rooms available. For example, a spa with 450 rooms has 164,250 rooms available per year (450 x 365 = 164,250). If in the same spa the rooms revenue was $14,131,142, its RevPar average rate would have been $86, but if this establishment ended the year with a 81 percent occupancy, the ADR would have been 106 (164,250 x .81 = 133,042 and 14,131,142 : 133,042 = $106). Thus, the ADR figure is not an indicator of how well the spa did selling rooms while the RevPar rate establishes a record for measuring optimum occupancy.

- **Total revenue change from budget:** *(Actual revenue – budgeted revenue) : budgeted revenue*

This ratio indicates the situation relative to budgeted sales. It reflects whether an individual division or department is ahead or behind its projected revenues. For instance, if the budgeted room revenue is $1,062,200 and the actual revenue for the same period of time is $1,115,300, the change percentage is + 5.0 (1,115,300 – 1,062,200) : 1,062,200 = 5.0).

- **Total rooms division payroll per occupied room:** *Total rooms division payroll : rooms sold*

This is a measure of productivity for the rooms division. The lower the number, the higher the productivity will be. If payroll cost is $206,331 and the number of rooms occupied for the same period is 12,136, the labor cost per occupied room is $17 (206,331 : 12,136 = $17).

CASH CONTROL

Cash consists of bills, coins, money orders and checks. Cash receipts are usually generated by cash sales transactions, advance deposits, **package coupons**, payments on folios made by guests or by credits to city ledger accounts. Only cashiers should be authorized to handle cash if they are to be made responsible for cash transactions that take place during their shifts. Generally, cashiers are provided with an **opening bank** or **float** to allow them to transact business and to provide change to guests. The bank also acts as **petty cash** to meet incidental expenditures. Cash disbursements or **paid outs** are payments made from the cashier's drawer on behalf of a guest or any department making a small purchase of merchandise. Examples of petty cash paid-out disbursements are these buying some ice for the lounge because the ice-making machine broke down, paying a taxi driver on behalf of a guest who didn't have enough cash to do so. In this last case, the amount is charged to the guest's folio as a cash advance. Payments made by the cashier on behalf of a guest should be supported by a **cash advance voucher** and those charged as petty cash disbursements by paid-out slips. In other words, cash disbursement vouchers are notices attesting that authorized reductions of cash held by the front office cashiers have taken place. All vouchers and paid-out slips should provide a record of the amount of cash withdrawn, the person receiving the cash, the signature of the person authorizing the disbursement, the date, and the purpose of the transaction.

Guests who pay cash at the time of checking in are usually given a copy of their folio showing the credit as proof of payment. If the cash payment is larger than the total of all charges and the folio shows a credit balance at the time of checking out, the guest should be refunded the difference. Credit balances from credit card payments or travel agency vouchers should not be refunded in cash. In the first case, the guest should be issued a rebate against the credit card; in the second, the guest should be told to contact the travel agent for the refund.

The actual cash on hand at the end of the three front desk shifts minus the opening bank amount should be deposited in a designated vault or safe. The total cash received and paid-out slips and vouchers constitute the **gross cash receipts.** This amount should match the reading of the PMS cash report consisting of all cash postings. **Net cash receipts** are the gross receipts minus paid-outs and vouchers. The net receipts amount is the cash that should be deposited in the drop (together with paid-out slips and vouchers). It is customary for another employee to witness the cash banking procedure. Often, cashier/clerks making the deposit are requested to fill out a **cash-count sheet** as shown on Table 13.4.

Shift _______________ **Date:**____________________

Opening bank	$ 150.00
Gross receipts (cash and paid-outs)	12,440.35
Cash to be accounted for	12,590.35
Cash on hand	12,589.35
Over (short)	(1.00)
Cash deposit	12,439.35

Cashier's name_____________

TABLE 13.4 SAMPLE OF AN END-OF-SHIFT CASH COUNT SHEET

A **due back** may occur when cashiers deposit more than they cash in and there is not enough cash to restore the float. This may happen if the final money count includes several large bill denominations or checks, making it impossible to keep the starting bank.

The following morning, all dropped deposits are audited by the general cashier– an employee who reports to the property's controller. The total amounts found in the deposited envelopes must agree with the final night audit cash reading at the end of yesterday's business cycle. Table 13.5 is an example of a front desk cashier deposit envelope.

Date_____ **Cashier's name**_____ **Shift**_____

Bills:		**Amount:**
	$1	$ 2.00
	5	0
	10	20.00
	20	0
	50	150.00
	100	0
Coins:		.20
Paid-outs:		45.00
Cash vouchers:		190.15

Gift certificates and coupons:	100.00
Checks:	11,932.00
Total amount enclosed	**12,439.35**
Receipts	12,440.35
Over/short	**(1.00)**
Due back	**0**

TABLE 13.5 SAMPLE FRONT DESK CASHIER DEPOSIT ENVELOPE

Cashiers should be trained to safeguard the content of the cash register by closing the drawer after each transaction. Other guidelines consist of asking cashiers to place the money above the clip in the drawer until the transaction is completed to prevent any dispute over the bank note tendered and the change to be returned to the customer. Some properties have a supervisor or a member of the controller's office conduct unscheduled audits of front office cash registers.

The training of cashiers should also include a course in false currency detection. Some signs of counterfeit bills are:

- The serial number in older notes doesn't correspond to the letter inside the Treasury Seal above the number.
- The serial numbers of a true bill are printed in the same ink color as the Treasury Seal.
- The portrait of the President doesn't stand out distinctly from the background.
- Seals on the bill may have uneven, blunt, or broken saw-tooth points (the fine lines in the border of a genuine bill are clear and unbroken).

Counterfeit money detectors on the market offer technology for easy visualization of the fluorescence of the security thread in U.S. notes and for checking their watermarks.

KEY TERMS

Cash advance voucher
Cash-count sheet
Consolidated rooms sales summary
Departmental income
Due back cash
Float

Gross cash receipts
Net cash receipts
Opening bank
Operating budget
Other expenses
Package coupon
Paid-out
Paid-out slip
Petty cash
Profit and loss statement (P&L)
RevPar
Rooms revenue
Salaries and wages
Variance analysis

DISCUSSION AND REVIEW QUESTIONS

1. On what day does a calendar year budget begin?
2. What division budget is the front office budget a part of?
3. The rooms division budget for the Royal hotel includes the following amounts:

    a) Revenue: $100,500
    b) Total other expenses: $6,532
    c) Total payroll: $18,090

    What is the budget **income percentage?**
4. If the annual rooms revenue is $6,004,800 and the "auto expense" for the same period of time $30,024, what is the expense percentage for this category?
5. For the same revenue, what would have been the variance percent for "auto expense" if $38,200 had been budgeted and the actual cost was $30,024?
6. Work out:

    a) The RevPar percentage for a 310-room hotel that sold 7,208 rooms in January for a total of $864,960.
    b) The ADR for the same month.

7. Find the revenue change from budget percentage for the rooms division of a resort that planned to generate a revenue of $783,432 for the month of June and ended up having a revenue of $994,200.

8. Jane is a cashier at a motel in Barstow, California. At the end of her shift, the PMS cash reading is $11,500 but she doesn't have enough change to make the exact deposit. She ends up putting checks and bills in the deposit envelope for a total of $11,770. Jane's initial bank was $150. What is the amount due back she will receive from the general cashier the following morning?
9. How can a front office manager determine quantitatively the productivity of her/his department?
10. If projected revenue for the upcoming year is $8,339,110 and the authorized percentage for "customer goodwill" is 1.1, how many dollars should be allocated to this category? What would be the cost percent for "customer goodwill" for the month of July of the same year if revenue was $691,666 and the "customer goodwill" expense was $6,225?

PRACTICAL SITUATIONS

Situation 13.1

Calculation of Departmental Profit

The results of last year's rooms division operations at the Royal Inn were:

Net Revenue:	$11,540,006
Front Office Salaries:	490,500
Housekeeping Salaries:	899,000
Taxes and Benefits:	375,000
Reservation commissions:	101,744
PMS-related expenses:	197,400
Cleaning supplies:	29,110
Linen replacements:	52,760
Guest supplies:	265,380
Digital communication:	96,550
Postage:	290
Printing and stationery:	25,640
Uniforms:	7,330
Laundry supplies:	24,300
Customer goodwill:	39,000
Auto expense"	109,300

ASSIGNMENT:

Calculate:

1. The percentages of all expense categories
2. The divisional income in dollars
3. The profit percentage

Situation 13.2

Cashier's report

Jay Hales is cashier at a hotel in Eureka, California. At the end of his shift, the "gross receipts" reading is $2,345. On counting the content of the drawer, Jay finds:

Cash	2,180
Paid-out slips	55
Vouchers	250

He started the shift with a $150 float.

Lobby Cape Girardeau Hotel
Courtesy of Drury Hotels

ASSIGNMENT:

Work out the shift's:

1. Net receipts
2. Over/short
3. Content of the drop envelope

Situation 13.3

Building the annual budget

As the front office manager of London's Royal Court Hotel, you are asked by the rooms division director to submit information about the upcoming yearly budget. An 85% occupancy has been projected for the year with an ADR of 225 pounds per room sold. After considering all variables regarding expenses, you decide to set cost percentages as follows:

• Reservation commission	2.0 of projected revenue
• PMS expense	1.5
• Limousine expense	.03
• Uniforms	1.1

ASSIGNMENT:

Project cost in Pounds for the expense categories listed above.

CASE STUDY 13.1

Financial ratios from income statements

The extract of the departmental income statement given below corresponds to the month of July for a 310-room motel in Denver, Colorado. In the interest of space, the expense categories have been combined. This information has been given to you for a test that you are taking in an attempt to land a job as rooms division director with a local hospitality management company.

Rooms Division Report

	Actual	Budgeted
Rooms Revenue	$473,979	$541,800
Total Payroll and Related		
Front Office	28,219	33,605
Housekeeping	48,833	57,283
Other expenses		
Front Office	16,754	18,411
Housekeeping	9,396	15,600
Departmental Income	370,777	416,901

ASSIGNMENT:

You are asked to work out RevPar, average daily rate, profit margin percentage, total revenue change from budget, front office labor cost per occupied room, total rooms division payroll per occupied room, variance percentage from budgeted and actual departmental income. The number of rooms sold for the month was 7,040.

CHAPTER 14

GUEST SECURITY AND SAFETY

CHAPTER OBJECTIVES

- Understand what to do in case of crime emergencies.
- Learn how to minimize theft.
- Explain procedures to be followed for lost-and-found property.
- Discuss the management of safety in the front office department.
- Explain the importance of safety training programs.
- Explain the risk of fire in lodging properties and discuss what to do in case a fire occurs.
- Learn about bomb and terrorism threats.

OVERVIEW

Safety and security are the greatest concerns of the lodging industry today. Employees must be trained to deter theft, eliminate safety hazards, prevent and contain fires, and to take proactive steps to prevent risk in lodging operations. This chapter deals with the reasons behind the need to involve front office personnel in safeguarding guests and their assets.

The responsibility for setting up and maintaining a security program often lies with the property's front office manager. The design of a sound safety and security program should be aimed at protecting guests as they expect a safe experience when they choose a specific lodging establishment for their stay. Security is most effective when uniformed service staff and front desk clerks participate in the property's security efforts and each employee has a definite role to play in the overall plan. Besides the need to deter common crimes, nowadays hospitality establishments must address the curse of international terrorism.

SECURITY IN LODGING OPERATIONS

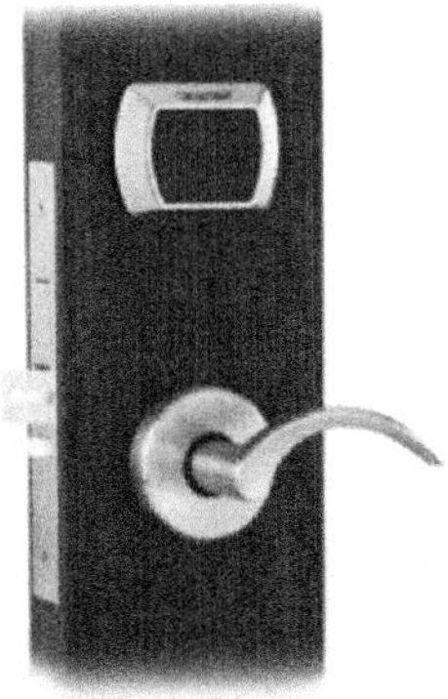

QUANTUM GUESTROOM DOOR LOCK

COURTESY KABA/ILCO

The goal of providing security in lodging operations is to protect guests, visitors, employees and assets. Lodging establishments can decide to have their own in-house security department or contract the security function to private companies or to off-duty police officers. By having an in-house staff, the property can exercise greater control over the security officers and train them to the specific characteristics of the establishment. Contracting the service to a security organization, on the other hand, can result in considerable savings because of lower payroll costs and freedom from administrative and supervisory responsibilities. However, the property cannot evade responsibility for the actions of contract security or off-duty officers because they are, in fact, the establishment's agents when on duty.

Smaller properties can resort to using off-duty police officers, who have already been thoroughly trained and usually are aware of the area's delinquents. Large lodging establishments generally have a security department managed by a director who reports directly to the rooms division director, resident or general manager; smaller properties with a reduced contingent of guards may report directly to the front office manager.

Besides security manpower, lodging properties should provide specific training for employees and invest substantial resources in closed-circuit TV surveillance, in-room safes, and impenetrable room-entry systems. Security awareness for guests and training of employees must be ongoing concerns of the rooms division management in order to prevent theft. Examples of guest security awareness are reminding travelers to keep valuables secure or to place them in the property's safe, asking them to use door locks and chains, and recommending that they look through the peephole before opening the guestroom door. Some specific training goals for the staff can be to close every guestroom door found open, to notify the security department of suspicious characters loitering in hallways, and to report anything unusual inside guestrooms, for example, weapons of any type or illegal drugs. Employees, especially the bellstaff, must be trained to be alert for objects left unattended in public areas and to report suspicious individuals present in areas for employees only. Conducting thorough checks on potential employees is also a must.

Uniformed personnel, front desk clerks, and parking attendants are in a privileged position to observe most people who arrive and leave the property. The design of modern lobbies allows for front office employees to monitor main entrances, elevators and staircases leading to guest floors. Employees should be trained to report any suspicious activity to the property's security or to management. Doormen must be trained to ensure that casual undesirables and prostitutes are prevented from access to public areas. Lodging establishments should do everything possible to discourage prostitution as it tends to upset other guests and affect the property's reputation. Front office employees should be made aware that lodging operations have the right to prevent anyone other than a guest from entering the sleeping areas; in other words, lodging properties have the right to require trespassers to leave.

Likewise, the front desk is entitled to refuse a room to persons in a drunken state on the grounds that they are not in a fit state to be lodged. The same applies to guests who misbehave as the establishment is not obliged to let them stay if they are quarrelsome or exceedingly noisy. If a guest calls the front desk to complain about being kept awake by loud neighbors, the clerk on duty should telephone or send a security guard to the room to quiet them down or, in the worst case, ask them to leave.

The eviction of anyone from the premises must be carried out with discretion keeping in mind that although the establishment is a private enterprise, it is at the same time open to the public. However, guestrooms and hallways are not open to the general public, and a person may be evicted who is not a house guest or has been invited by a guest to stay in these areas. On the other hand, the eviction of persons from public spaces, such as the lounges or lobbies, is allowed in accordance to the statutes of the locality and the liability law of the state where the operation is located.

Front office employees should be trained not to disclose any registration information to anyone nor say loudly the room number when handing the entry card to guests. In addition, a person calling for the room number of a certain guest should not be given the information but just connected to the telephone extension. When someone asks the front desk clerk for an extra door-opening card, the identity of the person should be verified to be sure he is a guest in the hotel. Written messages and parcels should be turned over to guests only after verification of identity.

BELL-STAND SECURITY

Parking valets and bellpersons should encourage guests arriving by car to conceal and secure any items that may appeal to robbers, such as suitcases, GPS devices or expensive clothing. All parked vehicles keys should be kept secure until they are returned to guests. Members of the bellstaff accompanying guests to their rooms should explain the use of door-locking devices and how to secure the opening door to the balcony (if any). Any luggage received by the door attendant should be kept secure until a bellperson gets control of it for transportation to guestrooms. Guests' personal belongings left in storage should be safely secured until they are returned to the owners.

In all cases, the security department of lodging properties should never assume the role that the regular police force represents. Establishments located in cities and towns usually need just a short period of time to have the local police arrive. While the people in charge of security can be very effective in deterring and restraining criminals, only the police department has the prerogative of enforcing the law.

EMERGENCY RESPONSE IN CASE OF CRIME

The establishment should be protected at all times from criminal threats. Travelers using lodging properties often carry many valuables and unscrupulous characters know it. Busy hotel lounges, swimming pool areas and even lobbies can be the target of pickpockets and bag snatchers. Some thieves may check in as regular guests and prowl the hallways in search of open guestroom doors or luggage pieces left around inadvertently. If a criminal act takes place, the manager or front office supervisor on duty should follow these procedures:

1. Call security and, if necessary, the police as soon as possible.
2. Designate only one person to speak for the property. Any other employee directly or indirectly involved in the act should not volunteer any statement.
3. Don't let anyone touch anything around the scene of a crime.

In the event of armed robbery at the front desk, service agents and cashiers should be instructed to comply with the robber's demands rather than resist and jeopardize themselves and others present. Some behavior guidelines include being cooperative, keeping hands in sight, and not attempting to disarm the robber. Employees should be trained to memorize the physical traits of the intruder such as build, color of eyes and hair, and any other outstanding characteristics of the individual. Doormen should be instructed to observe the direction of escape and obtain the license plate of the vehicle if one is used in the holdup.

MINIMIZING THEFT

Estimates of employee theft in the workplace are very high. While accurate statistics are difficult to obtain, it is believed that half of all employees steal from their employers. This is particularly credible in the hospitality industry where wages are low and working conditions leave much to be desired. Front office employees have opportunities to steal and pilfer—they can steal cash and they can pilfer company property, particularly office supplies. Often, employees steal because their part-time jobs and minimum wages are not sufficient for them to make ends meet. Other times disgruntled workers, feeling frustrated by the way they have been treated, decide to get even by taking the company's possessions. In other cases, employees steal simply because accounting control and security measures are lax.

Theft by employees can be curtailed by establishing theft-prevention measures in the department. One important step is to make sure that application forms are carefully scrutinized and that references of all employees hired are thoroughly checked. Gaps in employment history, for example, may indicate an attempt to hide a job from which the applicant was fired because of theft. References can be effectively checked by establishing an information network by phone with other front office managers in the area for mutual cooperation.

Once employees are hired, it must be clearly stated at orientation and in the employee handbook that theft will be an automatic cause for dismissal.

THEFT BY GUESTS AND INTRUDERS

Some cash-only guests are known for taking with them bathroom appliances, coffee makers, blankets, pillows, clock radios, telephones, TV sets and, in rare cases, the entire furniture of rooms by parking a van behind the room's sliding door/window. Guest theft can be reduced by not admitting travelers who don't use a valid credit card.

When the front desk is notified by housekeeping that items are missing from a room, the clerk on duty may ask the guest whether he/she has inadvertently taken any articles. Sometimes the departing guest will admit that he/she took the items as souvenir, in which case the cost of the articles should be added to the folio. If the guest denies taking anything, the front office manager will have a tough decision to make. If it is fairly certain that the guest has taken the items, the manager can request that the bags are opened although it is dangerous from a legal perspective to insist on this unless there is clear evidence to support the accusation.

SECURITY IN GUESTROOMS

TV sets and light appliances in guestrooms should be bolted down or secured to the wall, furniture, or an electrical socket. Entry doors should close automatically and be fitted with latching bolts to lock the door when it is closed. Besides the latching bolt, guestroom doors should have deadbolts, chains, and peepholes. Sliding glass doors on balconies should be provided with "charley bars" which, when extended down, prevent prying the door open from the outside. Special attention should be given to connecting doors between rooms. Besides the primary lock on the connecting doors, an additional security chain or deadbolt that can be activated by the guest from within each room should be installed.

Room keys, in use for decades, are not effective to deter crime; as a matter of fact, lodging properties using traditional guestroom keys are considered to be at a competitive disadvantage. That is the case because it is practically impossible to prevent crooks from keeping room keys if they rent a room, then keeping the key upon check-out, and coming back in the evening to enter the same room when the current guest has gone out. This problem can only be corrected by changing the locks each time keys are missing, which requires substantial labor costs and additional manpower.

Fortunately, most lodging properties in the US have abandoned the use of traditional keys, although this practice is still common abroad. Card entry systems, on the other hand, are designed so that every guest checking into the property receives a card with a combination different from that used the previous night. In fact, the computer terminal issuing cards at the front desk is capable of providing thousands of combinations for entrance to a room. Card entry systems can also register around the clock the time and what specific card was used to enter the room. That is to say, printed records can indicate the time guests and staff used the card at any time during the day or night. Besides, if a master card is lost, the entire floor or floors can be reset very quickly. Some entry card systems are designed to encode two different tracks, enabling the property to control not only guestrooms, but access to other designated areas such as pools, health clubs, elevators, and in-room safes. State-of-the-art cellular control systems can be programmed to issue cards that limit employee access to rooms by name, time, and date. For example, Saflok markets a Windows-based system that offers keycard management interfacing with the property's PMS. It provides centralized auditing and reporting features that can integrate with self-check-in kiosks. Saflok URL is www.saflok.com.

Guests' personal valuables can be protected by providing a small safe in the room. Most in-room thefts take place when guests leave jewelry, traveler's checks, cameras or credit/debit cards unattended while they are swimming in the pool or having a meal in the dining room. In-room safes can be operated with keys, cards, or touch-pads, on which guests can punch their own safe-opening codes. While the smallest in-room safes should be able to hold a camera, business properties need to install briefcase-size or larger units to accommodate portable computers.

LOST AND FOUND

Usually lost and found records are kept at the front desk as that is where persons claiming articles show up or telephone asking for their lost articles. If this is the case, all found items should be entered on a lost and found logbook. The record should include the date, time and place where the article was found, a description of it, and the person who found it. Once the identity of the owner is verified, the item is returned and a signature obtained on a receipt which should be kept as a record. If the article is mailed to the owner, the date of mailing should be noted. All articles of value, such as gold rings or necklaces should be placed in the property's safe deposit box at the front office until they are returned to the owner.

Management should make every effort to contact owners of mislaid or lost items to notify them of the finding. Items should not be sent to the guest's address stated at registration without first receiving his/her permission to do so. All articles should be sent using a "return receipt" option to prove that the parcel was received. If the owner cannot be reached after a reasonable period of time, the articles are usually given to the finder or raffled off at employee gatherings.

SAFETY IN THE FRONT OFFICE DEPARTMENT

There are three important reasons why safety for employees and guests is a function of management. The first is legal: the **Occupational Safety and Health Act (OSHA)** requires employers by law to keep their places of business free from hazards that may cause harm or injury to employees. The act assures every working person in the nation safe and healthful working conditions; therefore, front office managers must comply with OSHA regulations to keep workers safe. OSHA inspectors can enter an employer's premises without notice to conduct inspections, review records, and question workers about safety. When serious injury or death is involved, criminal charges can be filed against the property.

Another reason is financial: statistics provided by the **National Safety Council** indicate that the number of injuries that occur in the service sector is staggering, costing companies billions of dollars annually. In addition, thousands of lost workdays diminish human productivity significantly and are, therefore, the source of an even greater financial burden on organizations. Worker's compensation premiums go up whenever mishaps occur in the workplace. Worker's compensation is insurance required by the states to cover injuries sustained at work. The worker's compensation insurance premium payments are determined by his/her employer's safety and health records. Furthermore, courts of law tend to award substantial amounts of money when injured guests and employees file civil lawsuits against businesses for accidents or mishaps.

The third reason is ethical. As employees and guests expect to find a safe place to work and stay, lodging operators must see to it that their properties are free from harm, injury, danger, or risk and that the organizational climate is conductive to the personal well-being of their workers.

One way to minimize accidents is for front office managers to conduct **job-safety analyses** for those tasks that might involve any risk of injury. After describing the potential hazards that the task may involve, safety tips about how to perform the job should be provided to workers.

SAFETY TRAINING PROGRAMS

Safety-training programs are designed to instruct front office employees in safe working practices. Specific instructions to guard against hazards unique to their job assignments should also be provided. Some of the safety standards that can be adopted by the front office department may include the elimination of accident and fire hazards, providing first-aid supplies and equipment, having CPR-certified employees in the department, keeping stairs free from obstacles, and teaching employees how to handle weights (such as suitcases, trunks, and packages) correctly. Some specific safety tips for front office workers are these:

- Report all hallway obstructions.
- Keep loads close to the body when lifting.
- Bend knees and keep a straight back when handling heavy objects.
- Use ergonomic equipment at the front desk to avoid carpal tunnel syndrome.

Implementation of safety programs should start at orientation, when employees should be taught about the safety philosophy of the department, as well as what is expected of them in order to perform their jobs safely.

FIRE

Although most lodging properties are equipped with state-of-the-art equipment to suppress fires, they do occur. Fires in lodging operations are more complex to manage than those occurring in residential homes because of their high occupancy and guests' unfamiliarity with the building. Some travelers may even have difficulty understanding verbal or written directions in English. On the other hand, all establishments built in the US are constructed following strict codes which include fire and life-safety systems.

The role of front office personnel in case of fire must be clearly defined and understood by all employees as it is this department that is often in charge of monitoring the fire alarm and alert systems. The training of front office workers should include this information:

- A through description of how the fire control panel at the front desk works.
- A description of emergency procedures in case of fire.
- The identification of common fire hazards and how to prevent them.
- The correct manner to help with guest evacuation.

Fire alarm systems are generally required by local fire codes. A component of fire alarm systems is a panel, usually located at the front desk, which alerts of the location of the fire and permits prompt notification to local fire authorities. **Fire Alarm Control Panels (FACP)** receive information from the different alarm accessories located throughout the building, such as smoke, heat and carbon monoxide detectors, and pull-alarm stations. From the FACP, employees and guests can be alerted if smoke or fire occurs within the complex. Basically, the hardwired panel receives and processes signals from the different zones in which the establishment is divided and in turn triggers an alarm locally that can be set to dial it out to the fire department if necessary. It is important to emphasize to employees that delayed notification to the fire department and to guests has been the cause of major property fires in the past.

A copy of a fire emergency plan should be available to all employees, including those who work nights. Front desk and uniformed personnel should be able to identify fire and life safety hazards such as open fire doors, locked exit doors, blocked stairways, and burned out exit lights. All front office employees should also become familiar with the location of **pull alarms,** fire extinguishers, exit doors and stairwells, and how the **voice alarm system** works.

Generally, local emergency officials are in charge of ordering the evacuation of the premises. In other cases, a designated person within the establishment should be appointed responsible for making the decision to evacuate the building. Regarding the front office, evacuation plans should include:

- Only local emergency officials or a designated senior employee at location of fire who will give orders for evacuation.
- Printing of an occupancy report listing all checked-in guests with names and room numbers.
- Response to telephone inquiries as directed by the manager on duty or fire squad commander.
- Designation of assembly areas where employees and guests should gather after evacuation.

WHAT TO DO IN CASE A FIRE HAPPENS

It is imperative that employees understand that every alarm be treated seriously; that is, if the alarm sounds, or a fire is suspected, the fire department should be called immediately. After making the call, if it is determined that there is no fire because of equipment malfunction or a false alarm, the information should be relayed to the local emergency number (911 in the U.S.). However, the call to the fire department should never be delayed waiting for an investigation of the situation.

Fire safety programs should train employees to combat small, controllable fires such as a smoldering wastebasket. In a case like this, the use of a fire extinguisher or even a bucket of water can prevent the fire from expanding to other areas. Above all, employees must be trained not to panic in case of a fire but to remain calm. **Panic emotion** can cause people to feel disoriented, preventing them from acting rationally.

In case of fire, elevators should never be used because they may fail during the fire, trapping occupants. The elevator shafts may also fill with smoke and suffocate those in the car. Some steps for front office employees to follow before the fire department takes over could be these:

- Emergency exits locked for security reasons should be opened.
- Employees should assist guests to exits, particularly elderly persons.
- All guestrooms should be searched to make sure no one is left behind.
- Make every possible effort to contain or suppress the fire by closing certain doors, using extinguishers, etc.

Besides fire protection instruction such as how a fire extinguisher works and the location of fire exits and fire alarms, fire-safety programs should include fire drills. Fire departments in most localities will participate in employee training by showing videos on fire prevention, lecturing on the effects of smoke, and demonstrating the use of fire equipment. Guestrooms should be provided with diagrams of evacuation routes and instructions explaining what to do in case of fire.

THE THREAT OF TERRORISM

Attacks to lodging properties abroad have become only too common. While threats and attacks can occur in any establishment, overseas properties that cater to western diplomats, foreign tourists or military personnel can be especially attractive to terrorists. American companies operating abroad have reacted to calibrate their security efforts with government warnings; other hospitality companies are surely stepping up their terrorist-related security measures as well.

Tactics used by terrorists can be bomb threats, suicide bombings and armed teams infiltrating establishments to take hostages or cause as much harm as possible. This new reality is forcing lodging companies to supplement traditional security with security technologies, such as perimeter surveillance provided by cameras and, in sophisticated cases, ground-based radar and all-weather day-night laser-illuminated devices to vector in on and track approaching suspects. In selected areas within the property, networks can be configured to trigger an automatic alert for objects left behind or for intrusion in restricted areas. A command and control center with monitored visual displays is necessary for effective control if intelligence-enabled sensors, cameras, and ground radar are installed.

In case of bomb threats, procedures to respond should be included in the property's emergency plans. Persons likely to receive the threat are front office employees who should be trained to memorize the exact words of callers, to ask them when the explosive is set to go off and the reasons why the device was placed, and to remember the accent of the caller. Although potential terrorists are difficult to recognize, lodging employees should be trained to notice anything unusual, including potential terrorist scouts who try to case locations months prior to an attack, and to watch for abandoned packages. If approached with security questions about the property, employees must report such inquiries to management or security personnel.

KEY TERMS

Fire alarm control panel (FACP)
Job-safety analysis
National safety council
Occupational Safety and Health Act (OSHA)
Panic emotion
Pull-alarm station
Voice alarm system

DISCUSSION AND REVIEW QUESTIONS

1. Give three reasons why safety and accident prevention should be functions of front office management.
2. How would you describe OSHA?
3. What are the main advantages of implementing safety training programs in the front office department?
4. Why should front office employees be trained in security awareness?
5. What is most likely to be stolen by front office employees (front desk and uniform personnel)?
6. A bellperson enters a guestroom to deliver a dry-cleaned suit and discovers a cigarette was carelessly tossed into the wastebasket and it is smoldering. What should the bellperson do?
7. Do you believe that if a contracted security officer is negligent the property may be held liable? Why or why not?
8. Explain the implications involved in asking a departing guest to open her/his suitcase at the front desk because of suspicion of stolen property.
9. Is it correct procedure to send a ring found in a guestroom to the address on file for the guest in that room without getting his/her permission first to do so? Why or why not?
10. In which way(s) can uniformed personnel play an important role in guest asset protection?

PRACTICAL SITUATIONS

Situation 14.1

Sounding the fire alarm

Clay Douglas has been a bellperson at the Royal Hotel in Aspen, Colorado, for three years. Clay has been trained in safety and security procedures but has never experienced an emergency situation until today. It is early in the morning and he is delivering a package to room 511. As he is knocking on the door of the room, the fire alarm sounds and some guests, including those in room 511, open their doors to look into the hallway.

How should Clay react in this situation?

Situation 14.2

Crime outside the property?

On a late Sunday evening, an armed robber shot a registered guest a few feet outside the main entrance of a hotel. The victim was returning from dinner at a nearby restaurant and was approximately at the door of the establishment when he was confronted by two young men, one of whom had a gun. He was shot and fell dead on the sidewalk, his feet four feet from the glass rotating door at the entrance of the property.

The guest's widow brought a wrongful death suit against the hotel charging the defendants with negligently failing to provide adequate security to protect the decedent from assault by third persons and failing to warn him of the danger of being assaulted in the area. The plaintiffs introduced evidence to show that the hotel complex and its surroundings had been the scene of a number of crimes. The hotel company claimed that an innkeeper has no duty to protect its guests from assaults by third persons committed outside the environs of the hotel and, more particularly, it has no duty to protect its guests from assaults by third parties in areas where such protection is commonly owed by the local police department, such as on public sidewalks.

ASSIGNMENT:

Discuss the situation with other students in your class and decide whether the hotel exercised reasonable care to prevent this incident from happening.

Situation 14.3

Attack in a public restroom

The Northern Hotel, located in downtown Toledo, Ohio, was the object of a lawsuit following an attack on a female guest. One evening about 6:00 PM, a woman complained to the manager on duty that she had been assaulted by a male intruder in a ladies' restroom located behind the property's front desk. She told the manager that she saw nobody in the lower lobby or in the ladies' restroom before entering the cubicle where she was grabbed from behind by a man who sexually abused her. The attacker ran out of the restroom pursued by a uniformed employee who had just come out of the storage room where he had put luggage and heard the woman's screams. The front office clerk on duty also heard the shouting and joined the chase. The bellhop made the capture a few minutes later. The assailant was arrested, identified and eventually sentenced on a guilty plea.

Subsequently, the plaintiff filed a lawsuit against the hotel alleging that the defendant should have known of the possibility that an assailant might conceal himself in the restroom, and that it was therefore dangerous. The suit charged negligence in failing to provide a restroom attendant, failing to provide a uniformed security guard, failing to maintain s system of internal surveillance, and failing to alert employees and to provide them with security training. All witnesses agreed that nothing in the appearance of the attacker would have caused any hotel employee to detain him if he had been seen entering the hotel. On the other hand, there was substantial evidence that other persons, having no real business in the hotel, entered the premises with some regularity and were cause for concern to management. A former front office manager testified that prostitutes would sometimes take the elevators to upper floors and that vandalism occurred in the hotel's garage. A former employee who had worked as a security guard in the hotel said that petty theft in the gift shop was common. There was, however, no evidence of incidents of rape, assault, armed robbery or other violent crime in or near the hotel.

Drury Hotel Valdosta, GA
Courtesy of Drury Hotels

ASSIGNMENT:

Discuss the situation with a classmate and determine whether the plaintiff made an appropriate case of negligence and if the jury should vote in favor of compensatory damages to the plaintiff.

CASE STUDY 14.1

Robbery in a motel guestroom

Desert Inn was a medium-size motel located on the main drag of Winslow, Arizona. In the early morning hours of a February day, front desk clerk Patel, in charge of the graveyard shift, was working on the night audit when he was approached by two males who had entered the lobby by its only door. One of the men, a former employee of the motel, asked Patel whether Jake Lee was working that night, and after being told that he was not, the men exited the building. Without the clerk's noticing it, they took one bellperson shirt that was hanging in a corner.

Meanwhile, the activities of the men were being watched by a policeman who was routinely patrolling the motel's premises in an unmarked car. The officer became suspicious after seeing the men return to their car and drive to the rear of the parking lot near an adjacent block of motel rooms. The patrolman then entered the lobby and questioned Patel about the conversation with the men. Patel informed him that a short time previously a guest in room 125 had phoned the desk to report that a man knocked at the door claiming their room phone was out of order and that he had a message for them from the desk. Not recognizing the employee, the guest did not open the door. The patrolman, on hearing this information, suspected something unusual, called headquarters and requested the aid of additional support which arrived at the scene shortly thereafter.

The imposter "messenger," after being denied entrance to room 125, apparently went to room 190, occupied by Mr. Ogilvy. The man knocked on the door and repeated the same message, informing Ogilvy that the phone was not working and that he had a message from the desk. Mr. Ogilvy looked through the door's peephole and saw a man in the hallway wearing a bellboy's shirt, the type worn by the motel personnel. He opened the door, believing the message was the 6:45 AM wake-up call he had requested. Two men then pushed their way into the room and one held Ogilvy at gunpoint while the other searched his belongings. They found around $500 in cash and a set of keys. The intruders forced Ogilvy to accompany them, apparently intending further criminal action. He was pushed into his own car and at this time the police converged upon the vehicle and the two men were apprehended at the scene.

At the time of the assault, the outside entrance to the separate structure housing rooms 125 and 190 was neither locked, monitored by close circuit television, nor manned by motel staff or security personnel. The only security provided by the motel was a dead bolt lock on each room as well as a chain lock and a peephole. The hallway outside the guestrooms was well lighted at the time of the assault. The motel did not employ security guards, as in the past five years there had been few incidents requiring calls to the police for help and because the police routinely patrolled the motel parking lot.

In court, Mr. Ogilvy's attorney argued that the motel was negligent in permitting intruders access to his room that resulted in his being manhandled and robbed. He emphasized that a lodging operation has a duty to exercise ordinary care to provide adequate protection for its guests and their property from assault and other types of criminal activity.

ASSIGNMENT:

Based on a motel's duty to provide appropriate security, and the facts and circumstances that occurred:

1. Did the defendant motel provide adequate security? Did the presence of the assailants in the motel lobby, not for the purpose of renting a room but of looking for a certain employee, raise the question of suspicious circumstance requiring the clerk on duty to monitor the intruders' whereabouts?
2. Were security measures provided by the innkeeper sufficient to protect the personal safety of his guests?

Keycard console
Courtesy Saflok

CHAPTER 15

THE FRONT OFFICE AS AN INITIAL STAGE IN A HOSPITALITY CAREER

CHAPTER OBJECTIVES

- Develop strategies to plan a career in the lodging industry.
- Identify the best way to contact perspective employers.
- Explain the role of your college's career services.
- Prepare a perfect resume and cover letter.
- Describe what the first and second interviews mean.
- Explain what to look for in a job offer.

OVERVIEW

The semester is coming to an end and you are now much better prepared to assume a professional role in the lodging industry. You have learned how to handle many aspects of the front office including guest relations, personnel, accounting and technology. You may not be graduating yet but a summer job at the front desk is a great place to acquire work credentials and to begin your climb up the industry ladder. This chapter explains the strategies necessary to obtain a front office management-training position in the lodging industry. Students will be able to contact prospective employers directly or by using their college's career services. A perfect resume is indispensable in the search for a job. If the resume is sent by mail or submitted electronically, it should be accompanied by a cover letter explaining the purpose of the application. Students should also have a list of references to be provided to interested employers on request. The chapter also explains how to be successful at the time of interviewing for a position and how to select the most appropriate job offer.

STRATEGIES FOR PLANNING A CAREER IN THE LODGING INDUSTRY

The hospitality industry in general and the lodging industry in particular offer numerous career opportunities. Many job openings are aimed at filling positions in the rooms divisions of lodging operations; positions in other departments, such as accounting, and sales and marketing are fewer as these departments operate with a smaller number of workers. It is therefore advisable for seniors to accept any initial management-training job that is open at the time of the interview. By accepting a training position in the front office, for instance, the candidate will get a foot in the door with that company and, at the same time, start getting experience in management techniques. After the training period, individuals usually have opportunities to transfer to a position that better fits their personality, values, interests and aspirations. The career path in a lodging property, starting at the front office, could follow this sequence: trainee at the front desk, reservations, and night audit; shift supervisor; assistant front office manager; cross-training in other departments; front office manager; rooms division director; assistant general manager; and general manager.

Often, students wish to work solely in one aspect of the hospitality industry, for example in restaurants and not in hotels. If this is the case but they cannot find a position with a restaurant chain, they should start working in a large hotel, rather than reject such a work offer. The reverse is also true for students who plan to work only in, say, resorts and do not receive such a job offer. In this case, it would be to their advantage to accept a position with a hotel as trainee, thus beginning to gain some expertise in management.

Generally, a career in restaurants requires that beginning professionals work long hours in an environment where decision-making must be fast, whereas hotels or resorts run with more manageable schedules and fewer operational difficulties. Restaurants, however, usually offer college graduates fast opportunities for advancement and higher salaries than lodging establishments.

CONTACTING PROSPECTIVE EMPLOYERS ON CAMPUS

The most effective way of contacting prospective employers is through the on-campus career services office. Most colleges and universities provide this service to assist students in getting a job. Students should register with career services when they are close to graduation. Without cost, or for a small registration fee, the career services office usually offers help with the following activities:

- Career day and graduate school fairs
- Career resource center
- Job vacancy bank

- Recruiter information
- Finding-jobs-on-the-Web information
- Mailing of credentials to prospective employers
- Individual career counseling and guidance
- On-line listing of jobs
- Posting student resumes on-line
- Resume writing
- Job-interview practice

The career services office is usually in charge of sponsoring and organizing job fairs, where students have the opportunity of making direct contact with prospective employers. Often, the representatives of companies attending the fair are the same individuals that conduct job interviews. If recruiters organize seminars on campus about their companies, students should attend and ask questions relative to the positions open. It is important to dress professionally when attending these events. If students make a favorable impression, chances are they will be considered as potential candidates to interview. If the company is not interviewing at that time, students can follow up with a letter of intent addressed to the person they met on campus.

CONTACTING PROSPECTIVE EMPLOYERS THROUGH THE INTERNET OR DIRECT MAIL

Besides using the college's career services, students can directly contact hospitality corporations or individual properties to apply for a job, either by Internet or by mail, but this approach is not nearly as effective as interviewing on campus because letters or applications on line usually end up in the company's human resources department which receives a steady stream of job requests. The following list includes some websites where openings for hospitality jobs and careers can be found.

HOSPITALITY/HOTELS:

www.hcareers.com
www.hjo.net
www.hospitalityadventures.com
www.hospitalitycareers.net
www.hospitalitylink.com
www.hoteljobs.com
www.resortjobs.com

INTERNET ADDRESSES OF SOME LODGING CORPORATIONS IN THE U.S.:

Adam's Mark Hotels & Resorts	www.adamsmark.com
Best Inns & Suites	www.bestinn.com
Carlson Companies	www.carlson.com
Choice Hotels International	www.choicehotels.com
Country Inns & Suites	www.countryinns.com
Courtyard by Marriott	www.courtyard.com
Days Inns Worldwide	www.daysinn.com
Doubletree	www.doubletree3.hilton.com
Embassy Suites	www.embassysuites.hilton.com
Fairfield Inn by Marriott	www.fairfieldinn.com
Felcor Lodging Trust Inc	www.felcor.com
Four Seasons Hotels & Resorts	www.fourseasons.com
Hilton Hotels Corporation	www.hiltonworldwide.com
Howard Johnson International	www.hojo.com
Hyatt Hotels Corporation	www.hyatt.com
Interstate Hotels	www.ihrco.com
La Quinta Inns, Inc	www.laquinta.com
Lodgian Inc	www.lodgian.com
Loews	www.loewshotels.com
Marriott Hotels, Resorts & Suites	www.marriott.com
Motel 6	www.motel6.com
Omni Hotels	www.omnihotels.com
Radisson Hotels & Resorts	www.radisson.com
Ramada Franchise System, Inc	www.ramada.com
Red Roof Inns	www.redroof.com
Renaissance Hotels & Resorts	www.marriott.com
Residence Inn by Marriott	www.residenceinn.com
Ritz-Carlton	www.ritzcarlton.com
Sage Hospitality Resources	www.sagehospitality.com
Sheraton	www.starwoodhotels.com
Starwood Hotels & Resorts	www.starwoodhotels.com
Super 8 Motels, Inc	www.super8.com
Travelodge	www.travelodge.com
Wyndham International, Inc	www.wyndham.com

Many students are attracted to the hospitality industry because of its global scope. Although it is true that U.S. corporations have substantial interests overseas, including a great number of restaurants, hotels, resorts, and franchises, most of the employees in these establishments are local. Occasionally, a reduced staff may be from the United States, for example, the general manager, controller, and executive chef.

The best way to work for an American company abroad is to contact its international division in the U.S. Foreign corporations with headquarters overseas can also be contacted. They may be interested in graduates with a 4-year hospitality degree, particularly students who are fluent in the foreign language spoken in that country.

INTERNET ADDRESSES OF SOME WORLDWIDE INTERNATIONAL HOSPITALITY CORPORATIONS:

Accor	Worldwide	www.accor.com
AFM Hospitality Corp	Canada	www.hospitalitynet.org
Atlantica Hotels	Worlwide	www.atlanticahotels.com
Choice Hotels Canada	Canada	www.choicehotels.ca
Club Mediterranee	Worldwide	www.clubmed.com
Danubius Hotels	Hungary	www.danubiushotels.com
Dorint Hotels	Europe	www.dorint.com
Golden Tulip Hotels	Holland	www.goldentulip.com
Inter-Continental	Worldwide	www.igh.com
Jolly Hotels	Italy	www.nh-hotels.com
Kempinski Hotels	Worldwide	www.kempinski.com
Maritim Hotels	Germany	www.maritim.com
Mercure Hotel	Worldwide	www.mercure.com
Millennium Hotels	Worldwide	www.millenniumhotels.com
Minotel	Switzerland	www.minotel.ch
Nikko Hotels	Worldwide	www.jalhotels.com
Novotel Hotel Division	Worldwide	www.novotel.com
Orbis Company	Poland	www.accorhotels.com
Park Plaza Worldwide	Worldwide	www.parkplaza.com
Posadas USA	Mexico & US	www.posadas.com
Protea Hotels	South Africa	www.proteahotels.com
Ringhotels	Germany	www.ringhotels.de

Rocco Forte Hotels	Worldwide	www.roccofortehotels.com
Shangri-La Hotels	Far East	www.shangri-la.com
Sofitel	Worldwide	www.sofitel.com
Sol Melia	Worldwide	www.melia.com
Swiss International	Worldwide	www.swissinternationalhotels.com
Thistle Hotels	UK	www.thistlehotels.com

Students may decide to apply directly to individual properties for a position, either because they have visited or know about them or because they would like to work in a specific location.

INTERNET ADDRESSES OF A SHORT SAMPLE OF THE BEST HOTELS AND RESORTS IN THE UNITED STATES AND AROUND THE WORLD FOLLOW:

Los Angeles, CA	Bel-Air	www.dorchestercollection.com
Chicago, IL	Four Seasons	www.fourseasons.com
Honolulu, HI	Halekulani	www.halekulani.com
Rome, Italy	Hassler	www.hotelhasslerroma.com
Hong Kong	Intercontinental	www.intercontinental.com
Dallas, TX	Mansion on Turtle Creek	www.mansiononturtlecreek.com
Phoenix/Scottsdale, AZ	Phoenician	www.thephoenician.com
Laguna Niguel, CA	Ritz-Carlton	www.ritz-carlton.com
Positano, Italy	San Pietro	www.relaischateaux.com
New York	The Carlyle	www.thecarlyle.com
Sea Island, GA	The Cloister	www.cloister.com
White Sulphur Springs, WV	The Greenbrier	www.greenbrier.com
Bangkok, Thailand	The Oriental	www.mandarin-oriental.com
Paris, France	The Ritz	www.ritz.com
London, England	The Stafford	www.thestaffordhotel.co.uk

Cruise ships offer an exotic introduction to the hospitality industry. However, having been chief purser in cruise ships for several years, this author doesn't recommend that graduates plan to make a career of working afloat. Work aboard ship is very intense as cruises are usually booked back-to-back leaving no time to enjoy a normal social life. This frenetic lifestyle often leads to eventual job burnout. However, it is fine for a short time as the cruise-ship industry offers the best opportunities to visit fascinating destinations with landscapes to be remembered forever.

Some Internet cruise lines URLs lines are:

Carnival Cruise Lines	www.carnival.com
Royal Caribbean International	www.royalcaribbean.com
Norwegian Cruise Lines	www.ncl.com
Princess Cruises	www.princess.com
Disney Cruise Line	www.disneycruise.disney.go.com
Cunard Lines	www.cunard.com
P & O Lines	www.pocruises.com
Antarctica	www.polarcruises.com

Also, for information leading to employment, you should contact individuals you know or have met during field trips to hospitality properties, guest speakers or other experts in the field attending industry trade shows, and relatives, friends and alumni working in the industry.

THE PERFECT RESUME

The main purpose of a student handing a resume to a recruiter or sending it directly to companies is to be granted an interview. The resume can help candidates get a job or prevent them from getting a job. For this reason, resumes must be flawless in format, appearance, and content. In most cases, resumes should be limited to one page that includes the following components: objective, education, work experience, honors/awards, skills, extracurricular activities, and references. *Curriculum vitae* (extensive accounts of an individual's experiences) are not appropriate for students looking for an initial job. The following is a sample resume for a Northern Arizona University student looking for a job at a career fair on campus:

NATALIA FOSTER

Current Address
Northern Arizona University
P.O.Box 3333
Flagstaff, AZ 86011
(928) 774 1711
ncf22@nau.edu

Permanent Address
9292 El Rey Road
Los Trancos, CA 93004
(805) 647 2231

OBJECTIVE: An entry-level position in the hospitality industry leading to management.

EDUCATION:

20.. – 20.. **Northern Arizona University.** Bachelor of Science in Hotel and Restaurant Management. Cumulative GPA: 3.75.

Summer 20.. **Ecole Hoteliere Les Roches, Bluche, Switzerland.** NAU's Summer Studies in Europe Program.

INDUSTRY EXPERIENCE:

8/20..-present Drury Inn, Flagstaff, Arizona
Manager Trainee Internship, Rooms Division. Trained in front office, housekeeping, and reservations operations.

2/20..-8/20.. Chili's Restaurant, Flagstaff, Arizona
Line Cook. Mexican and American menu specialties. Supervised the evening shift on weekends.

6/20..-8/20.. Ritz-Carlton Hotel, Phoenix, AZ.
Manager Trainee Internship. Rooms Division. Trained in front office and reservations operations.

2/20..-6/20.. The Stafford Grill, Los Trancos, CA.
Part-time Server/Hostess. Fine-dining service. As hostess, performed restaurant closing duties when working the evening shift.

HONORS/AWARDS:

Phi Eta Sigma National Honors Society.
Academic scholarship from the American Hotel Foundation
NAU Dean's List. 20..-20..
The Stafford Grill Employee of the Month Award, 20..

SKILLS: One semester coursework in Spanish. One semester conversational Spanish.

EXTRACURRICULAR ACTIVITIES:

NAU Kayettes. 20..-present. *Corresponding Secretary.*

Big Brothers and Sisters. Active involvement.
IFSEA. Active club member.

REFERENCES: Available upon request.

THE OBJECTIVE: It should provide the company with a general idea of what the applicant is looking for. The objective should be all-encompassing rather than job-specific. If it is stated that a senior student is looking for an entry-level management position in the hospitality industry, prospective employers will consider her/him for all jobs being offered. On the other hand, if the student writes that she/he is looking, for a position in sales, the candidate may be automatically disqualified for any openings in other divisions or departments. In other words, applicants should be specific only if they plan to reject any other job that the company could offer them. Most industry professionals prefer resumes which state an objective so they can expediently find out if the candidate is willing to accept a position that is available at the time.

EDUCATION: Students should list first the hospitality degree they are about to receive, then any other relevant studies they have completed; for instance, studies done abroad or special certification obtained related to the industry. If the cumulative GPA is substantially lower than the major's, the latter should be listed. If the overall GPA is well below average, it is advisable not to state it and be prepared to answer questions at the time of the interview; perhaps mentioning (if this is truly the case) that the candidate had to pay his/her way through college by working full-time. Generally, hospitality recruiters do not put a lot of emphasis on grade point average, as they understand that low marks do not necessarily mean that the candidate will not be an excellent employee. Graduation from high school could be mentioned if the graduating GPA is superior.

WORK EXPERIENCE: Recruiters will be looking closely at the work experience students have had that is related to the position they want to fill. Experience in the industry can range from answering the phones in a travel agency and working in a McDonald's to having been an employee in a five-star hotel. Most recent employment is listed first and should include dates, positions held and any experience relevant to the job, such as having supervised other employees, ordered supplies or balanced the cash register. Internships in the industry while in college should also be listed. Students who have no industry experience should include all lab work required in courses taken; for example, in housekeeping, food and beverage, or front desk. The positions and dates of work performed must be verifiable as recruiters will conduct a background check prior to hiring the candidate. Students should be prepared to answer questions about unemployed periods, about switching jobs too frequently, and on the reasons for leaving a position.

HONORS/AWARDS: Academic honors, scholarships, and awards received in the workplace should be stated, such as Dean's List, student of the year, and employee of the month. Employers will be looking for scholarly and work-related signs of leadership.

SKILLS: Special abilities, such as knowledge of a second language, extraordinary culinary ability or exceptional experience with technological systems should be listed.

EXTRACURRICULAR ACTIVITIES: Some hospitality companies do look for activities other than those of having gone through college and having some experience in the industry. Having been involved in public and social activities is seen as a sign that the candidate will be willing to be involved in the social fabric of the community where the place of work is located. Membership in academic clubs, such as the National Society for Minorities in Hospitality, and community organizations like Big Brothers and Sisters should be listed.

REFERENCES: Because the main purpose of sending or handing out a resume is to obtain an interview, listing references on it doesn't serve any purpose. Stating that references are "available upon request" is sufficient. However, students should ask permission from academic instructors and industry managers they know well to use them as references and have a typed list ready to be sent or handed out to prospective employers upon request. Three or four individuals that know the student well should suffice. A sample list of references that includes two professors and two industry supervisors follows.

REFERENCES

Natalia C. Foster

Matt A. Casado
Professor Emeritus
School of Hotel and Restaurant Management
Northern Arizona University
P.O.Box 5638
Flagstaff, Arizona 86011
Telephone: (928) 523 1712
e-mail: matt.casado@nau.edu

Peter Fletcher
Lecturer
Hospitality Management
Tidewater Community College
1700 College Crescent
Virginia Beach, VA 23456

Telephone: (757) 321 7173
e-mail: ptchef@tc.cc.va

Eric W. Rande
Front Office Manager
Hyatt Regency at Macy's Plaza
711 South Hope Street
Los Angeles, CA 90017
Telephone: (213) 629 3230
e-mail: Erande@laxrlpo.hyatt.com

Anne P. James
Franchise Service Director
Choice Hotels International
23425 N. 39th Drive, Suite 104
Glendale, AZ 85310
Telephone: (623) 516 2980
e-mail: apgodi@choicehotels.com

THE COVER LETTER

When resumes are sent to companies by mail, they must be accompanied by a cover letter whose content and format must, like the resume, be very well done. Below is an example of a cover letter. If possible, the letter should be addressed to the person responsible for screening or who will do the hiring. The body of the letter should be divided into three parts: the first paragraph stating clearly the purpose of the letter, the second, explaining the reasons why the company should be interested in you. (Here, you should tout your industry experience, if any, personal traits and professional skills befitting the job in question. All statements should be truthful.) The last paragraph should reiterate your desire to work for the company. The cover letter should use the same typeface as used on the resume and be typed on at least medium thickness paper.

P.O.Box 3333
Flagstaff, AZ 86011
(928) 774 1711
dncf22@nau.edu

Kenneth V. Bailey
General Manager
Doubletree Resort
5401 N. Scottsdale Road
Scottsdale, AZ 85250
October 19, 2016

Dear Mr. Bailey:

I recently had the opportunity to visit your resort while in the Phoenix area. I was so impressed by the beautiful facilities and the excellent service you offer your guests that I thought it would be an exciting experience to work for a company such as Doubletree.

I will be graduating from the School of Hotel and Restaurant Management at Northern Arizona University in December of this year. Over the past four years, I have been exposed to the hospitality industry through academic and work experience. I am now seeking to gain industry know-how by joining a company that offers a good management-training program. My excellent work ethic and my desire to excel would make me an asset to your establishment.

I have included a resume listing my qualifications. I would appreciate an interview with you about employment opportunities in your resort. I look forward to hearing from you.

Sincerely,
Natalia Foster

LEARNING ABOUT THE COMPANY

Before interviewing, students should research the background of the company they intend to join. This preparation will help candidates answer questions asked by the interviewer, such as "what do you know about us?" It can also help them make comments indicating that they have made the effort to be prepared, such as "I understand that your company has opened six units in California in the last three years; how are they doing?" Information about corporations can be obtained on the Internet. The records and performance of privately-held companies can be found in reports published by trade magazines, such as Restaurants & Institutions. Calls or visits with people already working at a specific property can also provide students with a personal perspective of a company's operations and managing philosophy.

THE INTERVIEW

Countless books have been written about job interviewing, but the basic points to remember are these: be on time, be professionally attired and show a positive attitude. Most hospitality companies' executives interact with other professionals and guests dressed in business attire and they expect to see candidates dressed in a similar fashion.

At the time of the interview, it is important to remember that the persons you will be interviewing with are usually there to recruit graduates for their companies; that is, these companies need you as much as you need them. Your goal should be to sell yourself, to make clear that you are eager to learn about the industry and have a commitment to work hard. You should answer questions honestly, clearly, and concisely, without trying to dominate the conversation. Most interviews involve four types of questions:

- **Direct.** Usually beginning with what, when, where, who, why.
- **Open-ended.** Leaving the answer entirely to you.
- **Leading.** Usually to be answered with "yes" or "no."
- **Situational.** Asking about a hypothetical situation.

The following questions might be asked on a first interview:

What do you know about our company?
Why should we hire you?
In what ways do you think you can make a contribution to our company?
Why did you choose hospitality as a career?
What do you see yourself doing three years from now?
What motivates you to put forth your best effort?
Which is most important to you, the type of job we are offering or money?
Do you have plans for continued study?
What have you learned from the mistakes you made in the past?
In what kind of work environment will you be most comfortable?
Are you willing to travel?
Are you willing to be transferred often?
Why did you decide to seek a position with this company?
What are the most important rewards you expect with a hospitality career?
What are your long-range career objectives?
Will you relocate when necessary?

What qualifications should a successful manager possess?
How much do you expect to be earning in five years?
What do you consider to be your greatest strengths and weaknesses?
How do you determine success?

You should be able to answer each of these questions concisely and intelligently. The career services office in most colleges provides help in interviewing techniques. Candidates should be ready to answer professional questions (displaying knowledge they have about industry-specific situations), such as, "what do you understand for yield management in hotels?"; personal questions (regarding your plans for the future), for example, "would you mind being transferred to a location back east after your training period?"; and behavior-based questions (how you behaved in the past), for instance, "do you work well under pressure?" Conversely, candidates should ask the interviewer questions to clarify issues about the company, such as, "Can you describe the training-program you offer to first-time hires?" Asking questions about the company conveys to employers the feeling that you are interested in working for them. On the other hand, asking too many questions at the time of the first interview could be counterproductive, as you might come across as an over-anxious candidate.

Interviewers should be addressed by their last names, unless you are told to use first names as the interview progresses. Extra materials, such as a list of references, letters of recommendation or awards, and academic transcripts should be brought to the interview. After the interview, candidates should send a thank-you note to the interviewer expressing a desire to join the company.

CRITERIA FOR HIRING

The criteria for hiring on campus vary from company to company. In general, the ranking of attributes by recruiters is:

1. Verbal communication (fluent, concise statements)
2. Work experience (in the industry, internships, labs)
3. Personal appearance (professional attire and demeanor)
4. Prepared and enthusiastic about the company (research about the company, eager to join)
5. Extracurricular involvement (belonging to community and college organizations)
6. Grade point average (not critical to hospitality companies)

This ranking shows that interviewers will judge you first and foremost, from the way you communicate. If you are not an extrovert and have difficulty in expressing your thoughts clearly and concisely, you should practice with a career services expert or with a friend until you develop fluency in your answering patterns. A high academic grade point average, however, is not considered vital by most companies as it is generally accepted that there is no correlation between students' GPA and their future performance in the hospitality workplace.

SECOND INTERVIEWS

It is common for companies interested in hiring graduates to invite them to a second interview at corporate headquarters. Being invited to a second interview indicates that the company is seriously considering hiring you. Usually, the companies pay for transportation and lodging. In some cases, a panel of corporate officers will interview the candidate, asking general questions and observing his/her reactions to questions on specific industry situations. Some companies will ask you to spend one day on the job; for instance, preparing food in the kitchen or serving in the dining room. At this time, everything you do will be evaluated. The behavior of candidates will also be observed in informal settings, such as while having a drink at the bar or during dinner.

INTERVIEW FOLLOW-UP

Interviews and contacts made with prospective employers must be followed up with a thank-you message or telephone call. After the initial interview, a message thanking the recruiter for her/his time and stressing a desire to work for the company can be a helpful reminder that you are still interested in working for them. In some cases, students may get job offers while still being considered by a second company. After a discreet period of time, a phone call asking for their decision should be made.

ACCEPTING THE JOB OFFER

If you are lucky enough to receive multiple offers of employment, you should evaluate them carefully before making the final selection. The critical question is whether or not the position will fit your values, interests, and overall career goals. Issues like location, title of the position, salary, benefits, moving expenses, housing availability, opportunity for advancement, and so on should be considered very carefully. Often, alumni already working with the company can provide valuable information.

Candidates should keep in mind that **independently-owned companies** may offer a limited career scope if the number of properties they operate is small. On occasion, these companies belong to local individuals who intend to speculate on the real estate value of the establishments. It is common that independent owners franchise their properties from a national chain. You should understand that being hired by a **franchised property** does not mean that they will be working for the corporation holding the brand name; that is, being an employee of a Holiday Inn resort owned by a local doctor doesn't mean that you will be working for the Holiday Inn Corporation. Generally, **multi-unit chains** operating under the direct control of the chain's headquarters offer the best opportunities for graduates to advance in their careers. Usually, an employee that has been trained and has worked in a supervisory position for a large hotel chain is promoted to a management job after a reasonable amount of time. Opportunities for advancement with **management companies** also depend on the number of units the companies operate, as some of them have many properties, and others just a few units.

When you decide to accept an offer, you should request a signed contract or, at least, a signed letter confirming the initial position, salary, benefits and payment of expenses associated with the hiring. Sometimes recruiting companies want to test the ability of graduates working as hourly employees before they place them on a management-training track. In this case, students should obtain a firm commitment from the company that the job will lead to a management-track position within a reasonable period of time if they prove to be worthy employees. Accepting an hourly position, say front desk clerk, without a clear opportunity for advancement should be the last resort for a graduate of a 4-year baccalaureate program.

THE CAREER PATH

Some students are anxious to start a career in hospitality without having substantial previous experience. Their chances of success can be increased by planning their career path at the time they enroll in a higher education institution. Usually, the program will offer appropriate courses to prepare students with general and theoretical professional knowledge, but other aspects of the initial preparation should include practical experience by way of work while at school and from internships offered by the program. In cooperation with hotel schools, most hotel chains offer management-training programs that can last a summer, three or six months. Students are given the opportunity of working hands-on in several departments to gain experience in all aspects of the operation. These training programs also give interns the opportunity to prove themselves valuable to the company, increasing the chances that they will be offered a position at the time of graduation. The sample resume of Natalia Foster presented before, shows that she had made a point of working in a fine dining restaurant prior to enrolling at NAU, obviously while still in high school. Natalia also accepted a summer internship with a first-class hotel in Arizona and a job as a trainee in a lodging property on campus. Her training also includes working as a line cook at Chili's. Her work experience at the time of interviewing for a permanent job is impressive for a student about to graduate from college. Besides work, Ms. Foster was also involved in a professional organization (IFSEA), in a university sorority (NAU Kayettes), and with a child-mentoring organization

(Big Brothers and Sisters). This background would show the interviewer that Natalia worked hard to become a well-rounded candidate for a trainee position with the company.

In general, large **lodging chains** have more glamour but smaller companies may offer more opportunities for rapid advancement than larger ones. While it might take a new employee several years to become, say, a rooms division director in a large chain, the same person may be offered the position by a smaller chain in a much shorter period of time. In any case, through careful planning and diligent work a graduate joining a lodging company can move up the career ladder much faster than in other industries.

Once full-time employment has been secured, the new employee should first master the requirements of the job. After feeling confident in the position, it is helpful to cross-train in other departments as it is difficult to advance without experience in all aspects of operations. The Educational Institute of the American Hotel & Motel Association also offers independent learning courses leading to certification in subjects like food and beverage, housekeeping, sales or front desk which will increase the chances of climbing the career ladder towards reaching an executive position.

KEY TERMS

Career services
Cover letter
Curriculum vitae
Direct question
Franchised property
Independently-owned company
Job fair
Leading question
List of references
Lodging chains
Management company
Multi-unit chain
Open-ended question
Resume
Situational question

DISCUSSION AND REVIEW QUESTIONS

22. Name two activities career services offer to assist students in finding a job.
23. Why is it considered easier to find a job through career services than by contacting an employer directly?

24. What is the purpose of job fairs at colleges and universities?
25. What is the recommended strategy to apply for a job in a hotel located overseas that is owned by the Sheraton corporation?
26. What is the difference between a resume and a curriculum vitae?
27. Should the objective stated on a resume be very specific or provide a general idea of what the job applicant is looking for?
28. Is a student's GPA very important to hospitality recruiter? Why or why not?
29. Name two skills that students can include in their resumes.
30. Why do recruiters consider students' extracurricular activities important?
31. Is it critical to include three references on a resume? Why or why not?
32. When should a student include a cover letter with his/her resume?
33. In general, what is more important to a recruiter: a student's GPA or his/her work experience?

PRACTICAL SITUATIONS

Situation 15.1

Preparing a resume

Melanie S. Olson is a senior taking her senior seminar class at CSU, Denver, from which she will graduate in May, 2015. Her objective is to find a position with a hospitality company, preferably in the rooms division of a large golf resort. She attended Denver Community College in the fall of 2012 (one semester). She was an exchange student at Sheffield College, England, during the spring semester of 2014. Her cumulative GPA is 2.8 and her major GPA 3.76.

Miss Olson's professional experience is as follows: desk clerk from 1/15/15 to present at Rodeway Inn, Denver, Colorado; assistant manager at Woodlands Inn Bed and Breakfast, Boulder, Colorado, from 9/5/13 to 12/31/15; and line cook at Mecca Grill, Aurora, Colorado, from 2/2/12 to 12/15/12. Her honors received are Mortar Board Senior Honor Society, 2014; Eta Sigma Delta Honor Society, 2011/2012; and HRM Dean's List, spring 2014. Melanie understands and speaks Spanish quite well and knows how to operate a copying machine.

She has been a member of the Hospitality Entrepreneurs Club in college and has been active in the Denver Cancer Society League (DCSL). Two professors at CSU, one instructor at DCSL and the Rodeway Inn manager have volunteered to recommend her.

ASSIGNMENT:

Compile a resume with the information given.

Situation 2

Preparing a cover letter

Melanie is applying for the following position: reservations assistant manager at the Arizona Biltmore Resort & Spa, 2400 East Missouri, Phoenix, Arizona 85016, where George L'Heureux is general manager.

Drury Plaza Wichita, KS
Courtesy Drury Hotels

ASSIGNMENT:

Write a cover letter addressed to Mr. L'Heureux to accompany Melanie Olson's application based on her resume.

Situation 3

Preparing a List of References

From the information given in Situation 1, prepare Ms. Olson's list of references. Make up the titles, addresses, phone numbers and e-mail information of the persons involved but make sure that the list includes all necessary components.

CASE STUDY 15.1

Accepting the job offer

After several interviews with hotel and restaurant management companies on campus, you are offered three positions: two in the Rocky Mountain region and one in Texas. The first is with a management company, based in Denver, that currently manages 75 lodging properties, all franchised. The second offer is from the Marriott Corporation of Salt Lake City, and the third from Brinker International of San Antonio.

1. Assistant to the coffee shop manager of a 350-room Radisson-franchised hotel owned by a local insurance company in Denver, Colorado. The management company for which you are interviewing, you have been told, is going to need several F&B managers for new hotels being acquired next year. The company, that operates 75 properties in the U.S. and one in the Bahamas, offers a six-month management training period in which the employee will have to perform front-line work in the F&B department, housekeeping, and front desk. Promotion after the initial training is not guaranteed. Starting salary is $33,500 annually and includes medical and dental insurance. No participation in a retirement program is provided until employees reach department-manager status. The company doesn't offer a relocation stipend.
2. The job offer from Marriott is a rooms division manager-in-training position as assistant in the front office department of a Residence Inn in Salt Lake City. You have been told that you will be trained directly by the front office manager who has been ten years with the property. The salary guaranteed for the first year is $30,000. Full dental and medical insurance is covered by the company. A limited retirement plan is offered to new management-track employees. The company will pay $2,500 for moving expenses to Salt Lake and will provide housing in an apartment building near the hotel at $600 per month.
3. The third offer involves participation in an intensive training program at a Chili's Restaurant in San Antonio, Texas. The program is very well structured. The candidate will work the floor, the kitchen, and the cash register for six months before

being promoted to unit assistant manager. The company, you have been told, is expanding very fast. A friend working for Brinker International has told you that the company is excellent and that restaurant general managers in some locations are making over $75,000 per year. This particular unit, which is located near the airport, doesn't provide insurance or retirement plans until the first promotion. The starting salary is $36,000 annually and the company will pay all moving expenses to San Antonio.

ASSIGNMENT:

Discuss the advantages and disadvantages of accepting each one of the three positions offered.

FINAL ASSIGNMENT

Students will compile their own personal resume, a list of references and a cover letter addressed to an imaginary company applying for a management-trainee position in the rooms division. After the instructor has reviewed the last draft, students should have the three documents, ready for their personal use, typed in standard-size quality paper using 12-point font. Headings should be typed in bold and in regular typeface, not in italics. These documents should be updated as time goes by.

CONCLUSION

The practical situations and case study here give some possible scenarios you might encounter, but there are countless more. That is much of the excitement of the hospitality industry – no two days are the same. You will be meeting such a variety of people and be dealing with so many different situations, especially at the front office, that your insight and skills will continually be developing. With this start, I hope to give you confidence that you can deal with whatever challenge that confronts you calmly, capably and wisely.

GLOSSARY

A

Accounts receivable The total of the transient guest ledger and the city ledger. Amount that the property is owed at any given time.

Actual revenue The revenue realized in a given period of time.

Advance deposit Amount sent to the hotel to guarantee a guest's reservation.

Affiliate reservation networks A hospitality chain's reservation system in which all participating operational units are represented.

All-suite property A property where all rooms are suites.

AM guestroom check An inspection of guestrooms conducted as early as possible in the morning by the housekeeping department to ascertain whether the information provided in the night clerk's report was accurate.

American Automobile Association (AAA) A not-for-profit organization of clubs in the United States and Canada serving over 50 million members through a network of 1,100 offices.

American plan (AP) A price that includes room and three meals a day.

Americans with disabilities act (ADA) An act that mandates the elimination of discrimination against individuals with disabilities.

Application form A written or digital form filled out by prospective employees.

Aptitude test A measurement of an applicant's abilities such as to perform clerical tasks.

Arrival report A list with the names of the day's incoming travelers.

Authoritarian leadership style Management by which the manager dictates the tasks to be performed.

Authorization code A number issued by the credit card validator that provides approval of a transaction.

Average daily rate (ADR) The average rate obtained from the selling of rooms during a certain period of time.

B

Balancing up accounts The final calculation of the day's transactions done by the night auditor.

Bank deposit Amount collected in cash, checks, and credit card payments at the end of a shift.

Bell captain The supervisor of the front office uniformed personnel.

Bell staff The front office uniformed personnel.

Benchmarking Comparison of a company's costs of performing a business activity with the costs incurred by other companies for the same activity in order to ascertain competitiveness.

Bit A contraction of *binary digit*, a bit is the basic unit of information in computing that has only one of two values, commonly 0 and 1.

Block of rooms A number of rooms reserved for a particular incoming group or party.

Brand loyalty Tendency of some travelers to stay in establishments of the same company because of the special value or services they receive.

Business collusion An illegal secret business agreement.

Byte A unit of digital information that commonly consists of eight bits.

C

Call accounting (CAS) A system that identifies the extension from which a phone call has been made and the cost of the call. It is generally integrated into the property's PMS.

Career ladder program Plan to promote people from within the company.

Career services Office in most colleges that provides help to students to get a job after graduating.

Cash advance voucher A receipt for payments made by cashiers on behalf of a guest or for amounts charged as petty cash disbursements.

Cash count sheet A form filled out by cashiers that details the amount of cash to be included in the deposit at the end of a shift.

Cash-only basis This applies to guests who don't use any method of credit but cash.

Central reservation system An Internet location taking reservations on behalf of affiliated properties.

Chain website A central website of a lodging chain of hotels, resorts, etc.

Channel of distribution An Internet point that sells rooms or services on behalf of its affiliates.

Child assistance program A plan to help workers with child care such as nurseries in the workplace.

City ledger Account totals for customers not staying in the house.

Closing balance Total amount owed to the hotel at the end of the day's business cycle.

Cloud (The) A series of network-based services run by a virtual server.

Coercive power A manager's administration of punishment to modify a worker's behavior.

Competitive advantage A property's business opportunity that occurs when travelers are attracted to services or themes that are perceived as different, appealing, or superior to the competition.

Concierge An employee who provides assistance with information about the property's services, the city and surrounding area, entertainment, local tours and activities, church services, and other miscellaneous guest queries.

Concierge floor A floor dedicated to providing special services and security to guests.

Consolidated room sales summary A projection of revenues for the 12 months of the upcoming year based on the forecasted percentage of occupancy and average daily rate.

Contingency workers Employees who are not guaranteed enough hours to warrant benefits.

Cost-based rate The minimum room rate needed for the hotel to be financially sound. It includes all costs plus the expected return of investment.

Counseling session A face-to-face meeting between a supervisor and an employee when problems on the job are discussed.

Cover letter A letter sent with a resume to potential employers.

Credit denial A code issued by the credit card validator denying a credit transaction.

Credit floor limit The maximum credit amount a guest is allowed.

Critical incident method A method focusing on the observation of good or bad performance of employees to be discussed at the time of periodic evaluations.

Curriculum vitae A written document describing in detail the education, work-related history, and qualifications that a job-seeker possesses; en extensive resume.

Customer relationship management (CRM) A model that can be used to manage a property's interaction with guests and potential customers.

Cut-off date A designated time at which unbooked rooms from a block of reservations are released.

Cycle of Control A process which begins with setting standards, then operations take place, feedback is obtained, and an evaluation of results is conducted.

D

Date roll The change of date after the night audit is completed.

Day-use rate A price for guests who use the room for part of the day only.

Deficiency of execution Situation in which the employee knows how to do the task but decides not to perform it correctly.

Deficiency of knowledge Situation in which the employee doesn't know how to do the job better.

Democratic leadership style A type of management in which the manager seeks to reach consensus after group discussion.

Departmental income The result of subtracting the total of a department's expenses from the departmental revenue.

Department head An employee in charge of a department in lodging properties, such as the front office manager.

Departure report A list of guests which are scheduled to depart on a specific day.

Desk attendant An employee that provides service behind the front desk.

Direct billing Arrangement for an establishment to bill guests' charges to his/her company for payment.

Direct question In interviewing, a question usually beginning with what, when, where, who, or why.

Direct website A website operated by a single lodging property.

Distribution channels Intermediaries in the digital travel market that sell rooms for lodging properties.

Domain name system (DNS) An Internet protocol used in computers to identify domain names on the network; for example, "createspace.com."

Door attendant A uniformed employee who assists guests with their luggage when they arrive at the hotel's door.

Double Room A guestroom with a double-size bed.

E

Effort/compensation ratio A method of paying employees based on their work output.

Empathy The appreciative perception or understanding of another person.

Employee assistance program A plan aimed at retaining workers who are substance abusers.

Employee attitude training Educating employees to develop positive relationships with guests.

Employee handbook A list of rules and regulations about the property given to workers at the time of hiring.

Employee qualifications Minimum conditions required to ensure that applicants will be able to do the job for which they are applying.

Employee requisition form A request forwarded to the human resources department for hiring employees.

Employee security needs Maslow's premise that motivation is impossible if workers' basic needs are not fulfilled.

Employment checklist Document to ensure that no part of the new workers' induction process has been overlooked.

Empowerment of Employees A management approach that gives employees the necessary authority to provide effective customer service.

Emulation Effort to equal or excel the behavior of a superior.

English for vocational purposes Classes conducted, usually in-house, to teach foreign employees how to communicate with supervisors and peers on the job.

Equal employment opportunity Set up by the US Equal Employment Commission to protect against discrimination on the basis of race, color, religion, sex, or national origin.

European plan A room rate that includes no meals.

Evening shift (Front Office) Workers scheduled to work in the front office department after the end of the morning shift (usually between 3 and 11 PM.)

Executive committee The directors of divisions who, in large lodging properties, are involved in operational policy-making decisions.

Exit interview A technique used to find out the reasons why employees leave the company.

Extemporaneous speaking Speaking on the spur of the moment, without preparation or notes.

External recruiting The advertising of open positions outside the property, such as with newspaper ads.

F

Face-to-face selling Selling by front desk clerks at the time guests are checking out.

Field sales The solicitation and bookings of business door to door.

Fire alarm control panel (FACP) A panel, usually located at the front desk, which alerts of the location of a fire and permits prompt notification of local fire authorities.

Float A cashier's opening bank.

Floor limit The maximum credit amount a guest is allowed.

Forbes travel guide A company whose inspectors evaluate lodging properties on over 500 individual criteria to rate them by category.

Form I-9 Document used to verify employment eligibility.

Franchised property An establishment that contracts the right to conduct business displaying the logo of a particular chain while adhering to the company's requirements regarding service and amenities provided to guests.

Full house Term to express that a lodging property is one hundred per cent occupied.

Full-time employee An employee regularly scheduled to work more than 30 hours per week.

G

Global distribution system (GDS) A worldwide computerized reservation network structured as a single point of access for reserving lodging accommodations.

Graveyard shift (front office) The front office shift when the night audit is conducted, usually from 11 PM to 7 AM.

Gross cash receipts The total cash received, including paid-out slips and vouchers.

Group master account A folio where group guests can charge services to be paid by their company or organization after their departure.

Guaranteed reservation A reservation guaranteed for payment whether or not the traveler arrives at the property.

Guest folio The guest's invoice where different charges are posted.

Guest history record Computer-stored record of guests' stays and preferences.

H

Halo effect Appearance and smooth talk of job seekers that sway interviewers in their decisions to hire.

Hardware The physical parts or components of a computer, such as the monitor, keyboard, hard drive, and mouse.

Hard-wired locking systems A locking system that works through a console at the front desk and is interfaced with room key locks.

Head porter The bell captain or supervisor of the front desk's uniformed personnel.

High-balance report A printout that identifies guests who are nearing their credit floor limit.

Historical records (reservations) Number of rooms occupied in a property during a specific period of time in the past.

Hotel technology next generation (HTNG) A global trade organization dedicated to enhancing the deployment of technology in hotels.

House count Number of rooms available for sale at any given time.

HTTP The hypertext transfer protocol is used by the WWW to define how messages are formatted and transmitted and what actions browsers take in response to commands.

Hubbart formula A method of ascertaining cost-based room rates.

Human capital The sum of the competencies, knowledge, social attributes, and business acumen of a company's workforce.

Hyperlink A reference to data that the reader can follow. HTTP's contain hyperlinks. For example, in an online reference such as 'hospitality,' many words and terms are hyperlinked to the definitions of these words and terms.

Hypertext transfer protocol (HTTP) Structured text that uses logical links between nodes. It is used for data communication on the World Wide Web.

I

Impromptu speaking Speaking before a group without previous preparation.

Incentive program Technique intended to provide employees with such rewards as bonuses, recognition and appreciation for the good work they perform.

Incidence logbook A folder where problems, comments or suggestions are recorded at the front desk to be made known to management.

Independently-owned company Lodging establishments that are usually managed by their owners.

Inside sales Sales efforts directed to house guests.

Intelligence test A questioning of prospective workers to measure intellectual skills.

Interest test A questioning of prospective employees to measure the applicant's interest for a certain kind of work.

Internal recruiting The advertising of open positions inside a property.

Internet service provider (ISP) A company that provides individuals and organizations with access to the Internet.

In-the-hole Number of rooms oversold at any given time.

J

Job description A detailed statement of tasks required to have the job done.

Job fair A presentation, usually organized and sponsored by a college's career services office, where prospective employers display their job offers to students about to graduate.

Job safety analysis The identification of possible hazards in the workplace.

K

Key performance indicators (KPIs) Gathered data that measures customer satisfaction.

King room Guestroom fitted with a king-size bed.

Knowledge of the property Training of hired workers on the layout of the property and on services offered.

Knowledge of the surrounding area Training of front office employees on the area surrounding the establishment where they work.

L

Laissez-faire leadership style A type of management in which subordinates have complete freedom to make group or individual decisions.

Late charge A debt incurred by guests just before they leave not included in their final bill.

Length of stay restriction Restriction on which days of the week rooms can be reserved in an attempt to balance the property's occupancy.

Listening skills In communication, an ability that is critical to determine the needs, problems, and moods of the person who is speaking.

List of references A list of three or four individuals who know a job applicant well that is submitted to prospective employers along with a resume.

Load factor Percentage of seats sold by airlines to be compared with the revenue obtained from selling the seats.

Local area network (LAN) A network linking components together by interfacing computer systems that operate independently; for example, between the front office and a point of sales located in the property's restaurant.

Lodging chains Hospitality companies offering room accommodations.

Logbook A folder where problems, comments or suggestions are recorded at the front desk to be made known to management.

Long-range objectives Goals planned to be achieved in a long timeframe such as refurbishing a hotel within the next three years.

M

Maintenance checklist A form or computer program used to conduct maintenance inspections.

Management company An organization that manages lodging properties in exchange for either receiving a basic fee or retaining an agreed-upon percentage of the revenue or income.

Manager on duty (MOD) A manager scheduled to ensure that there is a person available at all times to solve operational problems and to take care of guest requests.

Marginal pricing Attempts to market lower-than-normal room rates to cover the property's operational expenses.

Market-based rate The average rate of guestrooms set after analysis of factors such as location, economic conditions, season, and direct competition.

Master account A folio where charges from different rooms are posted.

Master card A card that allows access to several sections of guestrooms.

Mechanical complaints Complaints by guests related to mechanical malfunction.

Meeting planner The person employed by corporations, organizations, or entities to book conventions or other functions.

Merchandising Sales efforts conducted in an establishment.

Microprocessor-based locking system A stand-alone system which consists of a battery-powered microprocessor and a card reader installed in every lock.

Mobile application (mAPP) A software application designed to run on mobile devices, such as smartphones and tablet computers, used to retrieve all kinds of information and link up with social media.

Modified American plan (MAP) Price that includes room, breakfast and one other meal.

Morning shift (front office) The front office shift that usually covers the hours of 7 AM to 3 PM.

Multi-unit chain Chain units operating under the direct control of the company's headquarters.

Murphy bed In-wall bed commonly used in parlor rooms.

N

National Safety Council A nonprofit nongovernmental public service organization dedicated to protecting life and promoting health in the United States.

Nature tourism Tourism aimed at visiting natural attractions, such Arizona's Grand Canyon.

Net cash receipts Gross cash receipts minus paid-outs and vouchers.

Network service provider (NSP) A business or organization that sells bandwidth or network access to the Internet.

News release Information provided to the press for publication free of charge.

Night clerk's room report A report prepared by the front desk at the end of the day's activity indicating the status of all the rooms in the house. This report is sent to housekeeping first thing in the morning.

Night shift (front office) Also known as the graveyard shift, this shift usually covers the hours of 11 PM to 7 AM.

Non-guaranteed reservation A reservation not guaranteed for payment. Usually, these reservations are held only until 4 or 6 PM.

Nonverbal behavior In communication, gestures that serve as expressions of emotions.

No-post status A notification in the computer to inform all outlets not to post any charges to guests with no in-house credit.

No-show A person or persons who have failed to register as scheduled.

O

Occupancy percentage The result of dividing the number of rooms occupied by total rooms available.

Occupational Safety and Health Act (OSHA) A part of the United States Department of Labor that assures safe and healthful working conditions for working men and women by setting and enforcing standards and by providing training, outreach, education and assistance to employers.

Older travelers The segment of the tourist industry comprised of senior citizens. It includes AARP members over fifty years of age.

On-call employees Workers who are asked to report to work when extra help is needed.

Online comment questionnaire A list of questions e-mailed to those guests who have patronized the property to measure their satisfaction with the establishment.

On-the-job training Method by which new employees are assigned to watch how jobs should be performed before they take over their assignments.

Open-ended question In interviewing, a question that cannot be answered with a simple yes or no, but requires some explanation.

Opening balance Amount provided to cashiers at the beginning of their shifts to allow them to transact business and to provide change to guests.

Opening team Employees selected by a company to open a new establishment.

Operating budget A budget that categorizes items that have a direct relationship to the day-to-day revenue resulting from the sale of guestrooms.

Operating costs Those costs related to running a property.

Organized tours Groups of people traveling together.

Orientation A sequence of the induction process to acquaint the new employee and the organization with one another.

Other expenses In operating budgets, other expenses include categories other than salaries and wages such as printing and stationery.

Outsourcing Contracting out to a third-party services otherwise performed by property employees.

Outstanding balance The total credit owed to the hotel at the closing of the day's transactions. It becomes the opening balance for the following day.

Overbooking Taking a larger number of reservations than there are rooms available for the same period.

Overstay A guest who decides to stay beyond the scheduled date of departure.

Over/under (cash) Any discrepancy between the amount of funds on hand and the PMS cash reading.

P

Package coupon A discount voucher.

Packaging Combining rooms and complimentary or discounted services into a single-price offering.

Paid-out Payment made from the cashier's drawer on behalf of a guest or for small purchases of merchandise on behalf of a hotel department.

Paid-out slip A chit for the amount of a disbursement.

Panic emotion Uncontrolled anxious behavior caused by a threat such as a hotel fire.

Paraphrasing Repeating the sense of a statement but using other words.

Parlor room Guestroom with a wall-bed concealed during the day behind a wall panel.

Participative management Practice aimed at creating worker satisfaction by allowing employees to take part in making decisions.

Part-time employment A job offering 30 hours or less per week.

Pay scale A method of compensation that starts with a probationary rate of pay and goes up in accordance with time on the job.

Per diem A daily allowance, usually for living expenses while travelling in connection with one's work.

Personal development Providing workers with opportunities to realize their potential and improve their ability to make positive changes in their lives.

Personal selling Sales efforts conducted either by telephone or face-to-face.

Persuasion power A manager's trait of convincing (rather than forcing) a worker to do something.

Petty cash A payment, usually small, made from the cashier's bank and vouched for by a paid-out slip.

Physiological needs Basic needs for survival such as food and shelter.

PM guestroom check A physical inspection of all guestrooms in the house conducted at the end of the morning shift. A report is generated from this inspection and sent to the front desk by housekeeping for room-status verification between the two departments.

Point of presence (POP) An access point to the Internet. It enables web users to connect to network service providers.

Pre-natal care assistance Help provided to female workers to assist them during pregnancy such as by providing sufficient time for visits to the doctor.

Pre-screening interview Interview conducted by the Human Resources department to screen out those applicants who don't meet the criteria for the job advertised.

Presidential suite Special living quarters offered by luxury hotels.

Press conference An event in which information of interest to the general public is released by an establishment to the media.

Preventive maintenance The inspection of guestrooms and other areas on a regular basis to identify repair and maintenance needs before major breakdowns occur.

Price gouging Charging unreasonably high prices during periods of high customer demand.

Probationary basis Period allowed for first-time employees to learn and perform their jobs efficiently.

Profit and loss statement (P&L) A financial report showing amounts earned from sales of goods and services, less costs incurred, for a certain period of time.

Property management system (PMS) Computerized applications designed to manage different aspects of lodging operations. PMSs consist of a series of computer software packages capable of supporting the various activities that take place at the property.

Publicity Public relations efforts conducted by an establishment to release relevant information to the media.

Pull-alarm station A pull-bar or button to be activated in case of fire that generally sends information to the property's fire alarm control panel.

Q

Quality circles A management technique in which worker involvement in the decision-making process is sought.

Queen room A guestroom equipped with a queen-size bed.

R

Rack rates Regular, not discounted room prices.

Random access memory (RAM) A form of computer data storage that allows stored data to be accessed directly in any random order.

Rapport In communication, the ability to communicate effectively while making others comfortable.

Rating scale Tool for employee appraisals consisting of a series of descriptors to which a numerical score is given to determine the effectiveness of workers.

Ready room A guestroom that is ready to be sold.

Regular maintenance Repairs performed when items break or malfunction.

Resume An abbreviated account of a job-seeker's education, job experience, and qualifications.

Retention bonus Extra compensation given to those employees who stay with the company.

Return on investment (ROI) A ratio obtained by dividing profit by the owner's investment.

Revenue-generating center A lodging property unit providing services that generate revenue such as the rooms division.

Revenue management Management of the sources of income by applying observations of consumer behavior. It is designed to raise revenues in the short term.

Revenue per available room (RevPar) The result of dividing the room revenue by the number of rooms available for sale.

Revenue potential (rooms) The optimum yield: selling one hundred percent of a property's rooms at the highest possible price.

Revenue report PMS reading detailing the amounts received by outlet.

Reward power A manager's administration of compensation to modify workers' behavior.

Road Scholar tours Educational travel and learning vacations for adults.

Rooming list Information on attendees provided to hotels by the trip organizer prior to the arrival of a group.

Rooming slip Printed information given to guests at check-in that contains descriptive information about the property.

Room on-change Guestroom that has been vacated but that has not yet been cleaned.

Room-rate report A list of all room prices charged the previous night.

Rooms division An operational unit that usually is comprised of the housekeeping and the front office departments.

Rooms division director Sometimes referred to as resident manager, this is the person in charge of managing the rooms division of lodging properties.

Rooms in the hole Number of oversold rooms.

Rooms revenue Amount obtained from selling rooms in lodging operations.

Room status report A list of the status of all guestrooms. It is generated at the front desk and is handed to housekeeping when this department opens early in the morning.

S

Salaries and wages Operating budget allocation for amounts paid to salaried and hourly employees.

Secret shopper An expert hired by hospitality companies to conduct service audits of lodging properties.

Self-check-out terminal A screen, usually located in the lobby, where guests can access their folio and review its content.

Self-esteem needs Psychological need for recognition and sense of accomplishment.

Servers Powerful computers that service a number of other computers; for example, the computer that your computer talks to when you do a Google search.

Service-related complaints Complaints by guests related to poor services they received.

Shop audit An inspection conducted by experts to gather information on products and services provided by an establishment aimed at measuring levels of efficiency and guest satisfaction.

Short-range objectives Goals planned to be achieved in a short timeframe, such as improving worker productivity in the next three months.

Situational complaint A complaint by a guest about an incident, such as a tactless employees interacting with other workers.

Situational question In interviewing, a question asking about a hypothetical situation.

Skipper A cash-only "guest" that decides to leave the hotel without settling his/her account.

Social needs Maslow's theory in which workers must feel a sense of being accepted by their peers before they can be motivated.

Sofa bed A guestroom couch that can be converted into a bed.

Software Electronic instructions that tell the computer what to do with data. It is used to encode and decode bytes.

Span of control The number of subordinates that a supervisor can oversee effectively.

Special interest travelers A visitor interested in a specific tourism offer or attraction.

Suggestive selling A selling technique in which products or services are advertised or displayed in-house.

Support center A lodging property unit that does not generate revenue, such as engineering.

T

Table d'Hôte A single-priced series of dishes served as a whole meal.

Technical skills training An instructional sequence in which new employees are taught how to perform the tasks listed in their job description.

Temporary help Workers that are hired for a limited time such as for the summer or ski season.

The International Customer Service Institute (TICSI) An organization that develops standards for service excellence with the objective of making them the global standard for quality customer service.

Toastmasters International An organization whose goal is to improve the speaking skills of its members.

Total cash and credit sales A report listing all cash and credit card sales.

Transaction report (reservations) Computer-generated information about the number of daily reservations, cancellations, and no-shows.

Transient guest ledger Account totals for guests staying at the property.

Transportation assistance A stipend given mainly to hourly employees to purchase train or bus passes.

Transportation drivers Employees in charge of driving the property's limousines and vans.

Transient room rates Listed, not discounted room prices. Rack rates.

Trial balance Test performed before the night audit report is finalized.

Turnaway report Tracking of reservations requests refused by the hotel because of lack of room availability.

Twin room A room equipped with two twin-size beds.

U

Uncollectable account An account where debit balances that cannot be recovered are posted.

Understay The departure of a guest before his or her scheduled checkout date.

Uniform resource locator (URL) Also called a web address, this is a string of specific characters.

Unity of command A management principle which states that workers should be given orders only by one supervisor.

Upselling Efforts made by sales agents or reservationists to obtain the highest possible price or room rate.

V

Valet parking A service provided by employees in charge of parking guests' vehicles and assisting with luggage.

Variance analysis Document with the changes in revenue, expenses and income from budget by category.

Verbal factors In communication, the words spoken and the tone of voice used.

VIP Very important person.

Voice alarm system A system used to alert people and give directions in case of fire.

Voice over internet protocol (VoIP) A protocol that converts analog audio signals into digital data that can be transmitted over the Internet.

Voucher A document issued by travel agents to cover the cost of a guest's stay.

W

Wakeup call Service provided to guests that consists in ringing the telephone in their guestrooms at a pre-determined time.

Walk-in A guest who asks for a room without having a reservation made in advance.

Walking a guest To reject because of overbooking a guest who has a reservation.

Web browser A form of software that provides access to resources available on the Internet.

Weekend travelers Segment of the tourist market, usually families, who travel on weekends for leisure purposes.

Wellness program A series of incentives provided by companies designed to prevent illness and enhance the well-being of employees.

Wide area network (WAN) Network designed to connect computers in a certain geographic area with computers across metropolitan, regional or national boundaries.

Wireless fidelity (Wi-Fi) A device that allows for the connection to the Internet wirelessly using radio waves.

Work order A request to the engineering department for repair or service of items that have broken down or that malfunction.

Y

Yield management A revenue maximization technique that aims at increasing revenue by allocating available room capacity at optimum price.

INDEX

E

I

O

P

Q

R

S

CPSIA information can be obtained at www.ICGtesting.com
Printed in the USA
LVOW03s2302240815

451321LV00021B/1065/P

9 781494 943646